No Crystal Stair

VISIONS OF RACE AND SEX IN BLACK WOMEN'S FICTION

Gloria Wade-Gayles

THE PILGRIM PRESS
New York

Printed in the United States of America

Library of Congress Cataloging in Publication Data

Wade-Gayles, Gloria.
No crystal stair.

Bibliography: p. 265
Includes index.
1. American fiction—Afro-American authors—History and
criticism.   2. American fiction—Women authors—History
and criticism.   3. Afro-American women in literature.
4. Race relations in literature.   5. Sex role in literature.
6. American fiction—20th century—History and criticism.
                                                I. Title.
PS153.N5W26   1984   810'.9'9287   83-27208
                                ISBN 0-8298-0714-4
                                ISBN 0-8298-0709-8 (pbk.)

WINNER OF THE PILGRIM PRESS MANUSCRIPT COMPETITION

The Pilgrim Press, 132 West 31 Street, New York, N.Y. 10001

To

JOE, JONATHAN, and MONICA,
*my very special loves, who paint the rainbow and
keep the colors vivid*

NOLA GINGER, *my proud grandmother, who
taught me how to struggle with dignity*

OLA, *my compassionate aunt, whose selfless
generosity surely comes from heaven*

But most especially to

MAMA, *my closest friend, whose wisdom stroked
me into a woman and taught me to grow tall in the
light of my own suns*

Well, son, I'll tell you:
Life for me ain't been no crystal stair.
It's had tacks in it,
And splinters,
And boards torn up,
And places with no carpet on the floor—
Bare.
But all the time
I'se been a-climbin' on,
And reachin' landin's,

And turnin' corners,
And sometimes goin' in the dark
Where there ain't been no light,
So boy, don't you turn back.
Don't you set down on the steps
'Cause you finds it's kinder hard.
Don't you fall now—
For I'se still goin', honey,
I'se still climbin',
And life for me ain't been no crystal stair.

—Langston Hughes, "Mother to Son," 1926

To be beautiful, to be petted, to bear children. Such has been women's theoretical destiny and if perchance they have been ugly, hurt, and barren, that has been forgotten with studied silence. In partial compensation for this narrowed destiny, the white world has lavished its politeness on its womankind,—its chivalry and bows, its uncoverings and courtesies. . . . From black women of America, however, . . . this gauze has been withheld and without semblance of apology they have been frankly trodden under the feet of men.

. . . This, then,—a little thing—to their memory and inspiration.

—*W. E. B. DuBois,*
Dark Water: Voices from Within the Veil, *1920*

CONTENTS

ACKNOWLEDGMENTS   ix

INTRODUCTION by Beverly Guy-Sheftall   xiii

A PERSONAL RESPONSE by Zillah Eisenstein   xix

TO THE READER   xxii

1

THE NARROW SPACE OF RACE, THE DARK ENCLOSURE OF SEX: The Case for This Book   3

2

A HISTORICAL OVERVIEW: Black Women in White America, 1946–1976   22

3

THE HALO AND THE HARDSHIPS: Black Women as Mothers and Sometimes as Wives   57

4

"GOING NOWHERE IMMEDIATE": Black Women of Hopelessness   114

5

"JOURNEYING FROM CAN'T TO CAN" AND SOMETIMES BACK TO "CAN'T": Black Women of Challenge and Contradiction   145

6

GIVING BIRTH TO SELF: The Quests for Wholeness of Sula Mae Peace and Meridian Hill   184

7

THE SPACE AND THE ENCLOSURE: The Collective Vision of Black Women   216

AFTERWORD by Alton Hornsby, Jr.   247

NOTES   251

SELECTED BIBLIOGRAPHY   265

INDEX   277

ACKNOWLEDGMENTS

I wrote this book when I did not have time to write it. As the mother of two teenage children, the wife of a college president, and a part-time college teacher, I had to find time to write. And so I wrote when I seemed to be doing other things. I wrote while I sat in rapt attention to speakers at college lectures, convocations, and commencements. I wrote during PTA meetings, swimming meets, my daughter's dance lessons, and my son's basketball practice (even some of his games). I wrote on the highway on trips to my in-laws in Birmingham and my family in Memphis, and to Emory University in Atlanta, where I searched for more books on black women. What I wrote in my head I put on paper when the children were asleep, the campus had been dark for hours, and my husband had finally turned off his desk light in the early hours of the morning. I never had time to write, but there was the promise to my mother, who wanted the book published "before I die" and there were the women characters in the novels who never stopped talking about their lives.

I *wrote* the book because I had to. I *finished* it because I received encouragement and assistance from many beautiful people during different stages of the project. I want to thank four dedicated teachers—Annette Hubbard Roberts, Velma McLemore, Juanita Williamson, and Lionel Arnold—who taught me to love literature and writing, and I want to pay respect to the memory of President Hollis F. Price, who inspired all LeMoyne College students to set high goals for their lives.

Delores Aldridge introduced me to the significance of sociology to women's studies. Gloria Blackwell gave me my first nineteenth-century black heroine, Ida Wells-Barnett. Darlene Roth raised the hard questions about "woman's place" and began my search for answers. Faye read the first draft and with a critic's eye guided me to significant revisions. Sandy and June cheered me on, and Naim remembered to send the vibrations. Beverly sensitized me to homophobia in black women's studies and consistently "talked up" my research. Fannie, who could

have and should have written many books, influenced the writing
of this one with her courage. And far away in St. Croix, Roseann
Bell (who should come home) reminded me that *Sturdy Black
Bridges* needed a companion. But it was Peter Dowell, my
graduate adviser at Emory University, who made this book possible. He is a brilliant critic, whom I affectionately call "my caring shepherd."

Affie Martin at the University of Alabama in Birmingham had
never heard of black women's literature until she put this manuscript on a word processor. I am grateful to her for her enthusiasm. I am grateful in a special way to friends at Talladega
College: to the group of women who gathered in my home to
discuss the culture of southern black women; to Shirley Ash,
Jeanette Davis, and Minola Ratchford, who typed the manuscript
and "liked" what they read; to Juliette Smith and Everlee Jones,
who turned the college library over to me and requested material
from places far from Alabama; to Nikky Finney, who was an
enthusiastic supporter and able assistant during her junior and
senior years; and to William Garcia and Maxine Parker, whose
consistent support kept me writing even when I did not have
time to write. No one at the college helped me more than Ella
Calhoun, a woman of quiet dignity, whose cheerful conversations
during the day and assistance in the house kept me sane. I love
her.

I was fortunate in having two talented and brilliant editors,
Nancy Guelich and Susan Converse Winslow. They cared about
the quality of the finished product, which bears marks of their
excellence. I am grateful to them.

The people who are responsible for the me that dared write a
book are the members of *my family*, remarkable for their
unselfish love. I want to name them, name them all, because each
one gave me something special that kept the pen moving for
three years: Grandmother, Aunt Mae, Faye, Loren, Uncle
Hosea, Uncle Jack, Chiquita, Bruce, younger Bruce, Kelli, Ginger, Aunt Cheney Mae, even Prince, and especially Mama. Dad
and Mom, whose daughter I am by marriage, celebrated the
coming of the book in quiet ways.

Love, support, thoughtfulness—all these my husband, Joe,
gave me. I thank him for being a vital part of my life without

stifling my personhood. I thank him for his pride in an accomplishment that comes from that part of me that is neither wife nor mother. I thank my children, Jonathan (now fifteen) and Monica (now fourteen), for giving me space when I needed it and for making me proud of their honesty, self-respect, and sensitivity to others.

Finally and in a class of giving all by herself is my dear friend, Erminel Love, whom we affectionately call "the other mother" and "the other wife." During the writing of this book, she stepped into my life, held back distractions and detractors, and kept watch over me as I realized a dream. Without Erminel I could not have written this book. She was angelic in her devotion and her desire to give without receiving. From her I learned the true meaning of sisterhood and love.

If this is one of the longest acknowledgments in the history of publications, it is only because I have been richly blessed with many friends, some of whom were not mentioned but who know that in my heart I remember them and give thanks for their support and encouragement.

GLORIA WADE-GAYLES
Atlanta, Georgia
January 1984

INTRODUCTION

No Crystal Stair is black feminist criticism par excellence despite Gloria Wade Gayles's assertion that her study is "not a platform for black feminism" and "doesn't attempt to explain feminist theory or feminist criticism." It is, she reminds us, "a literary study that calls upon history and sociology to explain dominant images of black women in selected novels written by black women from 1946 to 1976." Since the concept of black feminist criticism is elusive, I should like to explore the broader issue of what it means to be a black feminist critic in order to place *No Crystal Stair* in the appropriate context.

In her comprehensive review essay on feminist criticism, Cheri Register argues that the major task of the feminist critic is to illuminate the "female experience." More specifically, "feminist critics look at how literature comprehends, transmits, and shapes female experience and is, in turn, shaped by it."[1] Barbara Desmarais defines feminist criticism as a "corrective, unmasking the omissions and distortions of the past—the errors of a literary critical tradition that arise from and reflect a culture created, perpetuated, and dominated by men."[2] In the first theoretical essay on black feminist criticism, Barbara Smith describes her uneasiness as she attempts to write about black women writers from a feminist perspective, although she acknowledges at the same time that such an approach is urgently needed. Her painstaking definition of black feminist criticism is still useful:

> When Black women's books are dealt with at all, it is usually in the context of Black literature which largely ignores the implications of sexual politics. When white women look at Black women's works they are of course ill-equipped to deal with the subtleties of racial politics. A Black feminist approach to literature that embodies the realization that the politics of sex as well as the politics of race and class are crucial interlock-

> ing factors in the works of Black women writers
> is an absolute necessity. Until a Black feminist
> criticism exists we will not even know what
> these writers mean.[3]

The black feminist critic also works "from the assumption that Black women writers constitute an identifiable literary tradition," which means that "thematically, stylistically, aesthetically, and conceptually Black women writers manifest common approaches to the act of creating literature as a direct result of the specific political, social, and economic experience they have been obliged to share."[4]

Though feminist analyses of women writers became more prevalent during the late 1970s, the need for black feminist criticism became more urgent, according to Deborah McDowell.

> Not only have Black women writers been "disfranchised" from critical works by white women scholars in the "female tradition," but they have also been frequently excised from those on the Afro-American literary tradition by Black scholars, most of whom are males. . . . When Black women writers are neither ignored altogether nor given honorable mention, they are critically misunderstood and summarily dismissed.[5]

In her lucid essay on new directions for black feminist criticism, McDowell calls for a clearer definition of "the Black feminist aesthetic" and delineates the major tasks that confront the black feminist critic over the next decade.[6]

Not surprisingly, black women have been more drawn to black women's literature than has any other segment of the population. From the publication of Pauline Hopkins' article "Famous Women of the Negro Race: Literary Workers" (*The Colored American Magazine*, April 1902) to Claudia Tate's recent collection of interviews with black women writers, the black female literary tradition in America has been celebrated in some quarters (although it was ignored, for the most part, by the literary establishment). This celebration has taken place in two phases. The first phase is characterized by efforts to document that such a tradition exists. Frances Collier Durden's master's thesis, "Negro Women in Poetry from Phillis Wheatley to Margaret Walker" (Atlanta University, 1947) is probably the first work that falls into this category. One of the earliest doctoral dissertations to analyze the black female literary tradition (which is different from examinations of images of black women in literature) is Beatrice Horn Royster's "The Ironic Vision of Four Black Women Novelists: A Study of the Novels of Jessie Fauset, Nella Larsen, Zora Neale Hurston and Ann Petry" (Emory University, 1975). Sharyn Skeeter's "Black Women Writers: Levels of Identity" (*Essence*, May 1973) is better known and reached a broader audience.

The second phase was ushered in by the publication of Mary Helen Washington's scholarly article "Black Women Image Makers" (*Black World*, August 1974). Moving beyond the descriptive approach of Skeeter, she argued that black women writers are a distinct group not only because of their long history but because unique themes recur in their works. The introduction to her pioneering anthology *Black-Eyed Susans: Classic Stories By and About Black Women* (1975) contains a more detailed analysis of these major themes. Alice Walker's essay "In Search of Our Mothers' Gardens: The Creativity of Black Women in the South" (*Ms.*, May 1974) is perhaps the most eloquent and poignant account of the black woman artist ever written. I should also mention that Walker designed the first course on black women writers, which she taught in 1977 at Wellesley College. Another publication in the second phase was *Sturdy Black Bridges: Visions of Black Women in Literature*, edited by Roseann Bell, Bettye Parker, and Beverly Guy-Sheftall (1979), which was credited with being the "first book-length critical work devoted to a 'minority' literature."[7]

This second phase is also distinguished by the emergence of black feminist literary criticism, notably Smith's and McDowell's work and Barbara Christian's *Black Women Novelists: The Development of a Tradition 1892–1976*, (1981), the first full-length study of the novels of black women. The publication of *No Crystal Stair* links Gloria Wade-Gayles to a small but productive body of black feminist critics who "analyze the works of Black female writers from a feminist or political perspective."[8]

No Crystal Stair is a major contribution to the new scholarship on women. It is the first full-length, interdisciplinary study of black women's novels in the contexts of race, sex, and class. Like feminist critics in general, Wade-Gayles analyzes the novels she examines in the context of a particular set of cultural conditions at a given point in time. She subjects these important novels to "rigorous textual analyses," which McDowell argues is essential for the black feminist critic.[9] Although Wade-Gayles focuses on conceptual and thematic similarities rather than on stylistic and linguistic characteristics, *No Crystal Stair* provides fresh insights about the nature of black womanhood during the period 1946–1976.

Moreover, the book is revisionist, according to the author, because it deviates in many ways from previous analyses of black women writers. It does not, for example, make the case, as the critic Mary Helen Washington has done, that black women writers create new, nonstereotypical images of black women.[10] Wade-Gayles demonstrates that the uniqueness of the black woman writer is to be found in her complex treatment of race and sex, which is a manifestation of her more sensitive understanding of black womanhood. Wade-Gayles's approach is more similar to that of Barbara Christian, but it is more interdisciplinary because of its reliance on both history and sociology to analyze black women's visions.

Wade-Gayles's most outstanding contribution to black feminist criticism is that she provides a coherent conceptual framework for understanding what it has meant to be black and female (and heterosexual) as this experience is portrayed in the literature of black women of the mid-twentieth century. Her use of two central metaphors—the narrow space and the dark enclosure—to illuminate the double burden of race and sex, which is unique to black women, is stunningly perceptive. She describes three circles, asserting boldly:

> In one circle white people, mainly males, experience influence and power. Far removed from it is the second circle, a narrow space in which black

> people, regardless of sex, experience uncer-
> tainty and powerlessness. And in this narrow
> space, often hidden but no less present and real,
> is a small dark enclosure for black women only.
> It is in this enclosure that black women experi-
> ence . . . the unique marks of black womanhood.

Sensitive to the significance of gender, Wade-Gayles departs from traditional approaches to the study of black women that result in exclusively racial interpretations.

This study also reminds us that critical works or anthologies dealing with black or women's literature that fail to include more than token treatment of the writings of black women should be considered inadequate. *No Crystal Stair: Visions of Race and Sex in Black Women's Fiction* seriously challenges the male-focused literary canon. It also calls attention to the white focus, which has developed over the past decade in women's literature. To ignore such novels as Paule Marshall's *Brown Girl, Brown-stones*, Tony Morrison's *The Bluest Eye*, and Alice Walker's *The Third Life of Grange Copeland*, which are brilliantly analyzed in *No Crystal Stair*, is to deprive one's self of an extraordinary literary experience. Learning to know Silla Boyce, Pauline Breedlove, and Mem Copeland, to name only a few of the most memorable characters in this study, enables us to understand significant aspects of American culture and many of the most complex dimensions of the human experience.

To be sure, *No Crystal Stair* was written for black women and black men. It deals honestly and sensitively with the issue of sexism within the black community. It lays bare the problematic nature of black male/female relations; however, this thorny issue is always analyzed within the context of a racist, sexist, capitalist social order. *No Crystal Stair* also refuses to idealize relations between black women themselves; while it discusses the impor-tance of bonding among us black women, it reveals the fragile state of black sisterhood. Much too frequently class and color differences separate us and make painful our relationships. I hope that white women will also find *No Crystal Stair* useful, for it illustrates the radical ways in which the lives of black women and white women diverge in America, despite our common gender. Zillah Eisenstein's sensitive comments on the following pages make this point more eloquently. I hope too that black men will agree with Alton Hornsby's acknowledgment in the Afterword that this book is a significant contribution to scholarship and, I add, to dialogue between black men and black women.

Finally, *No Crystal Stair* is a celebration of black women writers and their collective vision of the human condition. They have much to say to all of us.

BEVERLY GUY-SHEFTALL
Director
The Women's Resource and Research Center
Spelman College
Atlanta, Georgia
January 1984

A PERSONAL RESPONSE

Gloria Wade Gayles's *No Crystal Stair* is an experience with black women writers and black women's literature that takes the reader inside the complex, painful, and struggling reality of black women. It is a study of the visions of black women by black women writers through the inside lens of a black woman. It is a gift to black women and, even more so, to white women because it shares the intimate thoughts, visions, and desires of black women. The intimacy is there to experience. You do not have to build it; you merely have to be willing to feel it. But to receive fully the intimate pain of racism and patriarchy in these black women's lives, we white women have to become conscious of our own white privilege; that we are part of black women's pain. Even when we do not mean to be we are part of what denies black women their lives. We, as white women, inevitably are in black women's way as they struggle for their own reality. If we can come really to understand what this means and focus on this tension, we can also build through it, around it, even in it. No (white) feminist has the right not to read this book.

No Crystal Stair was not written for white women but was written with us in mind. It was written in hope of erasing the dominance of white privilege. As such, the white woman is often the outsider, so that the inside of black women's lives can be seen. In order for white women to be able to hear and see black women we must explore these inner realms of black women's lives and accept that we are the outsider. We need to know—or to imagine—or try to imagine what it means to be a black woman. It is impossible for a white woman to know what it is to be black or to experience black women's realities exactly as they do, but we can come close. We must try to get as close as possible. *No Crystal Stair* helps us (white feminists) in that endeavor.

Gloria Wade-Gayles's book is a marvelous and much-needed literary study of the peculiar reality of black women as both black and female. The "peculiar" reality is defined by the specific way that both sex and race define black women, as different from, and yet similar to, white women. Wade-Gayles, as well as the authors she analyzes, is often angry at the way white women and their standards confine and define the understanding of black women's reality. She, as well as the black women writers she analyzes, has to construct their identity within the confines of racism and patriarchy, but they are never completely determined by the reality. It is the process of *how* they create their reality as black women against the backdrop of racism, patriarchy, and economic class privilege and how they feel about this situation that exemplifies the specific realities of black women. *No Crystal Stair* lets us experience these realities.

No Crystal Stair depicts black women in white America as "twice burdened" and "doubly invisible." They are twice burdened because they are both black and female and are doubly invisible because of the way a racist, white, patriarchal society tries to erase their presence. "Regardless of class, black women are defined in this nation as a group *distinct* from black men and *distinct* from white people *only* by the double jeopardy of race and sex." Wade-Gayles uses this idea of double jeopardy to present an insider's narrative of black women's lives. She constructs a vision of reality that recognizes and encompasses black women's complexities.

The discussion in *No Crystal Stair* moves back and forth between describing the reality of *the* black woman and constructing the realit*ies* of black women. This is partially done with a keen sensitivity for the way economic class further particularizes black women's experience, creating the harsh reality of triple jeopardy in terms of the way a person's economic class is bound up with her blackness and her femaleness. Although Wade-Gayles's focus is on the way sex and race define each other to limit black women's lives, her discussion always moves further along. She is wonderfully sensitive in her treatment of black motherhood. Black women, as mothers, have various and conflicting feelings about their motherhood—ambivalence, pain, strength, and so on, like Toni Morrison's Eva, in *Sula* who takes her son's life because "it was too painful for her." Wade-Gayles also discusses black women as domestics who "edge into life through the back door," who are surrounded by the darkness of racism and poverty. In the end she presents us with different visions of black women:

those going nowhere immediately who lead lives of submission and despair, those who are giving birth to themselves and challenge all limitations to do so, and those who try and sometimes make it and other times don't. She gives us a depiction of black womanhood and also makes clear that there is no such abstract category as the black woman.

Gloria Wade-Gayles as a black woman and a feminist lets black women speak for themselves. It is a time when black and white women's lives are becoming more similiar. As white women join black women in the labor force and as heads of single-parent families, it is terribly important for us all to understand the specific differences that exist within our similarities.

Black women speak for themselves in this book. White women need to read it, think it, feel it, act on it. It is a gift to us, whether it was meant to be or not.

ZILLAH EISENSTEIN
Author of *The Radical Future of
Liberal Feminism* (1981)
Ithaca College
January 1984

TO THE READER

This is not a book about joy and comfort, wealth and power, true romance and fairy tales, which end with everyone living happily ever after. It is not a book you can read dispassionately. It will anger some of you, surprise others, and please a few who, for the wrong reasons, want to say, "I told you so." It was a painful book to write; it is a painful book to read. It is a book about the impact of racism and sexism on the reality of black women in white America and indirectly on the reality of those whom black women love—black children, black men, and other black women. As such it is a book about all of us, for who in this country is not touched in some way by black women's lives? But since it examines black women in literature rather than those in real life, perhaps it is only a book about *fiction*. Perhaps.

1

THE NARROW SPACE
OF RACE,
THE DARK
ENCLOSURE
OF SEX

THE CASE FOR
THIS BOOK

But what's all dis here talkin' 'bout? Dat man ober dar say dat women needs to be helped into carriages, and lifted ober ditches, and to have de best place every whar. Nobody ever help me into carriages, or ober mud puddles, or gives me any best places . . . and ar'nt I a woman? Look at me! Look at my arm! . . . I have plowed, and planted, and gathered into barns, and no man could head me—and ar'nt I a woman? I could work as much as a man when I could get it, and bear de lash as well—and ar'nt I a woman? I have borne five chilern and I seen 'em mos' all sold off into slavery, and when I cried out with a mother's grief, none but Jesus heard—and ar'nt I a woman?

—Sojourner Truth, 1853, in Elizabeth Cady Stanton, History of Woman's Suffrage, *1881*

American capitalism is an oppressive system that divides people into groups on the basis of their race, sex, and class, creating a society in which a few have capital and therefore are able to influence the lives of many. There are three major circles of reality in American society, which reflect degrees of power and

3

powerlessness. There is a large circle in which white people, most of them men, experience influence and power. Far away from it there is a smaller circle, a narrow space, in which black people, regardless of sex, experience uncertainty, exploitation, and powerlessness. Hidden in this second circle is a third, a small, dark enclosure in which black women experience pain, isolation, and vulnerability. These are the distinguishing marks of black womanhood in white America.

Unlike other groups in white America, black women are twice burdened. Because they are *black*, they are denied the pedestals and petticoated privileges a racist and sexist society assumes to be appropriate "gifts" for women. Because they are *women*, they are denied the power and influence men enjoy as the "natural" (or God-decreed) heads of families and leaders of nations. Black women are thus confined to both the narrow space of race and the dark enclosure of sex. This "double jeopardy" has created a complex, painful, and dehumanizing reality in which they have struggled for both freedom and selfhood. Like the speaker in Langston Hughes's "Mother to Son," black women in real life have found it "kinder hard" to survive and achieve in places "where there ain't been no light," and often they have been able to measure their progress only by the "corners" they turn and the "landin's" they reach. Life for them "ain't been no crystal stair."[1]

And yet their unique position in American culture is often ignored or minimized in studies of the impact of race and sex on American values, lifestyles, and economic groupings. In histories of the black experience, for example, the women are either background figures refracted in a monolithic mirror of blackness and maleness, or they are extraordinary leaders such as Sojourner Truth, Harriet Tubman, Charlotte Hawkins Brown, and Frances Harper, who just happened to be women.

The picture is not significantly different in women's history. Works by white scholars—whether men or women—concentrate on the oppression of white women in a male-dominated culture and relegate black women to footnotes that can easily be missed. Even in contemporary feminist scholarship, however, the identity of black women as "women" is less important than their identity as "blacks," for white feminists often compare their own oppression to that of "the Negro." The truth of Gerda Lerner's statement is therefore irrefutable: "belonging as they do to two groups which have traditionally been treated as inferiors by American society—Blacks and women—[black women] have been doubly invisible. Their records lie buried, unread, infrequently noticed and even more seldom interpreted."[2]

If scholarship ignores black women, mythology makes them its most colorful subject. An intricate web of misconceptions and stereotypes defines black women in many roles and, simultaneously, creates the monolithic "black woman." She is

> Sapphire. Mammy. Tragic mulatto wench. Workhorse, can swing an ax, lift a load, pick cotton with any man. A wonderful housekeeper. Excellent with children. Very clean. Very religious. A terrific mother. A great little singer and dancer and a devoted teacher and social worker. She's always had more opportunities than the black man because she was no threat to the white man so he made it easy for her. Curiously enough, she frequently ends up on welfare. Not beautiful, rather hard-looking unless she has white blood, but then *very* beautiful. The black ones are very exotic though, great in bed, tigers. And very fertile. If she is middle-class, she tends to be uptight about sex, prudish. She is unsupportive of black men, domineering, castrating. Very strong. Sorrow rolls right off her brow like so much rain. Tough, unfeminine. Opposed to women's rights movements, considers herself already liberated.[3]

The problem of understanding the anomalous position of black women in America is further complicated by the tendency to interpret their reality exclusively in racial terms. As incredible as it might seem, images that are unmistakable sexual caricatures or that clearly relate to the sexual roles of wife and mother are often presented as interpretations of blackness, not womanhood. Such a reading of black women is tantamount to suggesting that the age-old problem of "woman's place" never took hold in the black experience. The suggestion is a gross misinterpretation of American history and culture, for race and sex are the main axes on which power and responsibility have always turned in this country.

Class is also an axis, if not the central one in a capitalistic society. For when groups are denied or given power on the basis of race and sex, the intent and the results are economic in nature. As Angela Davis writes in *Women, Race and Class* (1981), from the very beginning the reality of black women in this country was shaped by the synergistic relationship of race, sex, and class. During slavery, they were workers first, women second, and always black, and the three identities locked them into positions of vulnerability. After the abolition of slavery, they continued to be exploited as blacks and as women in the labor market and in the home. Black feminists of the Combahee River Collective write that "it is difficult to separate race from class from sex oppression because in our lives they are most often experienced simultaneously."[4]

"Double jeopardy" for black women is, therefore, triple jeopardy in white America. Zillah Eisenstein makes this point in her discussion of "capitalist patriarchy," which "requires racial oppression alongside sexual and class oppression." While all women are oppressed in a capitalist patriarchy, Eisenstein writes, "what they share as sexual oppression is differentiated along class and racial lines in the same way that patriarchal history has always differentiated humanity according to class and race." She cautions against our seeing "sex or class, or race or class, or sex or race." We need to "see the process and relations of power. If we direct ourselves to the process of power we can begin to learn how and why women are oppressed which is the first step in changing our oppression."[5]

While I agree with Eisenstein, I believe the uniqueness of black women's reality in a capitalist patriarchy requires that we have a full understanding of racial/sexual oppression before we can comprehend the "process and relations of power" as they affect the lives of black women. I say this because our conditioning in a racist society makes us think primarily of racial and class oppression in reference to black women—and rarely of racial and sexual oppression. What we think we know about black women comes from fiction and nonfiction on the ghetto experience. Indeed, we are all but blind to the machinations of sexual politics in the black experience, and blind as well to the sexual identity of black women. Even feminist scholars, as I mentioned earlier, write about blacks and women when they attempt to enlighten us on the oppression of white women, an error which has incurred the anger of black feminists since the beginning of the women's movement in the sixties. One solution to this problem is a clear understanding of race and sex in black women's reality.

Another reason I believe attention to class is not as urgent as attention to race and sex in black women's reality is that class oppression cuts across racial and sexual lines and is therefore not unique to black women. Indeed, it is only when we look at class oppression that we are able to discuss black men, black women, white men, and white women in the same context. When we do so, we can miss the uniqueness of black women in this country. I do not mean to suggest that race and sex are the heaviest burdens in our society. Poverty is the cruelest fate of all, and its stark face in America is a profound indictment of capitalism. Nor do I mean to suggest that we can always distinguish between class oppression and racial and sexual oppression, for the lines of distinction are sometimes faint or even nonexistent, and, as Eisenstein explains, they are made by the "process and relations of power" that affect the lives of all people in this country. I am emphasizing a point often missed in studies of the black experience and studies of class oppression: regardless of class, black women are defined in this nation as a group *distinct* from black men and *distinct* from white people *only* because of the double jeopardy of race and sex.

Since American culture is a mosaic of regional differences, I discuss black womanhood as it reflects such differences. Especially for southern black womanhood is this kind of focus necessary. As Beverly Guy-Sheftall explains, the South "has been and continues to be a predominantly bi-racial society. . . . The consequences of this bi-racialism . . . have been exaggerated forms of racial and sexual stereotyping and the creation of strong social constraints along race and sex lines." Moreover, because of the economic condition of the South, black women have been "relegated to a permanent domestic caste."[6] This fact has created tension between black women and white women and, even more unfortunately, caused many black women to cope with life as it is rather than seek to make it what it should be.

Whether they accept or challenge the negative images "others" have of them, black women are not blind to their position in this society, which has "taught" them that "the Negro's skin and the woman's sex are prima facie evidence of subjection . . . ,"[7] and they know that theirs is a triple subjection. In Maya Angelou's words, they "are caught in the tripartite crossfire of masculine prejudice, white illogical hate, and Black lack of power;"[8] and because they hear the loud thunder of this crossfire repeatedly, many black women have been forced to sacrifice their own creativity and lead severely circumscribed lives. As Alice Walker points out, where are the gardens of black women in America?

Writing a book about racism and sexism, two highly charged subjects in American culture, is like navigating between Scylla and Charybdis. There are many problems inherent in our assumptions about both issues. One such problem is a tendency to draw parallels between sexual oppression and racial oppression that obliterate the differences between the two. As early as 1860, Elizabeth Cady Stanton drew such a parallel in the Suffrage Movement. "Prejudice against color, of which we hear so much, is *no stronger* than that against sex [italics added]," she wrote. "It is produced by the same cause, and manifested very much in the same way."[9] Without equating racial and sexual oppression as Stanton did, Gunnar Myrdal, in a special appendix on women in *An American Dilemma* (1944), observed striking similarities between the mistreatment of woman and the mistreatment of blacks. And in the 1970s white feminists argued their case with the analogy of "women as niggers."[10]

Theoretically, the analogy is sound. Women and blacks "have shared a collective experience of being assigned a set of attributes and responsibilities on the basis of a physical characteristic and, as a result, each has been denied fundamental rights of citizenship, including access to political, economic, and educational opportunity."[11] But theory, like values, is not always true to reality. White women have never experienced the barbarity of slavery and the cruelty of racism. As whites, they have identified with the "master" and with the "majority race" that holds power. As women, they have vicariously experienced power and influence through their husbands and fathers. Black women, on the other hand, have been imprisoned because they were female and black. As Frances Beal writes, the black woman in white America has been "the slave of a slave."[12] The metaphorical equation of race and sex, therefore, comes dangerously close to minimizing the sufferings of black people in general and black women in particular and, in so doing, loses what relationship it has to truth. For this reason, I do not wish to discuss the parallel between racial and sexual oppression without emphasizing the significant differences between them.

A second problematic assumption is the tendency to see black women and white women as "sisters" in oppression. The difficulties here are obvious. White women have participated actively, and without coercion, in the oppression of black men and women. They have been "ladies" who lived in leisure because black women have been "mammies." They have been protected and pampered, while black women have been dehumanized, brutalized, and devalued as blacks and as females. Calvin Hernton writes:

> When any group of women has to submit to . . .
> atrocities, when they are denied the smallest privacy of body, when they have to stand in public
> before men and women naked on an auction
> block and be fingered in the most intimate
> places, it is absurd to ask them to esteem themselves. . . . The fiber of the human personality is
> not that independent of the milieu in which it has
> to struggle for sanity. It was in this way, then,
> that the Negro woman during slavery began to
> develop a depreciatory concept of herself not
> only as a female but as a human being as well.
> She did not have much of an alternative.[13]

White women were victims of the peculiar institution of slavery, but they were beneficiaries as well, and it is as beneficiaries that black women see them. In fact, the indictment of white women as racist is so prevalent in the thinking of most black people that even when white women put their lives on the line for black liberation, they are seen as the women who sleep with "the man," who give birth to new generations of "the man," and who socialize each new generation to take power.

Moreover, national images of white women, though sexist in nature, place an impenetrable barrier between them and their so-called sisters in oppression. White women are fragrant, dainty, and feminine ladies whom white America has placed on a pedestal. In the media, their hair moves like softly blown silk, accentuating blue eyes and aquiline features. Even when they are pictured at work ("woman's work," of course), they are immaculate in ruffled aprons and manicured nails. Black women, in contrast, are obese, bandannaed women who are neither dainty nor feminine and certainly not pretty. White women are "the driving forces behind every man . . . and the valued sex objects."[14] Black women are devalued sex objects and, as Sapphires and Caledonias, castrating women who exacerbate the powerlessness of black men. Since the history, present reality, and national images of black women and white women diverge radically along racial and class lines, it is sometimes necessary to speak of them as only "stepsisters" in one oppression and antagonists in another.

A third problematic assumption is the notion of "sisterhood," which implies that black women are as concerned about sexual oppression as white women are. It would be foolish to argue that racial oppression has vitiated the sexual consciousness of black women, for one's sex is the first syllable of one's name for self, and sexual roles are the very core of one's functioning in this society. Black women know this as well as any other group, if not more intensely, but since they have a collective history as blacks, they often perceive problems created by sex as endemic to their peculiar plight as blacks and/or poor people. More important, because they have suffered oppression along with their men in the narrow space of race, they often do not understand their peculiar pain in the dark enclosure of sex.

In the nineteenth century Frances E. W. Harper, a black abolitionist, wrote that the "lesser question of sex must go," for being "black is more precarious and demanding than being a woman; being black means that every white, including every white working-class woman, can discriminate against you."[15] A similar attitude is present in the writings of black feminists in the 1960s and 1970s. Toni Cade Bambara, noted writer and activist, speaks mainly of racial loyalty when she asks "sisters" to prepare themselves for the struggle. For Bambara, black womanhood, regardless of class, is measured by black women's commitment to the struggle for the nation. Women in the Combahee Collective do not see sex as "the lesser question," but their philosophy as feminists makes race a central question: "Our situation as Black people necessitates that we have *solidarity around the fact of race*, which white women of course do not need to have with white men unless it is their negative solidarity as racial oppressors [italics added]."[16] While it is clearly a matter of emphasis, differences in sexual consciousness are significant enough to justify placing black women and white women in separate camps on a number of issues.

A fourth problematic assumption is a tendency to emphasize conflicts between black men and black women, which automatically discounts the racial victimization of black men. Discussions of sexism must take us beyond attacks on black men (or any men, for that matter), which would misleadingly imply that sexism is biological or genetic.

An additional danger of focusing on men is that black women become easy targets for those who are opposed to women's liberation and can use an anti-male posture as "proof" that they are bitter, wounded-in-love women; power-hungry careerists; confused bisexuals; or latent lesbians. All these labels are pejoratively charged in national thinking. Women who are not feminists respond to them defensively. Marabel Morgan's *The Total Woman* is such a response. For most black women, being a "total" woman is virtually impossible, requiring as it does a life of leisure, membership in the right bridge clubs, an executive husband, and money for the best in negligees, fragrances, and coiffures, But black women have also been caught in the either/or game—either you are a "real" (as opposed to a "total") woman, or you are one of the questionable types in our society. When race is added, the game becomes more serious. Black women must prove that they are "real" women and also that they will stand by their men. Thus have many black women failed to appreciate the poetry of Ntzoke Shange's *For Colored Girls Who Have Considered Suicide When the Rainbow Is Enuf* because the play does not "stand by" black men. Just as the Moynihan Report attributes problems of the race to a deteriorating family structure, Shange's play locates black women's problems in the home with sexist black men rather than in the larger society. Why else, critics ask, has the play been an overwhelming success with white audiences? The question comes from black women's loyalty to black men and from their peculiar pain in the enclosure of sex. But the question is not without merit. While it is necessary to struggle against the sexism of black men, it is extremely important not to perceive them as the primordial or major oppressors of black women.

I do not attempt in this book to defend black men or set forth a platform for black feminism. Nor do I attempt to explain feminist theory or feminist criticism. This book is not a theoretical work or a history. Rather, it is a literary study that uses history and sociology to explain dominant images of black women in selected novels written by black women from 1946 to 1976. I believe that in lieu of a major book on racism and sexism in the lives of real black women, fictional treatment of race and sex is an accessible and useful avenue to a larger and more sensitive understanding of black womanhood. Moreover, I am inspired by the fact that double jeopardy has been a dominant theme in the fiction of black women novelists. For more than a century, they have "documented the feminine heart"[17] that beats in an ebony frame. From the publication of Frances E. W. Harper's *Iola Leroy* in 1863, the first known novel written by an American black woman, to the publication of Gayl Jones's *Eva's Man* in 1976, black women writers have created memorable characters who ask, either *sotto voce* or in a strident voice, "Ar'nt I a woman" and black?[18] Sometimes they speak in metaphors: "de nigger women is de mule uh de world."[19] Other times they release soul-drenched rage: "all I keep hearing is you all talking about the hard time a colored man's got. But what about the *colored woman?* What about her?"[20] Always they are aware that theirs is a double jeopardy.

As I use "feminist" in this book, it means any approach to black womanhood that identifies sexism as a problem, whether major or minor, and calls, either explicitly or implicitly, for wider options for women—for space in which they can create themselves as persons. I believe that the writers whose novels I discuss are feminists in this sense. I do not believe that they offer new names and new roles for women. They could not and render black womanhood truthfully in their art. However, they are writing out of their woman's consciousness. They are telling their various stories from the inside, and in the process they turn traditional images of black women inside out and upside down, exposing them as poor reflectors of the truths of black women's humanity. The writers take us into the minds of their women characters, where, in the silence of their thoughts the women define their own humanity as something far larger than the sum total of roles and images created by others.

My examination of black woman's literature does not suggest that fiction can substitute for a history of black women in real life. Fiction never equals fact, but it mirrors fact and in a profound way is "an interpretation and compilation of history, anthropology, sociology, psychology, and a host of other areas"[21] that puts us in touch with the sound and sense of real life. The highly respected historian William Chafe, makes this point emphatically when he defends his use of "the interior perspective of fiction" in *Women and Equality: Changing Patterns in American Culture* (1977). He writes:

> Despite the problems created by using a novel for purposes of historical analysis, the interior perspective that is offered outweighs the limitations of subjectiveness. . . . In the case of both women and blacks, novels provide a vividness of detail and personal experience necessary to understand the larger processes at work in the society, but for the most part unavailable in conventional historical sources.[22]

Barbara Smith, a black critic whose writing on black women's fiction has significantly raised the consciousness of many black women, uses the same reasoning as Chafe. She writes that "untraditional methods might be the only way to proceed in a field where there is barely any published data to consult." But unlike Chafe, whose use of fiction by black men betrays either an ignorance of black women writers and/or a male orientation to scholarship, Smith adds that "books by black women authors are the richest written source [of information on black womanhood] because in the creation of the work, we can assume that little has stood between the black woman and the telling of her story."[23]

It is significant for another reason to understand "the telling of her story." Black women writers, like white women writers, have suffered the "silences" of which Tillie Olsen writes. These "silences" are not

> *natural* silences—that necessary time for renewal, lying fallow, gestation, in the natural cycle of creation. They are unnatural: the unnatural thwarting of what struggles to come into being, but cannot. In the old, the obvious parallels: when the seed strikes stone; the soil will not sustain; the spring is false; the time is drought; . . . the frost comes premature.[24]

Because of double jeopardy, black women have suffered an "unnatural thwarting" of their creativity far more than white women; only twenty-six major novels by black women have been published over a period of three decades. And when their "seeds" have struck soil rather than "stone" and they have created memorable works, black women writers have been given recognition begrudgingly or not at all. Until the late sixties they were, in fact, second-class citizens in literary scholarship. Like most black male writers, they were excluded from the "mainstream" of literary scholarship because of their race. And because of their sex, they were not among the privileged few black writers chosen by the system as worthy of some attention. Even when critics began in the late fifties to acknowledge the existence of black women writers, they preferred, as Alice Walker has noted, to "talk about [their] lives . . . , not about what they wrote."[25]

Heightened interest in women's issues in the late sixties made black women writers legitimate, significant, and worthy of literary awards. In fact, some critics (most of them male) now say

that the black woman writer's double jeopardy has become a
double asset: she is potentially a major writer in the market of
women's literature and in the market of black literature. The
question they now ask is, "Where are the black male writers?"
Other critics, many of them black women, believe that the new
interest in black women's literature is only a fad, just as the
celebration of black writers during the Harlem Renaissance of
the 1920s was a fad. They are reminded of Langston Hughes's
words when the Renaissance ended:

> It was the period when the Negro was in vogue.
> I was there. I had a swell time while it lasted.
> But I thought it wouldn't last long. . . . For how
> could a large and enthusiastic number of people
> be crazy about Negroes forever?

Many women are concerned that interest in black women writers
has not had an impact on the lives of black women in this nation.
Again they are reminded of Hughes's observation:

> But some Harlemites thought the millennium
> had come. They thought the race problem had at
> last been solved through Art plus Gladys Bent-
> ley. They were sure the New Negro would lead a
> new life from then on in green pastures of toler-
> ance created by Countee Cullen, Ethel Waters,
> Claude McKay, Duke Ellington, Bojangles, and
> Alain Locke.
>   I don't know what made any Negroes think
> that—except that they were mostly intellectuals
> doing the thinking. *The ordinary Negroes hadn't
> heard of the Negro Renaissance. And if they
> had, it hadn't raised their wages any* [italics
> added].[26]

Perhaps black women writers *are* only "in vogue," and perhaps
when the national mood changes they will once again be ignored
as artists. But we cannot impose the past on the present or see
with certainty into the future. We know only that, for the first

time in the literary history of this nation, black women writers are receiving the attention and applause they deserve as artists. Gwendolyn Brooks, Ann Petry, Dorothy West, Carolyn Rodgers, Paule Marshall, Toni Cade Bambara, Mari Evans, Alice Walker, Toni Morrison, Gayl Jones, and other gifted black women writers are finding their way into anthologies, national magazines, learned journals and, most of all, into the consciousness of women in this nation. If in future decades—in the twenty-first century—they are once again ignored, the marks they have made on the consciousness of black women will remain bold and distinct. Many black women are able to understand the poignant statement in Alice Walker's poem, "On Stripping Bark from Myself":

> No. I am finished with living
> for what my mother believes
> for what my brother and father defend
> for what my lover elevates
> for what my sister, blushing, denies or rushes
> to embrace.
>
> I find my own
> small person
> a standing self
> against the world
> an equality of wills
> I finally understand.[27]

Not every woman character discussed in this book understands the need "to strip bark" from herself. Nor does every character understand that black women are "damaged persons by virtue of being Black women."[28] But all of the women are aware that theirs is a complex reality which requires struggles for freedom and dignity. As Claudia Tate writes, a dominant theme in black women's fiction "is the quest theme—a character's personal search for a meaningful identity and for self-sustaining dignity in a world of growing isolation, meaninglessness, and moral decay."[29] Tate continues:

Black women writers project their vision of the world, society, community, family, their lovers, even themselves, most often through the eyes of black female characters and poetic personae. Their angle of vision allows them to see what white people, especially males, seldom see. With one penetrating glance they cut through layers of institutionalized racism and sexism and uncover a core of social contradictions and intimate dilemmas which plague all of us, regardless of race or gender. Through their art they share their vision of possible resolution with those who cannot see.[30]

Of the twenty-six major novels written by black women between 1946 and 1976, twelve cut most brilliantly "through layers of institutionalized racism and sexism " and take us to the core of black women's humanity. Listed chronologically, they are as follows:

1946:   Ann Petry, *The Street*
1948:   Dorothy West, *The Living Is Easy*
1953:   Gwendolyn Brooks, *Maud Martha*
1959:   Paule Marshall, *Brown Girl, Brownstones*
1969:   Sarah Wright, *This Child's Gonna Live*
1970:   Louise Meriwether, *Daddy Was a Number Runner*
        Toni Morrison, *The Bluest Eye*
        Alice Walker, *The Third Life of Grange Copeland*
1973:   Toni Morrison, *Sula*
1975:   Gayl Jones, *Corregidora*
1976:   Gayl Jones, *Eva's Man*
        Alice Walker, *Meridian*

All the novels have been well received by the general reading public and by critics, and many have been excerpted in reputable anthologies of American literature in general and black American literature in particular. They are not novellas or novelettes, and they are not adolescent fiction. It is necessary to underscore this point because much of the fiction written by black (and white) women falls into either or both of these categories.

The twelve novels draw portraits of black women who accept their racial identity as distinct from black women who "pass." Our understanding of this painful decision is limited, for we have fixed in our minds the image of "Pinky" in the film *Pinky* (1946), who passes for white with the assistance of her black mother, who, ironically, serves as Pinky's maid. The reality is much more complex than Hollywood suggests. It can be argued that black women characters who "pass" should be included in this book because they are responding to the impact of race and sex on their lives. However, their existence in a white environment makes them inappropriate for a book of this kind. To understand the complexity of black womanhood, we must first understand the lives of black women who function in black situations; we cannot understand black women who "pass" until we fully understand the reality they choose to reject. Black women in black situations, then, are the subject of this book. They come from different regions, family sizes and structures, and economic conditions. They are southern/rural women and northern/urban women; married women and divorced women; women with one child and women with many; poor women and middle-class women; church-going women and whorish women—black women with individual frustrations, needs, and dreams.

With the exception of two minor characters, the women are heterosexuals. This sexual homogeneity does not mean that lesbianism is not a theme in black women's literature. To the contrary, there are significant black lesbian novels that are on the cutting edge of sensitivity to human sexuality. However, as a distinct group in black women's literary history, they were not written between 1946 and 1976.

For historical integrity, I begin with an overview of black women in real life from 1946 to 1976. In addition to considering the political and economic developments that shaped the lives of black women in these decades, Chapter 2 discusses national interpretations of black women in the popular media and in scholarship, and demonstrates how these interpretations of real black women are corroborated, qualified, extended, or seriously undermined by black women's novels.

Chapters 3–6 sketch the four levels of consciousness that so sharply define the postures of the women toward race and sex that they serve the aims of the book more effectively than would a chronological scheme. In Chapter 3, "The Halo and the Hardships: Black Women as Mothers and Sometimes as Wives," I look carefully at the experiences of women characters who are either wives or mothers or both. These roles dominate the visions of the novels discussed, but they are important for another reason: they are the roles in which women are always defined as women and often limited as persons. According to traditional myth, women who are married are "more woman" than women who are single, and mothers are the very epitome of womanhood, even if they are not married. In approaching the women from these perspectives, I am not suggesting that sexual roles define them and racial experiences are only minor points in those definitions. I focus on sexual roles quite simply as an effective way of locating the women where they are as women, and proceeding from there to examine their total reality.

Chapter 4, "'Going Nowhere Immediate': Black Women of Hopelessness," concentrates on women who are so burdened by their race, sex, and class that they resign themselves to their "place," wishing only to survive with as few problems as possible.

Chapter 5, "'Journeying from Can't to Can' and Sometimes Back to 'Can't': Black Women of Challenge and Contradiction," deals with women who wrestle with the ambiguities of their dilemma, articulating strong objections without ever finding the courage to sustain a struggle for change.

Chapter 6, "Giving Birth to Self: The Quests for Wholeness of Meridian Hill and Sula Mae Peace," examines the lives of two women who spit in the eye of the Furies and demand to define themselves and name their reality.

The concluding chapter, "The Space and the Enclosure: Analysis of the Collective Vision," moves in and out of the different novels to illumine further the narrow space of race and the small enclosure of sex in which the imaginative women are confined and in which many of them struggle to give birth to self.

The period of the study—World War II to the present—is a fertile one, mainly because the war had a tremendous impact on the reality of blacks and women in this country. In the case of blacks, the war precipitated a large-scale migration from the rural South to the industrial North, laying the foundation of to-day's black urban culture. And because the war was a struggle for "freedom and democracy" abroad, it intensified the impatience of blacks with the absence of freedom and democracy at home, giving rise to organized resistance to segregation. For women, the war opened doors to employment in munitions plants and other factories, temporarily suspending assumptions about the female role. By the time the war ended, the die had been cast, for many women refused to return to their "place" and even went on to explore wider options. The war so raised the level of consciousness of blacks and women that it needed the national soil for the Civil Rights Movement of the fifties and sixties and the Black Power Movement of the seventies, as well as the Women's Liberation Movement of the sixties and seventies.

The novels discussed in this book belong to a long tradition forged and defined by our collective consciousness as black women—a tradition that includes my grandmother's story; the story of black women of my mother's generation; the story of black women with whom I have studied, lived, and worked; and the story of those I know only from the annals of history or the back pages of our nation's newspapers. It is a poignant story in which race and sex are engaged in a *danse macabre* for control, and the women, seeing the dance, respond in various ways.

I believe the fascinating and complex imaginary women the writers have given us are counterparts of black women in real life, and we love them and hate them, learn from them, and grow in sensitivity and strength because we step, invited, into their lives and dreams. I write about them as a black southerner who learned the meaning of struggle from a proud grandmother who ran away from the cottonfields of Mississippi at the age of thirteen. Her dreams were too strong for dust-covered realities. I write as a remnant of the Freedom Movement, whose failures and successes taught me that we cannot eliminate racism with rhetoric, marches, or the senseless deaths of dreamers and fighters—both black and white, male and female. It is a deep illness, not simply a social problem, and as such it needs to be cured, cut out radically rather than treated topically and lightly bandaged. I write as a feminist who believes that we cannot dismiss sexism as a minor issue raised by women, black and white, who refuse to be content with their "place." It is a major issue that connects with racism and class exploitation to create a nation desperately in need of salvation. And finally, I write as a black feminist who believes that genuine bonding with white women (indeed, with white people) is both necessary and desirable, but it cannot be achieved until we as a people are able to love our own humanity as much as we love the dream of a free world.

The women artists discussed in this book created women characters who lead us through the narrow space of race and the dark enclosure of sex to a brighter day for black women in particular and all people in general. I bring their marvelous creations together in one place as a "little thing" to honor the "memory and inspiration" of real black women in white America.

2

A HISTORICAL OVERVIEW
BLACK WOMEN IN WHITE AMERICA, 1946–1976

I
am a black woman
tall as a cypress
strong
beyond all definition still
defying place
and time
and circumstance
  assailed
    impervious
indestructible

Look
  on me and be
renewed.

—Mari Evans, 1964

World War II forced the American tradition of sexual and racial discrimination to give way to the crisis of national survival. As soon as the war was in progress, Robert Brisbane explains, it was clear that victory was dependent on the country's willingness to make concessions to its minority groups. For blacks, these concessions were reflected dramatically in unprecedented gains in the labor market. Although early in the war years there was resistance to the employment of blacks in war factories, by the middle of the war, under pressure from the Fair Employment Practices Commission and other government agencies, blacks were visible in defense plants throughout the nation. In significant numbers they were employed in aircraft, shipping, iron, steel, and other industries that thrived in the wartime economy. Employment gains were not limited to defense plants, however. Blacks worked in various war-service agencies, in hospitals, in retail stores, and in civil service positions, doubling their number in the last category.[1]

The need for labor had an equally weighty impact on employment patterns for women. Indeed, there was such a drastic change in the nation's attitude toward "woman's place" that the "war marked a watershed in the history of women at work, and, temporarily at least, caused a greater change in woman's economic status than half a century of feminist rhetoric and agitation had been able to achieve."[2] Six million female workers were employed during the war years in jobs that had previously been identified as too strenuous for the "weaker sex"—hard labor in munitions plants, aircraft factories, the auto and steel industries, and others that met the needs of the war. "In eight of ten war-impacted cities surveyed by the Women's Bureau, the number of women workers doubled from 1940 to 1945."[3] Over a period of fourteen months, women made up 80 percent of new workers, and in many cities the number of women employed in factories by 1944 exceeded the number of women in the entire labor force in 1940.

Black women were well represented in these statistics, a major departure from the American tradition that had included them in the burdens of race and sex, but excluded them from gains extended to black men and white women. Involvement in the labor market, however, was not a new experience for black women. They were "twice as likely to be employed as [white women] but their economic horizons were severely limited. Over seventy percent worked as domestics in white private homes, and another twenty percent toiled in the fields, picking crops and hoeing gardens on small farms."[4]

During the war, however, more than 400,000 black women left their jobs as domestics to work alongside white women in defense plants throughout the nation. "Rosie the Riveter," the national symbol of female strength and patriotism, though depicted in the media as a white woman, was often black. As the percentage of black females who worked as domestics dropped from 72 to 48, and the percentage who labored on farms dropped from 20 to 7, the percentage of black women who worked outside those areas increased from 7.2 to 18.6.[5] Sociologist Delores Aldridge writes that the gains were not confined to factories. The number of "black women employed in clerical and sales positions quadrupled . . . and the number of black women in federal service positions also increased significantly."[6] No longer confined to domestic and farm work, black women experienced during the war what perhaps amounted to "economic liberation."[7]

These gains for blacks and for women did not mean that racial and sexual discrimination disappeared from American life. When discrimination could be practiced without directly jeopardizing America's success in the war, it was practiced. Many of the jobs held by blacks in war factories, for example, were the traditional ones of janitor and scrubwoman; while for white women, clerical and sales jobs remained high on the list of possibilities. Moreover, as John Hope Franklin documents, there were major differentials between the wages paid to whites and the wages paid to blacks. William Chafe, writing of the plight of women, makes the same point: men were paid more than women for the same jobs. And as visible as the two groups became in the labor market, they were not seen in upper-management positions.[8] They were the workers, not the policymakers. Since black women belonged to both minority groups, they were at the bottom of the labor hierarchy and they earned the least.

This high visibility of women in the labor market—for white women a new experience and for black women an old experience slightly upgraded—did not create a raised sexual consciousness or new cultural definitions of "woman's place." White women worked because war needs left vacuums in the manpower pool that, out of patriotism, they had to fill. And they worked because they realized, as did their husbands, that one income was hardly sufficient for a comfortable standard of living. After the war, when white female workers "were asked why they wished to continue on the job, a total of 84 percent cited 'economic need,' or the desire to assist with family support. Only 8 percent, in contrast, gave the need for self-expression or dissatisfaction with the traditional role of women in the home."⁹ This new reason for white female participation in the labor market was the old reason that had always forced black women into the role of "helpmate" for their struggling families. In one sense, then, the war and subsequent inflationary trends narrowed the gap between the reality of black women and the reality of white women. But the gap remained cavernous because black women, even in their so-called economic liberation, were discriminated against in the labor market, both in positions offered and in salaries earned. Barriers that had held them back for centuries had been only momentarily shaken and had then fallen back in place. It is not surprising, therefore, that at the end of the war "black women were the first to be fired . . . and through economic need were forced back into domestic and other service jobs."¹⁰

The late forties was a period of well-considered and carefully executed plans for racial progress as gains made during the war intensified the efforts of blacks to achieve complete integration in the nation. In fact, as Robert Brisbane documents, there was an aggressive black posture toward change even during the war. Black organizations, notably the National Association for the Advancement of Colored People (NAACP), pushed for desegregation in the armed forces, in employment, in housing, and in education. As early as 1946 President Harry Truman appointed a committee of nationally known black and white leaders (the majority of them men) to study ways to improve the status of blacks in the nation; and in 1948 he endorsed the committee's report, *To Secure These Rights*, and engineered its inclusions in the Democratic party platform of that year.¹¹

Acting often wthout support from established organizations, black women and men took their case for freedom to the nation. Though they did not brandish the Black Power fist that would become popular in the late sixties, they were no less insistent on power and change. In 1946 a black woman named Irene Morgan challenged segregation in interstate travel when she refused to move to the back of a bus on a trip from Gloucester County, Virginia, to Baltimore. Her challenge led to the Supreme Court decision of *Morgan* vs. *Virginia* in June 1946, which prohibited segregation in interstate bus travel. A year later the Congress of

Racial Equality (CORE) tested the strength of the decision by sending the first group of "freedom riders" in history into the South. In 1946 the Supreme Court ruled that "a state must provide legal education for blacks at the same time it is offered to whites." This ruling, like CORE's famous freedom rides, resulted from the courage of a black woman, Ada Sipuel, who in 1946 filed to attend the University of Oklahoma Law School.[12] There were other major rulings in the late forties, but what is often missed in the recitation of these landmark cases is the presence of black women as "movers and shakers."

While blacks and liberal whites sought to disrobe Jim Crow, Jane Crow was bedecked in pearls. For several reasons the pearls could not be removed, or even dulled in their shine. First of all, as discussed earlier, there had been no major challenge to sexual discrimination during the eventful years of "accomplishment" for women during the war. Second, the resurgence of racism after the war, as evidenced in race riots and demonstrations, minimized the significance of the woman's question for black Americans—indeed, for the entire nation. Any discussion of the woman's question by black women could easily have been perceived as "bitching" during a time when black men, still in uniform, were being brutally attacked in cities across the nation and, when not attacked, discriminated against in housing, employment, and public accommodations. And third, the exigencies of life in northern ghettoes pushed the issue of sexual liberation into a holding pattern.

Lured by jobs in the war industry, blacks left small southern farms to migrate in sizable numbers to cities in the South and, most especially, in the North, increasing the size and aggravating the problems of the "ghettos" that had come into existence at the turn of the century. Overcrowding, exploitation, poverty, crime, and violence were pervasive and unchecked in black communities in Chicago, Detroit, Cleveland, Newark, Philadelphia, and, of course, Harlem. But the existence of these large black communities gave blacks more political power than they had known since Reconstruction. In several northern cities they held the balance of power in close elections. Their votes were sought by politicians and, recognizing this, blacks established their own minimachines and made demands on the white political machines. It did not seem to matter to black women, who carried more than their share of burdens in the ghetto,[13] that black political leaders and black newly elected officials were male. Like the men of their race, they believed that political success for a few blacks would aid in changing the plight of all blacks.

The wartime gains for women were short-lived, for "almost immediately after the war ended, a concerted campaign developed among political leaders, the media and employers to persuade women to return to the home."[14] In 1947, the same year that President Truman set up the Civil Rights Commission, a special issue of *Life*, then a barometer of national opinion, called woman's confusion about her role a national crisis. "There was no middle ground, no way to combine marriage and a career, a job and motherhood," the article posited. "A woman became either a well-adjusted homemaker or a feminist neurotic."[15]

Just as white women such as Phyllis Schlafly and Anita Bryant would oppose women's liberation in the seventies, so did white women oppose new roles for women in the fifties. Helene Deutsch, a Freudian psychoanalyst, argued that women and men are "polar opposites whose spheres . . . ordained them to remain permanently separate."[16] Her work had a greater impact on the nation than did the profound scholarship and insight of Simone de Beauvoir's brilliant *The Second Sex* (1953), which was poorly received by critics and by the reading public. Two well-known critics "called the work paranoic," and Margaret Mead, though impressed with "its basic soundness, expressed annoyance with de Beauvoir's denigration of the role of mother."[17] Everywhere the signs were clear and the bell's tolling was resonant. The "feminine mystique," about which Betty Friedan would later write, muted the cry for women's liberation for more than a decade.

The postwar climate was symbolized by Adlai Stevenson's remarks to white women college graduates. This pillar of the liberal establishment advised young women that their task was to push their men into the seat of success by serving effectively in the "humble role of housewife."[18] Moreover, the issue of women's rights was not one to which black women were likely to be attracted. They were aware of the racism that had always marked feminist movements in America. Rosalyn Terborg-Penn writes that from 1830 to 1920, key years in the history of feminism, racism was an unhealing sore on the suffrage and feminist movements. "Discrimination against Afro-American women reformers was the rule," she emphasizes, "rather than the exception. . . ." Women of the stature of Frances Harper, Mary Church Terrell, Sarah Remond, Ida Wells-Barnette, and Josephine Pierre Ruffin spoke candidly of their experiences with racist white women reformers, even the legendary Susan B. Anthony, who discriminated against black male and female reformers because it was expedient to put aside racial equality in order to win the support of southern white women.[19] In the late forties and early fifties this attitude, printed indelibly on the psyches of black women, put white women and black women into separate and warring camps. Finally, the aggressive demands of blacks for racial equality militated against the creation of any large-scale organization involving black women and white women as equal partners in a common struggle.

A cursory examination of images of black women in the media during the late forties and early fifties furnishes another explanation for black women's muted interest in women's rights. For when we look beyond employment statistics and political gains to media images, we realize that World War II only scratched the surface of this nation's racist and sexist psyche. This was the era of the "scatterbrained maid or superstitious comic servant"[20] who added color and humor to insipid films about plastic people in plastic situations. This was the era when white America's fascination with the myth of Aunt Jemima made Hattie McDaniel and Butterfly McQueen[21] archetypal black domestics loved by white and black audiences alike. The Aunt Jemima myth had its origin in the South's need to create "passive, long-suffering and submissive" black mammies whose devotion would prove that slavery was not all bad. The myth persists in spite of the fact that, as historians have documented, the typical black mammy was a "young and attached" woman rather than "an aged mammy who remained in her antebellum place out of loyalty to a white family or because whites had a special concern for such women."[22] But overweight, submissive, devoted, older black domestics were the norm in American films of the era, such as *Song of the South* (1946) and *Pinky* (1946).

In the fifties Sidney Poitier began what later became a monopoly on nonstereotypic roles for blacks in the movies. In *No Way Out* (1950) he was a medical intern. In *Blackboard Jungle* (1952) he was a schoolteacher. For black women, however, the old stereotypes held on. In *Imitation of Life* (1951) a black woman appeared as the overweight, apron-wearing, self-sacrificing mother of a tragic mulatto. *Show Boat* (1951) also had its tragic mulatto, but the film was best known as a musical extravaganza that idealized the Old South: William Warfield sang "Old Man River," and black women in long skirts and red bandannas swayed, sang, and served white people. To the traditional images of Aunt Jemima and the tragic mulatto, Hollywood added the image of the black woman of sensuality and questionable morals. *Carmen Jones* (1954) and *Porgy and Bess* (1954) were laudable attempts to depict with sensitivity the complexity of black life, but both were variations on the old theme of the juice being sweeter when the berry is blacker.

It was in the fifties that "television became the most popular new form of entertainment. Whereas in 1947 there were 10,000 television sets in American homes, ten years later the figure was 40 million. Television had such a major impact on the 'leisure-time habits' of people in this nation that, in 1954, the 'TV dinner' was invented."[23] The effect for blacks was that larger numbers of Americans were indoctrinated with the old images on a regular basis. It was a television series, *Amos 'n Andy*, that presented the most negative and comical images of blacks. The black man in the series is a head-scratching, shiftless, and henpecked husband whose behavior is understandable because his wife is a "Sapphire." "Loud-mouthed, strong-willed, and practical," she makes a fool of her irresponsible and simple-minded husband. Barbara Christian writes:

> Sapphire's most salient quality is her ability to
> make black men look like fools, partly because
> she is unfeminine, that is, strong and independent, and partly because she is, by nature, emasculating. Although similar to the mammy, Sap-

phire is not so much maternal toward white folks
as she is unfeminine in relation to black men. To
them, she is, cold, hard and evil.[24]

Bell Hooks writes that "Sapphire's shrewish personality was
used primarily to create sympathy in viewers for the black male
lot" and in the present day "is projected onto any black woman
who overtly expresses bitterness, anger and rage against her
lot." Indeed, it is such a dominant image, Hook writes, that it has
caused many black women "to repress these feelings for fear of
being regarded as shrewish Sapphires."[25]

Given these pervasive negative images of black women, a national black agenda that ignored the reality of sexism, and
American preference for the "feminine mystique," it is not surprising that Frances Harper's nineteenth-century assessment of
the respective importance of race and sex in the reality of black
women of that day was equally applicable in the late 1940s and
early 1950s. When it came to choosing between sex and race, she
said, "the lesser question of sex [had to] go."[26]

It "had to go" in the fifties for yet other reasons. The outbreak
of the Korean War in 1950 fashioned new priorities for the nation,
but, more important, the acceleration of court cases, demonstrations, and racial violence heightened the black community's commitment to change. Thus when we study the historic Civil Rights
Movement of the sixties and the Black Power Movement of the
seventies, we must begin with a careful examination of the fifties.

In 1950 Ralph Bunche became the first black American to win
the Nobel Peace Prize, and a year later Mary Church Terrell took
her place in history alongside other black women activists when
she won a case against segregation in restaurants in the nation's
capital. In 1951 the worst northern race riot since the infamous
one of 1919 took place in Cicero, Illinois, when a black family
attempted to move into an all-white neighborhood; and a year
later, in 1952, racist bombings increased significantly in the
South. In 1954 the landmark Supreme Court decision in *Brown*
vs. *Board of Education* outlawed "separate but equal" educational facilities, thereby overruling the Court's earlier decision in
Plessy vs. *Ferguson* (1896); and in that same year, with the death
of Terrell, the nation lost one of its most valiant and persistent

black women reformers. In 1955 a wave of lynchings swept the South after the brutal murder of Emmett Till; and in that same year Mary McLeod Bethune, a creative black woman educator and shrewd political leader, died in Daytona Beach, Florida. It was also in 1955 that Rosa Parks, a black seamstress in Montgomery, Alabama, refused to give up her seat at the front of a city bus.[27] Her courage was the seed of the Montgomery Bus Boycott, which catapulted Dr. Martin Luther King, Jr., into national prominence.

By the beginning of the sixties the Montgomery Movement had given birth to a nationwide Civil Rights Movement that would have far-reaching effects on blacks and women in this nation. In 1960 four students "sat in" at a segregated lunch counter in Greensboro, North Carolina. After that first sit-in, others followed, and soon there were wade-ins, kneel-ins, and freedom rides—successful nonviolent protests against segregation all across the South. On May 6, 1965, with the signing of the Voting Rights Act, the hopes of the Movement for a new society were bolstered. Blacks and whites, committed to the philosophy of nonviolence eloquently articulated by King, came together for a common cause in greater numbers than at any other period in history. Students, Hollywood and Broadway stars, ministers, musicians, Ivy League professors, and professional athletes gave their time, talent, and, in some instances, their lives to the realization of the dream King immortalized in his "I Have a Dream" speech, delivered at the March on Washington in August 1963.

It was an exciting decade characterized by visibility for black male leaders: Andrew Hatcher, Robert Weaver, James Pearson, Thurgood Marshall, Edward Brook, Leroy Johnson, Carl Rowan, and Walter Washington, to name only a few. They took their places in history as the first blacks in various offices or positions. Black male leaders were also impressively visible in the Movement. The roll call included Julian Bond, Eldridge Cleaver and Huey Newton, Elijah Muhammad and Malcolm X, Stokely Carmichael and H. Rap Brown, Wyatt T. Walker, Ralph David Abernathy, Jesse Jackson, Floyd McKissick, and, of course, Dr. Martin Luther King, who received the Nobel Peace Prize on December 10, 1964. To this list we can add the names of Constance Baker Motley, only the second black woman in history to be appointed a federal judge, and Shirley Chisholm, the first black woman elected to Congress.

If the roll of black leaders was predominantly male, so, too, was the obituary page of American history in the sixties. In a wave of violence—lynchings, brutal beatings, and assassinations—black men were victims: Mack Parker, Medgar Evers, James Chaney, Malcolm X, and King. Violence also claimed the lives of activists Viola Liuzzo, Andrew Goodman, and Michael Schwerner, and President John F. Kennedy, all of whom were white. The "river of blood" that flooded the nation not only in assassinations but also in race riots (Watts in 1965, Cleveland in 1966, and Newark in 1967) explains why Dr. W. E. B. Dubois before his death on August 17, 1963, in Accra, Ghana, relinquished his citizenship in a nation that had ignored his wisdom of 1898:

> I still think today as yesterday that the color line is a great problem of this century. But today I see more clearly than yesterday that back of the problem of race and color lies a greater problem which both obscures and implements it: and that is the fact that so many civilized persons are willing to live in comfort even if the price of this is poverty, ignorance and disease of the majority of their fellowmen; that to maintain this privilege men have waged war until today war tends to become universal and continuous, and the excuse for this war continues largely to be color and race.[28]

The sixties was a decade as complex as it was violent. It was a time when students agitated for free speech on university campuses across the nation, forging into existence a new academe that would bear the scars of the students' rights movement well into the eighties. It was a time when revisionist sexologists such as William H. Masters and Virginia Johnson called the nation's attention to the need to redefine the sexuality of both men and women. And it was a time when the nation's image at home and abroad was marred by an irrational war in Southeast Asia.

These upheavals were, in large part, catalyzed by the Civil Rights Movement that had begun in 1955 with the courage of a black woman, but the Movement's agenda was all too simple to deal with "the problem of the color line." In retrospect, participants decry their emphasis on integration, which did little to alleviate the lot of the masses of black people in America and much to advance middle-class blacks, who would, in the seventies and eighties, become entrenched in the system. The ghetto, it seems, had become a permanent part of the reality of urban black people, and a culture of poverty limited the horizons of blacks on small farms. "Almost four out of ten . . . black families were living in poverty in 1965. This compares with a poverty ratio of about one out of ten in white families." Further, poverty was more likely in black families headed by women. "In 1965, sixty-two percent of the 1,132,000 [black] families headed by a woman were poor. Of the 3,860,000 white families headed by a woman [only] thirty percent were poor"[29]

In 1964, 32.5 percent of black female workers were employed in private households as domestics, compared to 4.9 percent of white women; and 23.4 percent were employed in service work (hotels and restaurants), compared to 14.5 percent of white women. Whereas 34.1 percent of white women were employed in clerical jobs, only 11.3 percent of black women were in this line of work.[30] After eight years of vigorous civil rights protests, the black thrust for integration and voting rights had not altered the position of black women in the labor market.

In the study "Family Roles, Occupational Statuses and Achievement Orientation among Black Women in the United States," Walter Allen corrects certain fallacies about black women workers. In 1964 black women, in spite of the era's myth of full employment, were "the most frequently unemployed and had the highest rates of unemployment *regardless* of occupational category." Also, black women earned significantly less than white men, white women, and black men in that order—again, Allen emphasizes, "*regardless* of occupation."[31] In the same year that the Civil Rights Movement began, the statistical profile of the black woman was that "she has a harder time finding a mate, remains single more often, bears more children, is in the labor market longer, has less education, earns less, is widowed earlier, and carries a heavier economic burden as a family head than her white sister."[32]

While it has been historically true that most (though not all) black women tended to identify all discrimination against them as racial in origin, in the late sixties more began to examine the burdens that were directly traceable to their sex. Ironically, they did so in Student Nonviolent Coordinating Committees (SNCC), the most militant of the civil rights organizations in the sixties. SNCC was a good starting place for black women's articulation of their dissatisfaction with sexual limitations because it was so blatantly sexist. Though black women were a majority of the membership, the leadership of the organization lay firmly in the hands of black males. One black worker complained that SNCC relegated women, and especially black women, to simple-minded, nonpolicymaking tasks. She wrote that "we run errands, lick stamps, mail letters and do the door-to-door."[33] SNCC's sexist attitudes toward its women members were manifested, but largely ignored by the nation, in the historic March on Washington in August 1963. All the speakers were men. All the delegates who met with the president were men. "This omission was deliberate," writes Pauli Murray. A group of women had asked for recognition in advance of the march, but their request had been denied because the male leaders of SNCC doubted that women could agree on a delegate—"a typical response from an entrenched power group."[34] A year later, in 1964, black women in SNCC staged a sit-in against sexist definitions of responsibilities. They made their point, but they had no intention of insisting on change.

Obviously, there were major problems in the relationship between black males and black females in SNCC, problems that could have generated a women's caucus in the organization, but no such caucus was formed because black women were not willing to jeopardize progress for their people by insisting on rights for their sex. Nor were they willing to embrace an issue that had always been dominated by white women, especially since relationships between black men and white women in the Movement had destroyed the sense of sisterhood black women and white thought they shared at the beginning of the struggle. It was only a short time before they came to admit that there were two problems: the "man" and the white woman. This was the subject of many poems written by black women during the sixties, one of the most poignant of which is Carolyn Rodgers' "I have Been Hungry":

> *and you white girl*
> *shall i call you sister now?*
> *can we share any secrets of sameness,*
> *any singularity of goals. . . .*
> *you, white girl with the head that*
> *perpetually tosses over-rated curls*
> *while i religiously toss my over-rated behind*
> *you white girl*
> *i am yet suspicious of/*
> *for deep inside of me*
> *there is the still belief that*
> *i am*
> *a road*
> *you would travel*
> *to my man.*

During the idyllic summer of 1964, white women risked their lives in the backwoods and small towns of Mississippi as they worked for the dream of a new South, but black women rarely let them forget their racial identity:

> *and how could you, any of you*
> *think that a few loud words and years*
> *could erase the tears*
> *blot out the nightmares and knowledge,*
> *smother the breeded mistrust*
> *and how could any of you think that i*
> *after being empty for so long*
> *could fill up on fancy fierce platitudes. . . .*[35]

Before they camped as a family of dreamers on Mississippi soil, black women and white women had already been positioned as antagonists by capitalism, which divides and therefore controls and conquers. The dream of the Movement and, no less, historic bitterness between black women and white women genuinely interested in bonding became catalysts for the white feminist movement of the sixties, just as the abolitionist movement was a catalyst for the suffrage movement of the nineteenth century.

When we discuss the cause-and-effect relationship between the Civil Rights Movement and the birth of the women's movement in the late sixties, we cannot ignore the historical animosity between black women and white women in SNCC, an animosity that had been temporarily mollified by belief in the dream and a genuine commitment to the creation of a humane society. Many black women activists were later to admit that their fires of anger burned silently even as they marched arm-in-arm with white female volunteers. They wanted bonding with white women activists, but as black women they had internalized the assumption that "being feminine meant being white."[36] Still, the difficulties of living in Mississippi during a summer of violence and fear made *any* definition of "feminine" seem irrelevant, for the experience was not, at least on the surface, about male-female relationships; it was a struggle that pulled together into one family poor black farmers (male and female) and college students (male and female, black and white). Black women and white women were equals—sisters—in the struggle. Even the old specter of the white woman's beauty as symbolized by straight hair was not a problem for black women activists, who walked tall and dignified in their Afros, a sign of self-acceptance and black pride.

The history of the synergistic relationship between race and sex, however, was stronger than the workers' commitment to the dream. There is never a time in this nation, Calvin Hernton explains, when the "sexualization of racism" can be ignored. It is a "unique phenomenon in the history of mankind," Hernton writes,

> an anomaly of the first order. In fact, there is a sexual involvement, at once real and vicarious, connecting white and black people in America that spans the history of this country from the era of slavery to the present, an involvement so immaculate and yet so perverse, so ethereal and

> yet so concrete, that *all race relations tend to be,*
> *however, subtle sex relations.* [italics added][37]

It was the "sexualization of racism" that made Mississippi during the summer of 1963 a veritable playground for many black men and many white women. As the black "buck" of phallic superiority and the white woman of beauty, femininity, and chastity played out their historic attraction for each other, black women were reminded that the nation *and* black men believed that "being feminine meant being white." They were participants in the freedom struggle and spectators of interracial "sex relations." Their pain was real, intense, and shattering—all the more so since black men and white women were coming together in the very region that had made black women mammies, mistresses, and breeders and white women "the center and circumference, diameter and periphery, sine, tangent, and sextant of all our affections."[38]

In the many articles and books published after the Civil Rights Movement was replaced by the Black Power Movement, black women wrote that they were angered by the menial assignments they were given and by the "extreme insensitivity" of white women, but their deepest anger was directed at the devaluation of black womanhood. This anger permeates Ruby Davis Smith Robinson's paper delivered at a SNCC conference, in which she attacked black men "for their failure to do justice to black women." The counterpart paper, written by two white women, Mary King and Casey Hayden, was one of the opening statements of the women's liberation movement.[39]

As white women were laying the foundations of a major women's movement, many black women were seeking security and an alternative to devaluation in organizations that idealized traditional definitions of "woman's place." In the Nation of Islam, Black Muslim women were required "to accept their men as 'first among equal' and in theory, at least, regard the man as the breadwinner and head of the family."[40] Bell Hooks, in an analysis of the devaluation of black women, discusses the ideology and rituals that made the Nation of Islam one of the darkest of enclosures for women members. Arguing that throughout history women have been viewed as evil, she sees the persistence of the idea of the purification of women in the Muslim requirement that they wrap their heads in cloth and cover their bodies in long skirts and dresses.[41]

The Republic of New Africa (RNA) went a step further—it required women literally to walk behind their men. Submission to black manhood, wrote founder Amiri Baraka, was a reflection of "the closeness, the completeness we are for each other, the expansion we provide for each other." "Expansion" was hardly what women experienced in RNA. Baraka preached that the salvation of the race could be realized if black men and black women together embraced "a value system that knows of no separation but only of the divine complement the black woman is for her man." He did not cloak in flattering rhetoric his belief that women should be men's helpmates rather than their own persons. His sexist arrogance, albeit in the interest of building a strong black nation, is unmistakable. He wrote:

> . . . we do not believe in the equality of men and women. We cannot understand what the devil and the devilishly influenced mean when they say equality for women. We could never be equals . . . nature has not provided thus. . . .[42]

Many black women were willing to walk behind their men because the women were hungry for the respect and attention they believed whole black men could or would give them. Also, they were sensitive to black men's hardships in the narrow space. But these were not the only reasons for their rejection of feminism. As Michele Wallace explains, "The most popular justification Black women had for not becoming feminists was their hatred of white women."[43] They were obviously caught in the historic dilemma of double jeopardy.[43] As females in a culture that placed white women on pedestals, they wanted a "crystal stair," a reality in which there were no "tacks" and "splinters, and boards torn up." As blacks, they wanted the movement for freedom to improve the lot of their people. Thus they brandished fists at white feminists and invoked the mercy of our ancestral gods for those of us who were feminists and therefore traitors to the race. They stroked the egos of black men, whose chauvinism they tolerated as a necessary display of manhood for the time being, and they accepted (and even advanced) the argument that black women would be free as blacks and as women only when black men were in full possession of their manhood. It was this kind of "liberation" for black women that made Don L. Lee's "BLACKWOMAN," one of the most popular poems of the Black Arts movement:

> *blackwoman*
> *is an*
> *in and out*
> *rightsideup*
> *action-image*
> *of her man........*
> *in other*
> *(blacker) words;*
> *she's together*
> *if*
> *he*
> *bes.*[44]

At the beginning of the seventies much of the rhetoric of the Civil Rights Movement had become tired, if not irrelevant to the building of "the nation." Stokely Carmichael's cry for "Black Power" had replaced the Movement's hymn "We Shall Overcome," and the glorious, media-supported image of blacks and whites working together in a nonviolent struggle gave way to the threatening image of blacks arming themselves and ousting "whitey" and "honky" from the Movement. In "Farewell to Liberals" Loren Miller wrote bitterly of the crisis within the Movement: Having brought the Movement to a position of power, white liberals received "a fond farewell with thanks for services rendered. . . ."[45] Charles Silberman, writing from a different perspective, contended that the break-up of the "friendship" was predictable. "Besides resenting their dependency [blacks] have never really trusted white allies; they have always had a nagging suspicion that . . . they could gain more . . . if they were only free to act on their own."[46] The decade of the seventies, then, like the decade following the abolitionist movement, was a period of tension between blacks and white liberals.

The seventies was also the decade that saw black mayors elected in cities such as Atlanta, Newark, Cleveland, Gary, and the District of Columbia. All the new black mayors were men. Some black women did enter national politics—Shirley Chisholm, Barbara Jordan, Patricia Harris, for instance—but they were a decidedly small minority. When black men were not going into politics, they were finding their way into upper-management positions in federal, state, and local programs. As one black woman scholar has observed, "When translated into actual opportunities . . . the Movement really meant rights for black men."[47]

The statistical profile of black women in the sixties, given earlier in this chapter, had not changed much. Black women were still paid lower salaries than white men, white women, and black men, in that order—"in the high paying positions . . . in the middle paying jobs, or the low paying jobs." Also, "there [was] proportionately more unemployment among black women than [among] black men . . . at each level of attainment."[48] Although black women had closed the gap between their educational attainments and those of white women, they were held to undergraduate degrees, whereas black men were encouraged to attain graduate and professional degrees. "Two surveys in all fields from all institutions in 1969 and 1970 show that black women hold roughly 21 percent of these degrees."[49] These statistics relate to middle-class black women, and they show that the "advantage" of a middle-class status did not alter black women's positions at the bottom of the wage ladder and the power structure. And for poor black women, who were the majority, the statistical profile Pauli Murray drew of them in the sixties was just as applicable in the seventies. They still had a "harder time finding a mate," stayed "single more often," received lower wages, bore more children, stayed "in the labor market longer," were "widowed earlier," and carried "a heavier economic burden as a family head than [their] white sister(s)."[50]

The seventies was also the decade when black women in greater numbers than ever before expressed explicitly and publicly an interest in their reality as women. *The Black Woman*, the first book in history that pulled together black women's views on black womanhood, was published at the beginning of the decade. Significantly, the anthology was edited by a black woman, Toni Cade Bambara. In her powerful preface to the book, addressed to black women, Bambara speaks of the need "to unify" and "to get basic with each other." This requires, she explains, that black women "find out what liberation for ourselves means, what work it entails, what benefits it will yield." It also requires that black women turn away from their traditional role of entertaining "the enemy: white people, whiteness, or racism; *men, maleness,* or *chauvinism* . . . [italics added]."[51]

Other important books or articles on black women followed. Gerda Lerner's *Black Women in White America: A Documentary History* was the first major work on black America to deal exclusively with women. Collected works edited by white feminists included landmark essays by black women on black women. Pauli Murray's "The Liberation of Black Women," for example, appeared in *Voices of the New Feminism* (1970), as did Shirley Chisholm's "Women Must Rebel." The 1973 issue of *Black Scholar* was devoted exclusively to the black woman and contained, among other major essays, provocative contributions by Barbara Sizemore and Mae King. The most controversial and courageous book on black women published in the 1970s was Michele Wallace's *Black Macho and the Myth of the Superwoman* (1978), which galvanized black women into discussing black men's sexism openly and fearlessly. It remains in a class by itself.

Other significant works written by black women in the seventies were *Beautiful, Also, Are the Souls of My Black Sisters* (1978) and *Sturdy Black Bridges* (1979), the former the first history of black women in America written by a black woman, and the latter the first study of black women as writers and as fictional subjects written from a positive perspective and edited by black women. Major black feminist scholars included Michele Wallace, Gloria Joseph, Toni Cade Bambara, Barbara Smith, Pat Scott, Gloria Hull, Beverly Guy-Sheftall, Bonnie Dill, Miriam Willis, Roseann Bell, and Bell Hooks.

Given such impressive scholarship on and by black women, it is not surprising that it was in the seventies that black women began to organize as feminists and not exclusively as blacks. As

186615

yet, no history has been written of the black feminist movement, for it is but an infant in the story of change in this nation. Therefore one can only speculate, but in an informed way, on the direct and indirect stimuli of the movement. Certainly high on the list of stimuli in this speculative investigation are the blatant sexism of SNCC, the impressive gains made by black women in the sixties, and the high visibility of the white feminist movement.

Less obvious stimuli are the courage, tenacity, and strength of several black women figures during the late sixties. Surely if black women could serve as role models for white women who were hampered by race, class, and culture in achieving total identification with black women, they could be real role models for black women. Angela Davis was such a model. She did not espouse the cause of the women's movement. Her involvement with the Black Panthers and her struggle on behalf of George Jackson left her no time for a cause that would not alter the plight of her brothers. However, she did see black women as a separate group within the race. Her courage in becoming a fugitive from America's capitalistic system of injustice afforded a renewing experience to black women, and her charge to her "sisters" to step forth as leaders and fighters is often seen as a call for black women to actualize themselves as persons:

> We, the black women of today, must accept the full weight of a legacy wrought in blood by our mothers in chains. As heirs to a tradition of supreme perseverance and heroic resistance, we must hasten to take our place, wherever our people are forging on towards freedom.[52]

Barbara Jordan, the brilliant and politically astute congresswoman from Texas, fearlessly pushed for truth in the Watergate proceedings until Richard Nixon was forced to resign. She did not speak about women's rights. Her behavior was her statement, and it carried a strong message about female independence, self-confidence, and assertiveness.

The statement of Shirley Chisholm, on the other hand, was explicit—perhaps too explicit for the times. A congresswoman from New York, she had the audacity as a black woman to run for

the presidency in 1972, and, in her campaign speeches, the bold-
ness to challenge the sexism of all men, regardless of color or
class. Before there were any formal organizations of black feminists, Shirley Chisholm exhorted black women to put aside their
loyalty to black men—a loyalty that demanded the postponement
of women's rights until black men had won "black rights"—and
recognize that racism and sexism are inseparable battles of equal
urgency: "I say there is no need to fight two battles; we should
fight [racism and sexism] at the same time."[53] She was the first
black woman to break publicly with the tradition of rating sexual
inequality as "the lesser question." In her autobiography, *Unbought and Unbossed* (1970), she wrote, "Of my two 'handicaps,'
being female put many more obstacles in my path than being
black."[54] It is worth noting here that the male members of the
Congressional Black Caucus were hostilely opposed to Re-
spresentative Chisholm's bid for the presidency.

A fourth stimulus for black feminism was Fannie Lou Hamer.
Uneducated, one of twenty children born into a Mississippi
sharecropper family, the mother of two, Hamer was a rare
woman. Race, sex, and class she pushed aside, asserting in
magnificent ways her personhood, her humanity. She was a
spokesman at the 1964 Democratic Party Convention and a candi-
date for Congress from her state. As an older woman in SNCC
and a leader in Sunflower County, she was not affected by the
sexism of the young black men in the organization. She was already a leader before she joined SNCC and was therefore useful
in pushing the Mississippi platform of the organization. She was
"not hung up on this thing about liberating myself from the black
man," however.[55] She was committed to working on behalf of
poor black farmers, regardless of their sex. She had great disdain
for white women, for they had abused black women domestics for
generations; and she had great disrespect for middle-class black
women because they disavowed any identity with lower-class
blacks.

Hamer's disclaimer of interest in women's rights aside, she
was one of the most liberated and forceful women leaders in the
sixties and seventies. She did not wait for black men to assign her
tasks in the struggle. On her own, like so many black women of
courage in history, she put her shoulders to the plow and pushed

where pushing was needed, refusing to take a back seat to anyone. She founded the Freedom Farm Cooperative, which grew from 40 acres of land in 1969 to 680 in 1971; which fed 1,500 people in 1969; and which owned 168 houses in 1971. Until her death, she was the head of the Coop. When Fannie Lou Hamer spoke of the kinds of roles black women should play in the racial struggle, she referred explicitly to leadership roles.

The growing body of major sociological studies of the black family, notable among them the work of Andrew Billingsley, should receive credit for the raised consciousness of black women in the seventies, for it provided significant scholarship on black women as wives, mothers, and workers. Daniel Patrick Moynihan's *The Negro Family: The Case for National Action* (1965) inadvertently created a new school of sociological thought. The countless articles and books written in opposition to Moynihan's thesis sounded the death knell for the theory of black female control and castration that had dominated sociology since the thirties. To be sure, some sociologists wrote, there *are* black matriarchs, for myth is never totally unrelated to truth. "Culture creates a mystique and real women fill its roles."[56] But the new studies of the black family went inside the myth and documented that the black matriarchy was not a deviant structure, did not explain the so-called deterioration of the black family, and did not reflect a penchant on the part of black women to castrate their men. Other studies disavowed the existence of a black matriarchy altogether and documented black women's powerlessness within the family, along with their response to burdens unique to their reality as wives and mothers.

And finally, the success of the white feminist movement contributed immeasurably to the formation of black feminist organizations. For if the sixties was the decade of black protest, the seventies was most assuredly the decade of women's liberation. The "feminine mystique" had been stripped of its apron, petticoat, pearls, and bra, and its mascara was conspicuously smeared. White women marched and petitioned, as black people had done in the sixties. They organized caucuses for the Equal Rights Amendment (ERA) in states across the nation, supported the right to abortion, agitated for a fuller understanding of rape, founded magazines, and wrote books on sexual oppression in America. History made room for "herstory."

The dialogue on women's issues was intense, full of energy and conflict, but often so abstract that critics of the movement called feminists Ivy League intellectuals who could not translate theory into concrete, realizable goals. Marxists, socialists, liberals, radicals, lesbians, or simply women activists—the groups were many, and their disagreements on priorities and perspectives resulted in brilliant books and articles that would guide the movement in the eighties to what Betty Friedan calls the "second stage." Friedan's own book *The Feminine Mystique* was popular among "laywomen"; the new books found an audience mainly among women scholars. They demonstrated that Friedan had raised only peripheral questions about sexual oppression in America and had failed to address head-on the issues that were at the core of a vision of a new society for all people, regardless of race or sex. Works by Zillah Eisenstein, Kate Millett, Shulamith Firestone, Susan Brownmiller, Sheila Rowbotham, and Adrienne Rich raised tougher questions for white women in the movement.

Still, herstory was essentially white. Many black feminists believed, as Bell Hooks writes, that "Every woman's movement in America from its earliest origin to the present day has been built on a racist foundation. . . ."[57] Angela Davis underscored the racism of the suffrage movement by printing in its entirety a letter to the *New York Times* from Elizabeth Cady Stanton, the preeminent suffragette:

> The representative women of the nation have done their uttermost for the last thirty years to secure freedom for the negro; and as long as he was the lowest in the scale of being, we were willing to press his claims; but now, as the celestial gate to civil rights is slowly moving on its hinges, it becomes a serious question whether we had better stand aside and see "Sambo" walk into the kingdom first.[58]

Such blatant racism was not present in the women's movement of the seventies, but white feminists, like nineteenth-century suffragettes, were "the representative women of the nation," and they were known to recite the "uttermost" they had done for blacks in the struggle for liberation. And they *had* struggled for black people in courageous ways, but black feminists were not impressed enough to ignore what they considered a tradition of racism in the women's movement. They insisted that white women own up to their racism, be held accountable for it, and exorcise it from their attitudes, platforms, and ideology. They did not accept Adrienne Rich's argument that charging white women with racism "impedes any real discussion of women's instrumentality in a system which oppresses all women and in which hatred of women is also embedded in myth, folklore, and language."[59] They would work toward bonding with white women only if white women dealt honestly with their conditioning as whites in a racist society. Bell Hooks's statement on this problem is particularly to the point:

> To black women the issue is not whether white women are more or less racist than white men, but that they are racist. If women committed to feminist revolution, be they black or white, are to achieve any understanding of (what Adrienne Rich calls) the "charged connections" between white women and black women, we must first be willing to examine woman's relationship to society, to race and to American culture as it is and not as we would ideally have it be. That means confronting the reality of white female racism.[60]

The case against white feminists was not helped by the fact that they owned the printing presses, that they had the "right" connections, that they were writing the books (and getting them published), and that they held positions of influence at white eastern universities. It did not matter that this edge, so to speak, was created by a racist system rather than by individual white feminists themselves. What mattered was their inability, or failure, to understand black women as women. What mattered, too, was the history of black women as devalued persons in the dark enclosure of sex and in the narrow space of race. Black women owned no printing presses, had no power to affect media images, had few "right" connections, and were in only a few rare instances in positions of power and influence in predominantly white eastern universities. Most black women were struggling with survival issues at historically black colleges and were so overextended by the workload at those institutions that they could not spare time for extensive research and scholarship. It is easy to understand why black feminists were reluctant to join a movement that was predominantly white in origin, leadership, attitudes, and ideology.

Moreover, black feminists could see little evidence that gains of the Civil Rights Movement and those of the women's movement had improved national understanding of black womanhood. Ironically, while white women were educating the nation on sexist images of women in the media, the media were thriving on negative images of black women. Some of the most popular shows during this period were ugly reminders that black women were still devalued in American society. In *Sanford and Son*, (Aunt Esther) and *The Flip Wilson Show* (Geraldine), the black woman was depicted as oppressive and disagreeable. In *Saturday Night Live* she turned up in various comical guises, impersonated by the token black *male* in the cast. In movies, black women were pitiful creatures hungering for the attention of a macho man *(Superfly)* or *(Cotton Comes to Harlem)* religious fanatics falling for transparently devious games played by men, and even sensuous women, powdered down, rouged, and/or nude. Melvin Van Peebles' *Sweet Sweetback*, a highly popular movie made during the sixties, used black women as minor characters without complexity and humanity, which was all the more painful since the film deals with a black man's obsessive desire for white women.

For all the reasons speculated on here (and many others as well), more than three hundred black women met in San Francisco in January 1973 and founded Black Women Organized for Action (BWOA). In December of that year four hundred black women founded the National Black Feminist Organization (NBFO) in New York. Both organizations acknowledged the relevance of many of the issues addressed by white feminists, but they rejected the idea that their reality was the same as that of white women. Black women live

> in structural opposition with a dominant racial
> and a dominant sexual group. In each subordi-

nate group they share potential common interests with group co-members, black men on the
one hand and white women on the other. Ironically, each of these is a member of the dominant
group: black men as men, white women as
whites.[61]

Their goals, however, were familiar. They would work in various
ways and with different groups to eradicate racial, sexual, and
class oppression. But they were emphatic about their identity as
a group separate from white feminists. In "A Black Feminist's
Search for Sisterhood," Michele Wallace expresses this idea in a
compact and poignant definition of black feminists.

We exist as women who are Black who are feminists, each stranded for the moment, working
independently because there is not yet an environment in this society remotely congenial to our
struggle—because being on the bottom, we
would have to do what no one else has done: we
would have to fight the world.[62]

Many black men were uncomfortable with both black feminist
organizations and the national emphasis on the rights of women.
Both were often perceived as evidence of a conspiracy against
black men, robbing them of jobs and positions as the nation began
to use black women to meet racial and sexual quotas at the same
time. They were also concerned that assertive black women
would exacerbate existing tensions between black men and black
women. Robert Staples, who in the sixties had argued convincingly against the theory of the black matriarchy and the emasculation of black men, seemed to contradict himself when he
cautioned black women against becoming feminists. "Any movement that augments sex-role antagonism extant in the black community," he wrote, "will only sow the seed of disunity and hinder
the liberation struggle."[63] For feminists, this advice was only half
a step from Imamu Baraka's declaration in *Muanamke Mwanan-
chi* that women were created to be submissive to men. Or it

seemed an intellectual expression of the exploitation of women's bodies that was rampant in SNCC in the sixties: "the only position for women in SNCC is prone."[64] Black feminists countered that they had been in the "prone" position throughout history and they intended now to stand tall and give birth to themselves as black persons.

They believed that, unlike white feminists, they would be able "to transcend and eradicate labels."[65] The composition of the groups who founded BWOA and NBFO supports this claim. They included domestics, operatives, welfare mothers, unemployed women, businesswomen, college teachers, scholars, and politicians. Because of the social constraints on black women in the South, most of the women were from the urban North. Frances Beal applauds this cross-section of classes and occupations, but she sees both organizations as black versions of the National Organization of Women (NOW). "They never raise the question of the basic exploitative nature of the capitalist system," she writes.[66] Although they see the interrelationship of race, sex, and class, they essentially want "their piece of the pie" as women. The court is still out on BWOA and NBFO, and on white organizations as well, since fundamental changes in the workings of a system take more than a decade to accomplish.

Once black feminists were organized, sexism and the black man and sexual politics in the black experience were no longer verboten topics. Women discussed them openly, and often with anger, at conferences, in college classrooms, and in their writings. With the exception of Shirley Chisholm's comments in speeches made in 1971, Barbara Sizemore's "Sexism and the Black Male" was the first statement on a problem that had been hidden under the debris of racism and poverty. Black women, especially poor black women, Sizemore writes, have suffered greatly in the black community because black men have been insensitive to them as persons. Having "embraced the values held by" the white male culture of America, black men "have been socialized into male superiority."[67]

Poetry written by black women reflected this change in attitudes toward black men's sexism. In the sixties, when sexism was not a talked-about subject among black people, "brothers" were beautiful men wearing Afros, walking "baaad" and "taking care of business." They were a new breed of black men with their "heads on right." Nikki Giovanni wrote in 1968:

> *I wants say just gotta say something*
> *'bout those beautiful beautiful outasight*
> *black men*
> *with they afros*
> *walking down the street*
> *is the same ol danger*
> *but a brand new pleasure.*[68]

In the seventies the Afros could not conceal black men's sexism. Even in their beauty, black men had to be held accountable for their treatment of black women. Alice Walker wrote the cutting-sharp compact poem "He Said Come":

> *He said come*
> *Let me exploit you;*
> *Somebody must do it*
> *And wouldn't you*
> *Prefer a brother?*[69]

To indict black men for a history of sexist behavior was one thing, to call them "the enemy" was quite another. Whereas some white women identified men as just that, black feminists moved the cannon of their battles away from black men. They did not make excuses for black men's sexism. Indeed, as mentioned earlier, they wanted to get the issue out in the open, clear the air, and move "with all deliberate speed" to their liberation. However, they consistently viewed black men as their *brothers*, with whom they shared a collective history of racial oppression and with whom they would enjoy whatever victories were achieved by the feminist movement. Any rights they gained as women, they pledged would "not be made at the expense of black men."[70]

Michele Wallace, however, does not take this position in *Black Macho and the Myth of the Superwoman*. Like Ntzoke Shange's play *For Colored Girls*, Wallace's exposé of black men's sexism plunged deep into the troubled waters of black male-female relationships. She is angry at black men and refuses to suppress her anger because of the collective history of oppression black women share with black men. She attacks "the narcissistic macho of the Black Movement," who expected a "big Afro, a rifle, and a penis in good working order" to be all the weapons he needed "to lick the white man's world. . . ."[71] She writes with disdain of the black man who

> has made himself a living testament to the white man's failure. He must continue to suffer, to be brutalized, and to brutalize his peers until whites are able to become the better people that will be required to deliver him from his condition. He has become a martyr . . . not because of the dependency inflicted upon him in slavery, but because his black perspective, like the white perspective, supported the notion that manhood is more valuable than anything else.[72]

The poor black man caught mercilessly in the narrow space of race, where brutality and dehumanization are rampant, is "implicated in this as well. Yes, forces conspire against him," Wallace writes, "but he *allows* life to happen to him. . . ." It would be unfair to Wallace's scholarship and her fine writing to suggest that she does not place sexism within the larger context of a capitalist society. She does, but that is not the focus of her book. She is not speaking to white America about its sins. She is speaking to black men about their sexism, which pours salt into the open wounds that racism cuts into the souls of black women. She writes with honesty and courage, capturing the pain black women share with one another in small groups or many in the privacy of their thoughts. She writes with a sense of urgency for change.

> Do we like what he has done? Are we satisfied to ride the tide of the changing interpretations of black manhood? Can it sustain us and the nearly fifty percent of black children who depend upon us? Can we afford to sit by and allow *him* to orchestrate *our* future?[73]

Whether black women spoke out in rage against black men or in rage against a racist system that victimizes both black men and black women, they spoke as feminists who would never embrace darkness again. They were not speaking as a minority among black women, for "black women have been stronger supporters of the idea of women's liberation than white women," a fact not commonly known. A 1972 Louis Harris poll for Virginia Slims showed blacks outscoring whites 62 to 45 percent in support of efforts to change women's status and 67 to 35 percent in sympathy with women's liberation groups." Black women have been affected in fundamental ways by "a constellation of social and economic factors" that forecast "a transformation of woman's 'place.'"[74] The Department of Labor predicts that in the year 1990 women will marry at a later age, will have fewer children, will be more involved in careers outside the home, and will support, in various ways, the idea of sexual equality.[75] That these projections do not exclude black women is easily supported by the new images of women that fill the pages of black publications, even those as conservative as *Ebony Magazine.*

Looking back at our early involvement as black feminists in the women's movement, we should question our priorities, just as we questioned our priorities in the freedom movement. In the latter movement, we gave too much attention to integrating black people into situations and places that excluded the masses of working-class blacks. In the women's movement we placed too much emphasis on making speeches to white feminists about their racism. Although we never removed "black" from our identity as feminists, we inadvertently neglected our communities, institutions, and organizations. There *were* projects and activities that addressed the immediate needs of working-class black women, but we spent too much of our energy stating our case for and against white feminists. Instead of working to reform the agendas of NAACP and the Southern Christian Leadership Conference (SCLC), to name but two black organizations, we struggled to make the agendas of white feminist groups reflect our unique reality and our special needs. Instead of working to strengthen the College Language Association (CLA), which for decades was the only professional organization that recognized us as legitimate scholars, we rushed to the Modern Language Association

(MLA) because the once-closed door had been left slightly ajar. Instead of pushing black magazines to create more space for our point of view, we held *MS.* close to our bosoms, only to be disenchanted a decade later with its slick, commercial, moderate, and white face. Instead of founding a printing press (where would we find the funds?), we were dependent on the Feminist Press for a minuscule number of black women's books annually. Instead of organizing conventions accessible to the black community, we organized black caucuses at annual conventions supported by the power, influence, and capital of white feminists. Instead of achieving a bonding with white feminists, some of us became highly respected and admired tokens in what was essentially a white movement in complexion, if not always in ideology or attitude. Most regrettable of all, we black feminists devoted more time and energy to charging white feminists with racism than we did to educating black women and black men on the need for a new struggle which would challenge race, sex, and class oppression. The result of all these choices of emphasis was that we became known by name, works, and ideas mainly in the white community and only rarely in the black community.

There are several reasons why we did not communicate as well as we should have with other black women. The challenge was a difficult one. As black women in the Combahee Collective explain:

> The material conditions of most Black women
> would hardly lead them to upset both economic
> and sexual arrangements that seem to represent
> some stability in their lives. Many black women
> have a good understanding of both sexism and
> racism, but because of the everyday constric-
> tions of their lives cannot risk struggling against
> them both.[76]

Then, too, because most black feminists do not live in the South, and also because some feminist organizations added freedom for lesbians to their platforms, the larger black community greeted us with fear, disapproval, or suspicion. Finally, we had to make an effort to communicate with white feminists, for as believers in the eradication of racial, sexual, and class oppression, we could not be true to our vision of a new society if we did not address racism in the women's movement—if we did not seek bonding with white women just as blacks in the Civil Rights Movement sought bonding with white liberals. But we were naive to expect the small house to be totally different from the mansion in which it was cloistered. If one of the most difficult challenges facing white feminists in the early seventies was establishing their credibility with black women, one of the most difficult and important challenges facing black feminists in the decades ahead is building our credibility with the larger black community. We must go to the people where they are—even in sexist black institutions—or we will never experience true bonding with our own. If we cannot work with our own people, we have no *self*, no *identity*, and no *name* to take to bonding with other groups.

As we move toward the twenty-first century and what is now called the "second stage" of the women's movement, we must answer many questions about our priorities as black feminists during the decades of the sixties and seventies, questions that are raised by various groups in the black community. Are our organizations essentially black liberation organizations that have added dignity and self-actualization for women to an otherwise familiar agenda for change? What is our distinguishing philosophy of struggle, of love, of personhood, of blackness? If we say that our collective history of racial oppression makes it impossible for us to be liberated as women without the racial emancipation (and sexual as well) of black men, how do we relate to black men from our position as feminists? How do we demonstrate that we are not involved in a conspiracy against black men and, at the same time, stand firm on the need for major changes in black male-female relationships? How do we frontally attack sexism without making our liberation as women separate from a struggle for a new society in which all people, regardless of sex, are liberated? How can we convince the black community, on whose behalf we struggle, that we are not selfish women bent on getting our slice of the American pie? How can we keep conflict over homophobia from dominating our dialogue with one another? How do we find our way from white universities (where black women and black men are in the minority) to historically black colleges, where the black macho's peacock-spread dominance is virtually uncontested? If we do not reach black college coeds in these institutions, where do we expect to reach them? If bonding with white women is a goal, can we achieve this goal before we have learned to love ourselves as black women and found our place as feminists in the black community? When and how do we translate our ideology, now presented mainly in university settings and in books, into concrete goals the black community can understand and work to realize? When do we leave the printed word and take our struggle into the field, where people, regardless of race, sex, or class, are in need of liberation?

We have tilled the soil, planted the seeds, and in various ways are working toward a new harvest for black women as persons; we believe such a harvest will be instrumental in the creation of a humane society for all people. But as *black* feminists we face the dilemma that black women reformers faced in earlier decades—the harmonious blending of the struggle for racial freedom with that for sexual liberation.

In spite of my commitment to the goals of feminism, I believe that although sexual liberation has been our chant, racial freedom has been our historic song. It was so with our predecessors—Sojourner Truth, Anna Cooper, Frances Harper, Ida B. Wells-Barnett, Josephine Ruffin, and others. They were aware that race, class, and sex worked together to create a painful reality for black women, but the hardships of the race often claimed their energies. If it came to choosing between race and sex—between struggling for brighter horizons for black women or struggling for dignity and freedom for black people—they saw sex "as the lesser question."

Everywhere the signs are evident that the American nation is turning away from the drive toward black equality and affirmative action. If racial polarization and racial violence intensify, we may be forced to adjust our agenda and, in the process, inadvertently choose sex "as the lesser question." This does not mean that black women, whether they are feminists or nonfeminists, will step back into darkness as women. Rather, some of us might become black women leaders like Sojourner Truth in the nineteenth century, who "wanted to tell . . . a mite about Woman's Rights . . . came out and said so," and then, committed to solving increased problems for the race, sat "to watch."[77]

The women whose novels I discuss wish to tell about black womanhood no less than Sojourner Truth "wanted to tell . . . about Woman's Rights." Since they wrote between 1946 and 1976, their telling was affected by the reality discussed in this historical overview, for fiction is often a "mirror of reality." But fiction does more than reflect reality; it particularizes it. It makes us familiar with imaginary counterparts of real black women, living in an imaginary world that is strikingly similar to the real world. We see the women functioning in relationships with other black people. We hear them breathe and sigh. We learn the rhythm of their walk and the melody of their song. We become familiar with the intangibles and the particulars of their lives, and thus do we come to know them as individuals. And as we discover them by name, need, and dreams; as we move with them through their victories and defeats; and as we hear them speaking for themselves in a clear voice, we are made more sensitive to the anomalous position of real black women in white America from 1946 to 1976.

THE HALO AND THE HARDSHIPS:

BLACK WOMEN AS MOTHERS AND SOMETIMES AS WIVES

"I didn't mean that, Mamma. I know you fed us and all. I was talkin' 'bout something else. Like. Like. Playin' with us. Did you ever, you know, play with us?"

. . .

"No time. They wasn't no time. Not none. Soon as I got one day done here comes a night. With you all coughin' and me watchin' so TB wouldn't take you off and if you was sleepin' quiet, I thought, O Lord, they dead and put my hand over your mouth to feel if the breath was comin' what you talkin' 'bout did I love you girl I stayed alive for you. . . ."

—Toni Morrison, Sula, *1973*

Because women are biologically capable of bearing children, it is assumed that all women look to motherhood for fulfillment in life. Nine months of discomfort, hours of painful labor, years of physical and emotional exhaustion—all this women endure and welcome because motherhood, they are told, more than any other experience they can have, makes them "beneficent, sacred, pure [and] . . . nourishing."[1] It is "a sacred calling"[2] that confers upon women an untarnishable halo. And once is not enough, for "what is more precious in all this wide world/than a baby—unless it is two?"[3]

The myth of the "sacred calling" was one of many sexist assumptions that Simone de Beauvoir challenged in *The Second Sex*

(1953). Writing of the cultural conditioning of women for an "inward, passive, and simply present existence,"[4] de Beauvoir posited that the institution of motherhood assists in the conditioning. She was well ahead of her times, for it was not until the late sixties that her ideas struck a responsive chord among women scholars. By the decade of the seventies, these ideas were dominant themes in many works of "herstory." Adrienne Rich's *Of Woman Born: Motherhood as Experience and Institution* (1970) is one of the most provocative of these works. It examines "cracks in [the cultural mask] of motherhood"[5] and makes mockery of the myth of the "sacred calling." Distinguishing between the "institution" of motherhood and the "experience," Rich argues that there are profound differences between what women are programmed to expect in motherhood and what they often experience. The institution of motherhood is a "system which recorded civilization has never actively challenged, and which has been so universal as to seem a law of nature."[6] The institution confers on men the titles of father, breadwinner, and protector, but it demands of them few of the responsibilities associated with parenting. The care of children and the home are assigned mainly to females—either mothers, grandmothers, neighborhood women, or female children. The work entailed is neither recognized nor recompensed, for "what a woman does as wife or mother in her own home is considered a labor of love, is not defined as work by the society, and is not done for direct wages."[7] This is as it should be, according to the myth, for why should one be paid for responding to one's "sacred calling"?

Moreover, the institution of motherhood paints a picture of "Sistine tranquillity" and creates images of mothers as "Madonnas who are . . . calm in their fulfillment."[8] When we look beyond these myths into the reality, we often find, Rich writes, the opposite of tranquillity and fulfillment. For in the experience of motherhood many women are besieged by supreme boredom, frequent depression, recurring rage, and an unsettling feeling that their intellectual powers are atrophying. The institution of motherhood is based on the sexist assumption that women have "maternal instinct rather than intelligence, selflessness rather than self-realization, relation to others rather than interest in self."[9] While the experience necessitates maternal care, understanding, and service to others, it does not quiet the stirrings in women's souls for self-actualization and for personal accomplishments outside the role of mother. Indeed, it often pushes women from the center of their dreams.

The theory of motherhood as both institution and experience is applicable to the reality of black women, but in the alembic of race, sex, and class, it is altered significantly and enmeshed in complexity: black women are "mammies," but they are no less imbued with "maternal instinct rather than intelligence, selflessness rather than self-realization, relation to others rather than interest in self."[10] Indeed, racist interpretations of the black experience, undergirded by sexist interpretations of motherhood, place the myth of the "sacred calling" in high relief in national images of black mothers. Just as "all black people can dance," so can all black women become superhuman mothers, not only for their own people, but for white people as well. More than white women, it is assumed, black women look to motherhood as their chief justification in life; and more than white women, they are physically and emotionally capable of handling the responsibilities associated with it.

In *Tomorrow's Tomorrow* (1971) Joyce Ladner writes that black women are "legendary figure(s) in American thought . . . , stronger than other women and certainly stronger than black men."[11] In many sociological studies of the black family, the legend seems to be a documented fact of life for a large majority of black women. Robert Staples argues this point in "The Myth of Black Matriarchy" when he states that giving birth to a child is "the high point" of a black woman's life and that "motherhood represents maturity and the fulfillment of one's function as a woman."[12] Daniel Thompson makes a similar assertion. In a sociological study of women in a New Orleans ghetto in the seventies, he found that his subjects, almost to a one, were self-sacrificing women who saw motherhood "as the only honorable, creative role in which they can reasonably hope to participate."[13] Because of the exigencies of black life in white America, black women have been forced to function heroically in the role, and their heroic functioning is often perceived as fulfillment.

In literature, as in sociology, the strength of the black mother is a dominant theme. Maya Angelou writes of a

> kind of strength that is most frightening in Black
> women. It's as if a steel rod runs right through
> their heads down to the feet. And I believe that
> we have to thank Black women . . . for keeping
> the Black family alive. . . .[14]

Andrea Benton Rushing, in a study of images of black mothers in poetry, refers repeatedly to a long tradition celebrating "poor and pious women whose outstanding characteristics are self-sacrifice, hard work, and fierce maternal love."[15] To this tradition belongs Langston Hughes's well-known "Mother to Son," written in the twenties and quoted at the beginning of this book. "Well, son, I'll tell you: Life for me ain't been no crystal stair." And to it also belongs Carolyn Rodgers' frequently anthologized "It is Deep," written in the seventies:

> . . . she pushed into my kitchen so she could
> open my refrigerator to see what I had to eat,
> and pressed fifty bills in my hand saying, "pay
> the talk bill and buy some food; you got folks
> who care about you. . . ."

> My mother, religious-negro, proud of having
> waded through a storm, is very obviously, a
> sturdy Black bridge I crossed over, on.[16]

Daryl Dance has done a similar study of the images of mothers in black American fiction, but she chooses to examine "two anti-thetical views" rather than a "tradition." Using mainly works by black male writers such as Richard Wright, James Baldwin, Leroi Jones, and John Oliver Killens, to name a few, Dance discusses the black mother who "brings death and destruction" and the black mother who "brings life and salvation." The former, whom Dance calls "Eve," was created by the racist culture of white America. She represses

> the spirit and vitality of her Black men, whether
> as a result of her blind acceptance of the dictates
> of white America or her subservience to them.

> [In the] emasculation of the Black male . . . the
> Black mother has been unwillingly forced into
> the role of accomplice.[17]

Having written of the black mother's "emasculation" of black
males, Dance immediately defends the mother's repressive spirit
by arguing that it is an expression of her maternal devotion and
love. In Dance's description of the black mother, whether she is
depicted as an "Eve" or as a "Madonna," we see similarities with
the self-sacrificing mother on whom civilization throughout history has bestowed a halo. A more truthful rendering of black
mothers, Dance writes, should balance their repressive spirit
with their magnitude of character. Speaking almost in monolithic
terms, she writes that the black mother

> is unquestionably a Madonna, both in the context
> of being a savior and in terms in giving birth and
> sustenance to positive growth and advancement
> among her people. It is she who has given birth
> to a new race; it is she who played a major role in
> bringing a race from slavery and submission to
> manhood. It is largely because of her that we can
> look back on the past with pride and look for-
> ward to the future with courage.[18]

When we turn our attention to black women's novels written
between 1946 and 1976, we find that the writers as a group pay
tribute to black mothers who are committed to their families and
who are remarkable for their strength, endurance, and achievement. There is no question that black women writers value
motherhood in the same way that real black women do—that is,
in Thompson's words, as "the only honorable creative role in
which they can reasonably hope to participate."[19] We will see this
point developed in the novels I discuss in this chapter. We will
also see that black women novelists are familiar with the legendary, self-sacrificing, monolithic black woman of history and
sociology.

Given these similarities, the contribution of black women
novelists to our understanding of black motherhood must lie else-

where. It lies unmistakably in the fine details of the portraits of mothers rather than in the captions that label them. Able to create fully developed characters in a way that poets are not, the novelists examine the tension that exists between the institution of motherhood and black women's experience of it, keeping central to their vision the interdependence of race, sex, and class. Imbued with an inside understanding of the tension, black women novelists are able, as their male counterparts are not, to distinguish between the mothers' feelings about the role and their functioning in it. They question whether devoted mothers are pleased with their realities, and they search for hidden explanations of the posture of an "Eve" as well as the posture of a "Madonna." In essence, they are concerned with black women not only as they function in the role of motherhood but also as they dream for themselves outside the role, reject the role, or carry it like an iron-heavy cross.

In this chapter we examine the reality of Mrs. Hill in Alice Walker's *Meridian* (1976), Pauline Breedlove in Toni Morrison's *The Bluest Eye* (1970), Eva Peace in Morrison's *Sula* (1973), and Mem Copeland in Walker's *The Third Life of Grange Copeland* (1970)—and use as corollary details of motherhood the realities of Maud Martha in Gwendolyn Brooks's *Maud Martha* (1953) and Henrietta Coffin in Louise Merriwether's *Daddy Was a Number Runner* (1970). The complexity of black motherhood becomes apparent as we listen to these women speak for themselves.

Mrs. Hill is perhaps the most articulate mother in this group, though she is the least studied. Part of the explanation lies in the fact that she is only a minor character, but the larger reason is that critics often fail to see the woman's vision in the work. Because *Meridian* is Alice Walker's journey into the South during the Civil Rights Movement of the sixties and, in many ways, an autobiographical statement of Walker's life as a child of the South and a participant in the Movement, critics see mainly the vision of race. It is the one novel, they write, that brilliantly uses the Movement as artistic subject matter and sensitively examines the triangle of the black woman, the black man, and the white woman. This interpretation is easily supported, for the major question raised in the novel is "the nature of social change and its relationship to the past and the future, a question that [was] at the crux of the Civil Rights Movement."[20] Walker answers the question by examining the relationship between the Movement and Meridian Hill's "quest for wholeness."[21] But early in the novel, she establishes that the major stimulus for Meridian's quest is not the Movement but rather the sense of emptiness that engulfs Mrs. Hill. Walker writes, "[Mrs. Hill] was not a woman who should have had children."[22]

As a single woman and a schoolteacher in a small Mississippi town, Mrs. Hill enjoys the "freedom of thinking out the possibilities of her life" (p. 39). It does not matter that these possibilities are rather limited: she can stay in this small town and teach, or she can move to another town and teach. They are her possibilities, and they represent her independence and her personhood. However, the patterns of the lives of the other women in the town raise unsettling questions for Mrs. Hill about her own life as a woman without a man or children. It is a selfish life, she feels, devoted entirely to sleeping late on the weekends, teaching during the week, and enjoying the material things her life as a professional woman makes possible. The lives of the other women, by contrast, are devoted to the daily tasks associated with the nurturing of children and husbands, and perhaps this devotion gives them that glow of excitement her life lacks. In the glances of other women and of men, Mrs. Hill believes she sees respect, but not approval, and the unalterable judgment that a woman does not have the right to live for herself. She is not eager to marry and has no genuine interest in rearing children, but she is conditioned to the cultural expectation that makes the role of mother a necessity in the life of a woman. Unable to live outside the culture, she marries. Within the space of a few years, she gives birth to Meridian.

The portrait of Mrs. Hill is a small masterpiece in American fiction, although it occupies only a few pages in the novel. It reveals how a woman's sacrifice of a life of independence leads to a life of frustration and emptiness. For once she experiences motherhood, Mrs. Hill realizes that the "mysterious inner life . . .

she had imagined gave women a secret joy, was simply a full knowledge of the fact that they were dead, living just enough for their children" (p. 41).

This view of motherhood is not an uncommon theme in black women's fiction, as subsequent discussions will show, but it often operates as a comment on the dynamics of race and class, not on sex. It is also present in sociological studies of real black mothers that are at odds with the stereotypic picture of black women basking in the joys of motherhood. When Camille Jeffers, for example, writes in *Living Poor* (1966) of the frustrations of mothers in a Washington, D.C., housing project, she documents the impact that racism and economics have on the women's aspirations both in the role and outside it.[23] Walker's statement is a departure from this thesis, however, for Mrs. Hill is not poor by the standards of her small Mississippi town. She is, in fact, a privileged woman in her training, speech, manner, and possession of "things" and leisure.

Comparative security, Walker suggests, does not save Mrs. Hill from the fate of her poorer sisters, for she is as limited as they are in what she can do with her life once she becomes a mother. Certain fundamentals about the institution cut across class lines:

> The primary role to which black women have been assigned and for which they are perpetually praised is also, paradoxically, the means by which they are cut off from life. Since, in principle, society places motherhood on a pedestal, while, in reality, it rejects individual mothers as human beings with needs and desires, mothers must . . . love their role as they are penalized for it. True for all mothers, this double-edged dilemma is heightened for black women. . . .[24]

The dilemma is a painful one for Mrs. Hill, who had known independence and the pleasure of "thinking out the possibilities of her life" (p. 39). As a mother, she has no independence. She may dream, but she cannot take time to actualize her dreams.

One of the several strengths of Walker's analysis of the frustrations of motherhood is the attention it gives to the physical fact of pregnancy. A woman's body changes during pregnancy, and with these changes comes the psychological conditioning that her value as a person depends on her ability to nurture the growing seed into life. For Mrs. Hill, however, pregnancy is but an uncomfortable prelude to a life of emptiness. As she carries Meridian, she feels that she is "distracted from who she is" (p. 40). Therefore, even before she experiences motherhood, she is convinced that "her personal life is over" (p. 39). Once she becomes a mother, she is enraged by the fact that she is not even allowed the right to resent that her life is over. In maternal chores she releases the woman's rage that society believes should be repressed:

> In the ironing of her children's clothes she expended all the energy she should have put into openly loving them. Her children were spotless wherever they went. In their stiff, almost inflexible garments, they were enclosed in the starch of her anger, and had to keep their distance to avoid providing the soggy wrinkles of contact that would cause distress. (p. 73)

Alice Walker's vision challenges the assumption that black women are a monolithic group with the same needs, the same strengths, the same weaknesses, and the same dreams. They are, instead, variegated flowers in a garden of humanity. Some of them have the personality makeup to handle well the experience of motherhood in a sexist culture. Others, like Mrs. Hill, need to be "unfettered by the needs of dependents, or the demands, requirements of a husband. Their spirit is of such fragility that the slightest impact on it [could] cause a shattering beyond restoration" (p. 39). For such women there should be alternatives to motherhood. Walker develops this point convincingly when she writes that Mrs. Hill has "no interest in children" (p. 41) and, having seen the darkness that the halo of motherhood conceals, no desire for the cultural accolades the role generates. In her opinion, motherhood is like "being buried alived, walled away from one's own life, brick by brick" (p. 41).

The image of "being buried alive" poignantly encapsulates Walker's thesis that throughout history black women have suffocated under layers of racist and sexist assumptions. For those who were artistic, the suffocation amounted to a life of "spiritual waste." Because there were no outlets for their talents, these women were often driven "insane." Mrs. Hill's realization that her talents are "unused and unwanted"[25] is like a barbed coil twisting within her. She receives limited pleasure from doing woman's arts and crafts, but she understands that what she has become is a distortion of what she wishes to be and could be. Walker writes that Mrs. Hill

> learned to make paper flowers and prayer pillows from tiny scraps of cloth, because she needed to feel something in her hands. (p. 41)

She is defiant toward the system that ties her to sexual definitions of labor—to "woman's" work:

> She never learned to cook well, she never learned to braid hair prettily or be in any other way creative in her home. She could have done so, if she had wanted to. (p. 41)

The central idea is made explicit: "creativity was in [Mrs. Hill], but it was refused expression" (p. 41).

Walker's vision of motherhood surpasses in depth and compassion the vision in Toni Morrison's *Sula* (1973), which critics of black women's fiction often call the most profound statement on the desire of imaginative black women to give birth to themselves and not to children. Sula is explicit about her life's goal: "I don't want to make somebody else. I want to make myself."[26] Whereas Mrs. Hill is "buried alive" by the burdens of motherhood, Sula escapes those burdens. But because her assessment of motherhood comes from first-hand experiences, Mrs. Hill makes a more convincing statement about the institution.

In the structure of *Meridian* an inside rendering of black motherhood is an integral part of Walker's aalysis of Meridian Hill, a participant in the Civil Rights Movement of the sixties, who gives up one child, aborts another, and eventually has her tubes tied. These acts are more clearly related to Walker's vision of black womanhood than to her vision of the Movement. Indeed, motherhood is at the center of the novel. As a Civil Rights activist,

> Meridian found, when she was not preoccupied with the Movement that her thoughts turned with regularity and necessity to her mother, on whose account she endured wave after wave of an almost primeval guilt. (p. 71)

Walker balances well these two emotional poles in Meridian's life—the Movement and black motherhood—but her strongest insight is how motherhood cuts black women off "from the possibilities of life and growth."[27] This knowledge is, in fact, the source of Meridian's guilt. When her mother asks with a vacant stare in her eyes, "Have you stolen anything?" (p. 41), Meridian understands that she has stolen her mother's life.

Theft of another woman's life is also a theme of Morrison's first novel, *The Bluest Eye* (1970), but in Morrison's work it is the mother who steals the daughter's life beyond rescue, beyond salvation. The novel is an example of the piercing art of Toni Morrison that cuts open the heart and accelerates its beating. Instead of the chant of anger and bitterness we hear in *Meridian*, there is Pauline Breedlove's hymn of resignation. She also resents that her personal life is over, but she has learned to cope with the emptiness by believing that her real life will begin in heaven, where God will reward her for carrying the crosses of wifehood and motherhood.

The novel is really the story of Pauline's daughter, Pecola, who covets blue eyes as a symbol of beauty and worth. This bold statement of theme does nothing to suggest the tragic complexity of Pecola's desire as it is worked out by Morrison. As Barbara Christian writes, "how Pecola comes to want blue eyes demands more than just telling Pecola's story." It demands telling the story of "three hundred years of unsuccessful interface between black and white culture in a small Ohio town."[28] It also demands telling the story of Pauline Breedlove's life as it is shaped not only by this interface but also by sexist assumptions about black women and by the class and racial restrictions that undergird those assumptions. As we cannot understand Meridian Hill's guilt without understanding Mrs. Hill's feeling that she has been "buried alive" by motherhood, neither can we understand Pecola's desire for blue eyes without understanding the equally insane fantasies of Pauline Breedlove.

The novel begins with Claudia McTeer, Pecola's friend, speaking of the tragedy of 1940–1941. In that year Pecola's baby by her father was born dead, and the marigolds failed to bloom. "The seeds shriveled up and died," Claudia says, "her baby too."[29] It is Claudia's voice as an adult woman remembering the past that guides us through the incidents in the small Ohio town that tell the full story of Pecola Breedlove—how she was raped by her father, how she desired blue eyes, and how she eventually plunged into insanity. In the telling of this story Morrison uses nature images as headings for the four chapters in the novel. Within each chapter she devotes sections to characters who in some way participated in Pecola's tragedy. Each section begins with familiar lines from Dick and Jane primers that were used in schools throughout the nation in the forties, but Morrison runs the familiar lines together to emphasize how far this all-American fantasy is from the reality of Pecola Breedlove. The section that introduces us to the Breedlove family distorts the Dick-and-Jane picture of a very pretty green-and-white house that has a red door:

HEREISTHEHOUSEITISGREENANDWHITEIT
HASAREDDOORITISVERYPRETTYITISVERY
PRETTY PRETTYPRETTY (p. 30)

Immediatelfy after these lines Morrison describes the "abandoned store" that is the home of the Breedlove family. Like its occupants, the house is "irritating and melancholy" (p. 30) and ugly. It is in this house that Pauline Breedlove fights with her husband, Cholly, beats her daughter, Pecola, and her son, Sammy, and sings her hymns of resignation.

Then Morrison travels back in time and place to Pauline Breedlove's childhood. As the ninth of eleven children in a poor Alabama sharecropper's family that lived seven miles from the nearest neighbor and the nearest road, Pauline Williams knows "only separateness and unworthiness."[30] Her parents, consumed as they are by the responsibilities of rearing a large family on meager earnings, have no time for parental embraces. It is Pauline's lot to be virtually ignored. Unable to understand her parents' lives, Pauline believes her predicament stems from a slight limp in her right foot, the result of a wound she suffered at the age of four. Slight as it is, this "deformity" becomes Pauline's crutch, explaining "many things that would have been incomprehensible" (p. 88).

Because her mother is forced by economics to work outside the home, Pauline is taken out of school to care for the younger children. Thus prematurely initiated into the reality that will define her in adulthood, Pauline performs interminable "woman's work" with efficiency. The quick rhythm of Morrison's description of this work heightens the reader's appreciation for the extent to which a woman's life is consumed by housework:

> She kept the fence in repair, pulling the pointed
> stakes erect, securing them with bits of wire,
> collected eggs, swept, cooked, washed, and
> minded the younger children. . . . (pp. 89–90)

When Pauline enters puberty at fifteen, the biological development produces a change in her desires and interests. Instead of the pleasure she once experienced in keeping house, she feels an unsettling emptiness. Something is missing, she thinks, and as she responds to her sexuality, she names that "something" in fantasies about "men and love and touching." In all of these fantasies she is a passive, solitary figure waiting for a man to complete her—to validate her existence. When Cholly Breedlove comes into her life, her deformity becomes an asset: "instead of ignoring [Pauline's] infirmity . . . he made it something special and endearing" (p. 90). His touch, his interest in her, his presence in her life, salve her damaged psyche. Pauline remembers her first meeting with Cholly as the day of her salvation:

"When I first seed Cholly, I want you to know it
was like all the bits of color from that time down
home when all us children went berry picking
after a funeral and I put some in the pocket of my
Sunday dress, and they mashed up and stained
my hips. My whole dress was messed with purple, and it never did wash out. . . . I could feel
that purple deep inside me. And that lemonade
Mama used to make when Pap come in out the
fields. It be cool and yellowish, with seeds floating near the bottom. And that streak of green
them june bugs made on the trees the night we
left from down home. All of them colors was in
me. Just sitting there. So when Cholly came and
tickled my foot, it was like them berries, that
lemonade, them streaks of green the june bugs
made all come together." (pp. 91–92).

Morrison's colorful and moist images of "down home" call our
attention to Pauline's alienation in the steel-mill town of Lorain,
Ohio, to which she and Cholly move shortly after their marriage.
Cholly is able to find work in the mills and, fully employed, he
should be able to keep the "bits of color" in Pauline's life vivid.
But there are no colors in the cold Midwest. Once she leaves
Alabama with its warm springs, its "berry picking," and its
"streak of green them june bugs made on the trees," Pauline
reexperiences the separateness she had known as a child. Cholly
begins to drink heavily. He leaves for work every day, and she
remains home in isolation. Their life together, once filled with
pleasure and companionship, is perforated with quarrels and
fights. She fights Cholly and calls on Jesus to "strike the bastard
down from his pea-knuckle of pride" before she kills him, but she
looks forward to the fights. They gave substance to the minutes
and hours otherwise dim and unrecalled. They relieved the
tiresomeness of poverty, gave grandeur to the dead rooms"
(p. 36).

In much the same way Cholly needs Pauline and their marriage
of conflict. When he was "four days old, his mother wrapped him
in two blankets and one newspaper and placed him on a junk heap

by the railroad" (p. 105). He was reared by Aunt Jimmy, a poor woman, who belonged to the group of women whom Morrison described as "edging into life from the back door. Becoming. Everybody in the world was in a position to give them orders" (pl 109). When she died, Cholly, only a teenager, went in search of his father, Samson Fuller. The experience is traumatic. Cholly's attempts to claim his father cannot compete with Samson Fuller's interest in a crap game.

> He bent down to toss a bill on the ground, and waited for a throw. When it was gone, he stood up and in a vexed and whiny voice shouted at Cholly, "Tell that bitch she get her money. Now, get the fuck outta my face!" (p. 123)

Morrison writes sympathetically of Cholly's boyhood: "Abandoned in a junk heap by his mother, rejected for a crap game by his father, there was nothing more to lose" (p. 126). But she writes most movingly of Cholly's psychological castration at the hands of white men who come upon Cholly in his first sexual act with a young girl.

> When he was still very young, Cholly had been surprised in some bushes by two white men while he was newly but earnestly engaged in eliciting sexual pleasure from a little country girl. The men had shone a flashlight right on his behind. He had stopped, terrified. They chuckled. The beam of the light did not move. "Go on," they said. "Go on and finish. And, nigger, make it good." (p. 37)

Cholly does not struggle against the men, for he had long ago learned from "myriad other humiliations, defeats and emasculations" (p. 37) that he could not win against their power and their predilection for violence. So he mounts the girl and makes "it good" in the beam of the flashlight. Morrison writes, "Cholly had not hated the white men; he hated, despised the girl" (p. 37). It is the taste of this remembered humiliation that shapes Cholly's attitude toward Pauline. "He poured out on her the sum of all his inarticulate fury and aborted desires. Hating her, he could leave himself intact" (p. 37). And so they fight with a "darkly brutal formalism that was paralleled only by their lovemaking. Tacitly they agreed not to kill each other" (p. 37), but they knew that they must fight as if they would. During this difficult period in their marriage, Pauline discovers that she is carrying Cholly's child.

The consummate maternal joy that Staples and Thompson document in sociological studies is very far from Pauline's expectations and feelings. The notion of motherhood as a sacred calling lived out in Sistine tranquillity is a rhetorical lie in Pauline's culture. Pauline had seen no gratifying maternal experiences in her mother's life, since each new birth—and there were eleven—meant more work for a woman already exhausted by her responsibilities as farmer, wife, and mother many times over. The only joy the unplanned pregnancy brings Pauline, ironically, comes from Cholly, who treats her with more tenderness because his male ego is enlarged by this proof of his virility. "They eased back into a relationship more like the early days of their marriage," Pauline recalls (p. 97). This fictive picture connects with the cultural pattern of escorting women "with child" into "an atmosphere of approval"[31] It was this atmosphere that pulled Meridian's mother into marriage and then into motherhood, and it is this atmosphere that gives Pauline her only joy as an expectant mother.

Like Mrs. Hill, however, Pauline Breedlove quickly discovers the difference between what she expects and what she experiences. She is not ushered into bliss but thrust into loneliness. All day she keeps house and hears the sounds of life outside. She returns, out of desperation, to her earlier dreams of escape from melancholy into bliss, and she escapes by experiencing vicariously the lives of white men and women on America's silver screen. At the movies, she sees beautiful white women and servile black women. The polarities never change—white luxury and black powerlessness, white beauty and black ugliness. It is at the movies, Morrison writes, that Pauline Breedlove is introduced to "the idea of physical beauty." This idea, and that of "romantic love," which has long shaped Pauline's fantasies, are "the most destructive ideas in the history of human thought. Both originated in envy, thrived in insecurity, and ended in disillusionment" (p. 97). Together they convince Pauline that she is irredeembly ugly. As she watches a Clark Gable and Jean Harlow film, she loses a tooth—a front tooth at that—and the loss plunges her into self-hatred. Her telling of the incident is one of the most moving moments in the novel, and it is written with Morrison's brillance for creating mood. I reproduce it here at length, for it is such a compelling statement on the impact that images of black women in America's white media have on Pauline Breedlove's dreams and frustrations:

> "The onliest time I be happy seem like was when I was in the picture show. Every time I got, I went. I'd go early, before the show started. They'd cut off the lights, and everything be black. Then the screen would light up, and I'd move right on in them pictures. White men taking such good care of they women, and they all dressed up in big clean houses with the bathtubs right in the same room with the toilet. Them pictures gave me a lot of pleasure, but it made coming home hard, and looking at Cholly hard. I don't know. I'member one time I went to see Clark Gable and Jean Harlow. I fixes my hair up like I'd seen hers on a magazine. A part on the side, with one little curl on my forehead. It looked just like her. Well, almost just like. Anyway, I sat in that show with my hair done up that way and had a good time. I thought I'd see it through to the end again, and I got up to get me some candy. I was sitting back in my seat, and I taken a big bite of that candy, and it pulled a tooth right out of my mouth. I could of cried. . . . I don't believe I ever did get over that. There I was, five months pregnant, trying to look like Jean Harlow, and a front tooth gone. Everything

went then. Look like I just didn't care no more
after that. I let my hair go back, plaited it up,
and settled down to just being ugly." (p. 98)

The tragedy of the incident is not Pauline Breedlove's loss of the
front tooth but her use of fantasies to help her cope with reality.
These fantasies, which can never become realities, remove her
from the healing memories of the Kentucky spring. Tragically,
she resigns herself to being an ugly women whose only hope for a
better life lies in serving the Lord. She serves by carrying two
crosses—her children and her husband.

For Pauline, the experience of motherhood is a mixture of
maternal rage and maternal regret. Thus she beats her children,
feels guilty that she had beaten them, but beats them again. She
understands why she does this, and her understanding echoes
Camille Jeffers' observation that poor black women's functioning
in the maternal role is shaped "by the lack of sufficient money and
its irregular flow."[32] Pauline's lucid words, "perhaps it was having
no money or maybe it was Cholly, but [the children] sure worried
the life out of me" (p. 98). The daily needs of her children are like
lighted matches to the fuse of her disappointment as a black
woman denied beauty and romantic love. Like Pauline, Cholly is
frustrated, for he is a black man in a white-controlled society that
keeps his sense of self turning in the wind. But he is free from
having to care for the children, a privilege conferred on men by
the laws of the institution of motherhood.

An interesting dimension of Morrison's portrait of Pauline
Breedlove is the character's desire for a second child despite the
bitter disappointment of her first experience with motherhood.
Pauline does not know why she "actually tried to get pregnant"
(p. 98), but she believes it was because she knew what to expect
this second time and was therefore not afraid. Morrison offers a
different explanation. In a culture that limits woman's creativity
to the single act of childbirth, Pauline naturally chooses to become pregnant in a moment of deep depression. She experiences
a sense of power and possession in this second pregnancy because
she made it happen and because, unlike the first child, this one of
her making will be her special friend. The myth of maternal
service is reversed here. Instead of taking up a "sacred calling"

to which she will give a lifetime of unselfish devotion, Pauline sees her second venture into motherhood as a retrieval from the pits of loneliness. Her attitude is touching and pathetic. She sees the child within her womb as the "other self" who understands her, as Cholly does not, and who makes her happy, as her reality does not:

> "I used to talk to it whilst it be still in the womb. Like good friends we was. You know. I be hanging wash and I knowed lifting weren't good for it. I'd say to it holt on now I gone hang up these few rags, don't get froggy; it be over soon. It wouldn't leap or nothing. Or I be mixing something in a bowl for the other chile and I'd talk to it then too." (p. 98)

Because this special child deserves more than the hands of a midwife and the ugliness of the Breedloves' house, Pauline plans her first hospital delivery. To suggest the ironic contrast between her expectations and reality, Morrison first describes the comfort Pauline anticipates—she is "eased" back into her earlier bliss, her pregnancy is a "state of ease"—and then moves immediately into the horror of Pauline's labor in the sterile, insensitive white hospital. As a *woman* in this world, Pauline feels life breaking forth from her with urgency and force, but she cannot communicate what she feels to the team of white male doctors who are sexually outside her experience. As a *poor* woman, Paulines lies defenseless, her nakedness exposed to a group of interns who callously treat the nameless patients in the charity ward. And as a *black* woman, she is humiliated and debased by the racist assumptions these doctors make about her. She observes them using gentle hands on the white women, conveying concern with their "nice friendly talk," and she is outraged and deeply wounded when they push her legs open and jam rough hands inside her body. But it is their talk that cuts with deep sharpness into her soul "Now these here women, you don't have any trouble with. They deliver right away and with no pain. Just like horses" (p. 99).

Pauline is wrenched by the experience because it is so radically different from her expectations, but she does not comprehend why it is different. She understands, of course, that economics placed her in a charity ward, but the presence of white charity patients makes the matter of class insignificant. Since the medical profession then systematically excluded blacks and women, she expected the doctors to be white men. She believes she suffers not because she is female and poor, but only because she is black. She reasons that if the ability to endure pain in silence distinguishes her from white women, she should scream out in excrutiating pain:

> "I moaned something awful. The pains wasn't as bad as I let on, but I had to let them people know having a baby was more than a bowel movement. I hurt just like them white women. . . . Wht'd they think? That jus' cause I knowed how to have a baby with no fuss that my behind wasn't pulling and aching like theirs." (p. 99)

Pauline *is* stronger than the white women because she can endure pain in silence. She knows "how to have a baby with no fuss," but she is too overwhelmed by racism in the delivery experience to understand that her quiet endurance of pain is an expression of her dignity, not an indictment of her as a lesser woman (p. 99). Seeing herself, however, through the eyes of others, she attempts to express her humanity by imitating the very women whose behavior calls her humanity into question. She "moaned something awful."

Myths spawned by the institution of motherhood suggest that women, because of their experience with "creative pain,"[33] immediately approve of their newborn child. The experience of motherhood sometimes teaches us differently. If beauty is in the eye of the beholder, there is sometimes a direct relationship between the mother's image of herself and her image of her child. Thus Pauline Breedlove sees her newborn as "a cross between a puppy and a dying man" (p. 98). Nevertheless, she makes a commitment to the child, and in that is unlike the hundreds of black mothers in real life who, according to Jesse Bernard, "disappear once they have delivered."[34]

Pecola Breedlove is the tragic character in the novel. She is victimized by both parents because they are made incapable of nurturing her by the limiting phenomena of race, sex, and class. Out of a deep well of self-hatred and psychic pain, they give Pecola the fullest measure of their misery. Pauline loves Pecola, but she beats her, teaching her

> fear of being clumsy, fear of being like their father, fear of not being loved by God, fear of madness like Cholly's mother . . . fear of growing up, fear of other people, fear of life. (p. 102)

Cholly loves Pecola, but he rapes her. The rape scene makes us aware of Cholly's damaged self and Pecola's tragic vulnerability. Cholly sees his daughter bent over the sink washing dishes. "The sequence of his emotions was revulsion, guilt, pity, then love. His revulsion was a reaction to her young, helpless, hopeless presence."

> Why did she have to look so whipped? She was a child—unburdened—why wasn't she happy? The clear statement of her misery was an accusation. . . . Guilt and impotence rose in a bilious duet. What could he do for her-ever? What give her? What say to her? What could a burned-out black man say to the hunched back of his eleven-year-old daughter? . . . What could his calloused hands produce to make her smile? (p. 127)

He "loves" her physically, but his "hatred of her slimed in his stomach and threatened to become vomit" (p. 127). He rapes her, breaking into her virginal tightness, and when he finishes his "hatred would not let him pick her up, the tenderness forced him to cover her" (p. 129).

Pauline's beatings, Cholly's rape, and daily reminders that *white* girls are beautiful reinforce Pecola's belief that she has been assigned to the "bottom category in the scale of absolute beauty."[35] She wishes to disappear.

> "Please God," she whispered into the palm of her
> hand. "Please make me disappear." She
> squeezed her eyes shut. Little parts of her body
> faded away. Now slowly, now with a rush.
> Slowly again. Her fingers went, one by one; then
> her arms disappeared all the way to the elbow.
> Her feet now. Yes, that was good. The legs all at
> once. It was the hardest above the thighs. She
> had to be real still and pull. Her stomach would
> not go. But finally it, too, went away. Then her
> chest, her neck. The face was hard, too. Almost
> done, almost. Only her tight, tight eyes were left
> They were always left. (p. 39)

But she wishes most intensely for blue eyes. She is a "little black
girl who wanted to rise up out of the pit of her blackness and see
the world with blue eyes" (p. 137). Pecola is her mother's child,
for in a real sense Pecola's desire for blue eyes is not unlike
Pauline's desire to be Jean Harlow with a "little curl" on her
forehead, but Pecola suffers from self-rejection more tragically
than Pauline because she has never seen the "bits of color" in a
Kentucky spring, tasted the sweetness of lemonade prepared by
a mother who greets her husband at the end of the day, or felt the
"deep purple of berry picking" within. She has not been "down
home." She has never known "home" in the Breedlove house.
Alone in her pain, she goes to a community recluse known for his
strangeness, his madness, his rejection of the traditional ordering principles of the community: "I'd like a pair of new blue eyes"
(p. 142). His understanding of her pain makes him an accomplice
to her insanity.

> I, I have caused a miracle. I gave her the eyes. I
> gave her the blue, blue, two blue eyes. Cobalt
> blue. A streak of it right out of your own blue
> heaven. No one else will see her blue eyes. But
> she will. And she will live happily ever after.
> (p. 143)

White America's definition of beauty and its effect on black women's self-images are handled differently in Gwendolyn Brooks's *Maud Martha*, which was published two decades before *The Bluest Eye*. Set in Southside Chicago, the novel is a "series of lyrical, perhaps autobiographical, vignettes of life"[36] in small kitchenettes during the late thirties and early forties as it is experienced by Maud Martha and those with whom she interacts. "We hear through her mind's voice the sounds of her family, her community and the unknown white world," and we see Maud Martha receiving love and guidance from a strong, cohesive black family and support from the nurturing "communal rituals" that make the black community a large extended family. "Her world is a cocoon in which she has protection and nourishment to find herself."[37]

The self she finds is decidedly different from Pauline Breedlove's self, for Maud Martha never knows the separateness Pauline feels so acutely. Whereas Pauline is one of eleven children in a sharecropper's family that lives miles from the nearest neighbor, Maud Martha is one of two children in an urban family that shares doors, walls, steps, stoops, schools, and churches with other people of like circumstances. This explains why Pauline Breedlove's reality is suffocating and Maud Martha's is a warm cocoon. One woman is the product of a southern/rural experience; the other of a northern/urban experience. One woman is uneducated, isolated, and afraid of life; the other is educated, involved in a world of activity, and eager to embrace life. Pauline escapes at the movies. Maud Martha finds pleasure and beauty in "candy buttons, and books, and painted music . . . and dandelions."[38]

> She would have liked a lotus, or China asters or the Japanese iris, or meadow lilies—yes, she would have like meadow lilies, because the very word meadow made her breathe more deeply, and either fling her arms or want to fling her arms, depending on who was by, rapturously, up to whatever was watching in the sky. But dandelions was what she chiefly saw. (p. 5)

Brooks's image of dandelions as "yellow jackets for everyday, studding the patched green of the back yard," reflects Maud Martha's picture of herself as ordinary woman. She prefers dandelions to more exotic flowers because of their "demure prettiness" and "everydayness," proving that "what was common could also be a flower" (p. 5). The theme of "everydayness" is related to Morrison's theme of blue eyes for Pauline. While Pauline Breedlove, after comparing herself to white images of beauty, decides that she is irredeemably ugly, Maud Martha, less damaged by the comparison, considers herself "sweet . . . but certainly not what one would call pretty" (p. 41).

Other comparisons between Pauline Breedlove and Maud Martha alert us to the different ways the problem of color has been treated by black women writers. Even on this issue—almost a given in the reality of black women—there is no monolithic statement. For Pauline Breedlove, white women are the symbols of beauty. For Maud Martha, "high-yellow" (light-skinned) black women with straight or curly hair serve the purpose. Of course, it can be argued that what is involved here is only the flipside of the same coin because admiration for high-yellow black women is but a reflection of the black community's acceptance of the white ideal. But intraracial color prejudice is a different dynamic. This is not to say that the preference for light skin within the race does not pierce the souls of black women. It does. Brooks describes the deep injury Maud Martha suffers because she is darker than her sister, Helen, and, for this reason, teased by her peers and disregarded by her father:

> It does not please [Maud Martha] . . . to watch her father . . . think . . . how daintily [Helen] ate, how gracefully she sat in her chair, how pure was her robe and unwrinkled, how neatly she had arranged her hair. (p. 29)

Brooks even seems to suggest that Maud Martha's interest in "candy buttons," and certainly her interest in books, is created by her status in her family and among her peers as an unattractive girl. However, admiration for high-yellow black women produces less intense rage than admiration for white women. The latter are always outside the culture. The former are often biological sisters, as in Maud Martha's case, and always racial sisters. This fact, along with sustaining family love, explains why Maud Martha's sensitivity to her "everydayness" is an irritant in her soul rather than an Achilles' heel in her life.

As an irritant, it shapes Maud Martha's attitude toward her relationship with Paul, a gentle man and a fairly sensitive husband. Here again, there are similarities and differences between Pauline Breedlove and Maud Martha. Pauline waits for a man to touch her and make her whole because she is lacking in self-esteem. She is, therefore, grateful for Cholly's love. Similarly, Maud Martha is grateful for Paul's love because she is convinced that she is not a prize catch. Therefore she promises to give in love and understanding what she cannot give in beauty. She will be like the women of old who were

> strong women, bold; praiseworthy, faithful, stout-minded; with a stout light beating in the eyes. . . . Women who would toil eminently to improve the lot of their men. Women who cooked. She thought of herself, dying for her man. It was a beautiful thought. (p. 146)

Neither Pauline nor Maud Martha considers the possibility of giving birth to herself without a man in her life. Pauline waits by the roadside for that someone special. Maud Martha "hooks" (p. 43) Paul into marriage. Just as dandelions prove that "what was common could also be a flower," so does Paul's troth prove that a woman who is not what a man "would call pretty" can also be desired. Still, Maud Martha is never free from the feeling that Paul thinks he "can do better than this black girl." Since a man wants more than "everydayness" in his woman, Maud Martha is convinced that

> even with all this hair . . . even with whatever I have that puts a dimple in his heart, even with these nice ears, I am still definitely not what he can call pretty if he remains true to what his idea of pretty has always been. Pretty would be a

little curly-haired thing the color of cocoa with a
lot of milk in it. Whereas, I am the color of cocoa
straight, if you can be even that *kind* to me.
(p. 41)

Brooks's portrayal of Maud Martha's life is on one level a sensitive picture of problems in the lives of black people in an urban
ghetto. On another level, it is a hymn to the beauty of "everydayness" and the beauty and character of ordinary black people.
Maud Martha is perhaps the only one among the characters analyzed in this book who is neither a heroine nor a victim. She has
her share of problems, however. She lives with the knowledge
that she is an unattractive woman. She faces the cutting
superiority of upper-class Negroes. And she copes with the condescension of the white woman who employs her as maid when
Paul cannot find a job. Her life is not all "candy buttons," but it is
a life of flowers because Maud Martha plants them in her vision of
possibilities. Her knowledge that white America circumscribes
her reality as a black woman does not deprive her of her ordinary
joys or lessen her pride in the unique beauty of the kitchenette
culture of black people. Her knowledge that marriage and par-
enthood demand more of her than of Paul because she is a woman
does not diminish the joy she receives in bathing her child, cooking baking powder biscuits for her man, washing, ironing, and
cleaning. These responsibilities incorporate her into a community
of women she admires and respects. In her "everydayness" she is
a tribute to her own dreams of life.

Brooks imbues her portrait of Maud Martha with genuine admiration for the character's humanity, humility, intelligence, and
ability to see the beauty in small things. Indeed, she depicts
Maud Martha as a "spiritually pretty" woman. Predictably, Maud
Martha's response to motherhood is one of warmth, enthusiasm,
and joy. The childbirth scene is wrapped in all three emotions.
Maud Martha screams out in pain, but she sees the pain as an
experience that is creative in the fullest sense of the word. She
would have everyone in the building know that she, Maud
Martha, is giving birth to a child. Her screams, then, are not like
the screams of Pauline Breedlove. They come from her sense of
her own worth. Whereas Pauline Breedlove is surrounded by

white male doctors, Maud Martha is surrounded by supportive black women—her mother and a neighbor—and she is aware that Paul has rushed to find the doctor. Whereas Pauline gives birth in the hostile environment of a white-run charity hospital, Maud Martha gives birth in the warmth of her home. These differences in the two experiences explain why Pauline Breedlove screams to prove her humanity, and Maud Martha screams to announce her joy in being a woman. She feels as if

> her whole body were having a bowel movement. The head came. Then, with a little difficulty, the wide shoulders. Then easily, with soft and slippery smoothness, out slipped the rest of the body and the baby was born. (pp. 71–72)

The painful labor gives Maud Martha a "handsome child" (p. 73) and a feeling of triumph. Brooks does not romanticize motherhood, for she writes that Maud Martha does not dwell long on "the fact of the baby." Responsibilities for this "fact" would "be [hers] all her life long" (p. 73). Rather, Maud Martha prefers to enjoy "the bright delight that had flooded through her upon hearing that part of Maud Martha Brown Phillips expressing itself with a voice of its own" (p. 73). It is significant that Maud Martha's triumph, as her long name for the child indicates, is an expression of her own achievement as a woman. It is a triumph that never diminishes, for throughout the novel, Maud Martha is the most marvelous of dandelions.

Henrietta Coffin in *Daddy Was a Number Runner* (1970) is also an "ordinary woman," but she rarely feels good or triumphant about it. Set in Harlem during the difficult years of the Depression, her story is one of frustration, fear, and unrelenting struggle. She and her husband struggle to rear three children into wholeness in a community that is "nothing but one big garbage heap."[39] They have no way out of Harlem. Mrs. Coffin has no skills and has been prevented from getting a job by her husband's wish to be the acknowledged head of the family. Mr. Coffin is a number runner who barely earns enough to keep his family. All around, in the streets outside and in the various apartments within their tenement, the Coffins see devastation and, most frighteningly, the victimization of black teenagers in a world of drugs, violence, and crime. In this world there are no dandelions or candy buttons.

The novel is told from the point of view of fourteen-year-old Francie Coffin, who is too young to understand the complexity of her mother's life. In Francie's eyes, only "Daddy" truly loves her. She compares him to the "knots of men" who sit on Harlem stoops or stand "wide-legged in front of . . . storefronts, with their black ribs shining through shirts limp with sweat. They spend most of their time playing the single action," and "Daddy" is the one to whom they give their bets. She is glad "Daddy [is] a number runner" because people come to her for tips as if she were "somebody special" (p. 15). Her description of her father is a touching tribute of love:

> Mother was always telling me that men were handsome, not beautiful, but she just didn't understand. Handsome meant one thing, and beautiful something else and I knew for sure what Daddy was. Beautiful. (p. 20)

Mrs. Coffin is not "beautiful." She is an unattractive woman, "short and dumpty dumpty" with "long breasts and wide hips" that run together, hair that is "short and thin," and teeth that are "rotting yellow" (p. 18). Consumed by motherhood and poverty, she has "let herself go." Indeed, Francie's description of her mother would fit any number of poor black women in black American novels—and in real life as well—on whom the exigencies of black life in the ghetto have taken their toll. But for Francie, the problem with "Mother" is not simply that she is unattractive. Rather, it is that she is unaffectionate, and, in personality, stern and sour: Mrs. Coffin "seldom" smiles. "Daddy shouted and cursed when he was mad and danced around and hugged you when he was feeling good," but Mother does not show her feelings at all. "It was hard to know what Mother was sensitive about. . . . She didn't curse you but she didn't kiss you either" (p. 18).

Instead of the sterotypic image of the strong black mother who pulls children to her all-embracing bosom, Louise Meriwether develops the image of the distant mother who has no time for embracing. Mrs. Hill in Walker's *Meridian* is also a distant mother, but her distance is not to be confused with that of Henrietta Coffin. Mrs. Hill is distant because she is sensitive to the unfairness of motherhood, its theft of her "emerging self." Mrs. Coffin, on the other hand, is distant because she is sensitive to the unfairness of a racist system that divides society into blacks and white, have-nots and haves, respectively. Meriwether's portrait of Mrs. Coffin is singularly absent of references to sexual consciousness. Although the novel was written in 1970 and is a rather obvious response to the sociological controversy over the black matriarchy, it does not reflect the concurrent controversy over women's rights. All the details of the portrait are racial and class details, drawn boldly to dramatize the impact that poverty and racism have on intact black families that are spiritually strong. The key to Meriwether's interpretation of such a family is her emphasis on Mrs. Coffin's posture as a supportive wife. She walks behind "Daddy" because she loves him and also because, sharing with him a history and, more acutely, a present experience of oppression, she supports his right to be a man. She therefore submerges herself in the roles of wife and mother and sacrifices her life for her children's future.

It is her commitment to maternal sacrifice that explains Mrs. Coffin's distance, a fact that Francie comes to understand only later in the novel. As the mother of three children, Mrs. Coffin is engaged in the miracles of "making a way out of no way"— altering cast-off clothes so that they fit her children, shopping for bargains of "cardboard" shoes, planning menus on a shoestring budget, and cleaning the apartment so that the bedbugs do not take over. Repeatedly, Meriwether pushes Mrs. Coffin's maternal aspirations to the center of the novel. The children will get a college education. Even when the Depression and the welfare system succeed in pushing Mr. Coffin out of the family, even when potted meat can no longer be "stretched from here to yonder with mayonnaise" (p. 89), Mrs. Coffin remains committed to her maternal aspirations. Even when her sons drop out of school, she is confident that her daughter will succeed. And so she preaches to the girl the only sermon she knows: "You don't be no fool, you hear? You finish school and go on to college. . . . You hear?" (p. 173).

It is appropriate to follow a discussion of Meriwether's *Daddy Was a Number Runner* with Paule Marshall's *Brown Girl, Brownstones* (1959), since both novels deal with the experience of growing up black and female in a black community in New York. Interestingly, the female adolescents in both works love their fathers and must struggle to understand their mothers. These are only surface similarities, however, for Marshall writes about a West Indian family living in Brooklyn during the forties and fifties, and Meriwether about a black American family living in Harlem during the thirties. The differences in time and location are of less importance than the cultural differences. As Marshall's novel teaches us, West Indians are black, but they are not to be confused with black Americans. They have their own values, lifestyles, rituals, dreams, and problems and they have a different history. In her story of the Boyce family, Marshall translates the proverbs, interprets the conversations, and renders the poetic language and rhythm of Barbadian culture. She writes specifically about Silla and Deighton Boyce and their two daughters, Selina and Ina, and generally about a people who have a strong sense of themselves as a distinct group and a passion to acquire things—especially property. The controlling symbol in the novel is the brownstone. To be Barbadian and to own a brownstone is to possess status and security—to have arrived in "this mahn's land."

Marshall begins her book with a poetic description of the "unbroken line of brownstone houses down the long Brooklyn street" on which the Boyce family lives. The brownstones resemble "an army massed at attention" with their "uniform red-brown stone" and "high massive stone stoops and black iron-grille fences staving off the sun." They are "formidable" structures "draped in ivy as though mourning. Within their larger rooms, yawning endlessly one into the other,"[40] is a history of migration or white flight common to this nation. Whites built the brownstones and lived in them for a century, but slowly abandoned them as new immigrants—black immigrants—"edged" themselves into the community. "Like a dark sea nudging its way onto a white beach and staining the sand, they came" (p. 4). In 1939 the last of the whites were "discreetly dying" (p. 4), or simply running as their tradition had taught them to, and Bajans were replacing them as landlords and tenants, loving the brownstones with "the same fierce idolatry as they had the land on their obscure island" (p. 4).

Just as they claimed the land as theirs but had no power on their "obscure island," so do they claim the brownstones as theirs but have no security in white America. They share with black Americans the peculiar reality of acquiring things while remaining outside the circle of power and influence in this country. The brownstones the Bajans work hard to own are for Selina Boyce, who is wise beyond her ten years, museums "of all the lives that had ever lived there" (p. 5). We see her alone at the beginning of the novel, interpreting the "aged and inviolate silence" of the brownstone her parents are renting. She imagines the white family who had once served tea in this house and rustled long dresses across the "parquet" floor imploring "her to give them a little life" (p. 5). She imagines, too, that she is "no longer a dark girl alone and dreaming at the top of an old house, but one of them, invested with their beauty and gentility" (p. 5). This child's fantasy is like Pauline Breedlove's desire to be Jean Harlow and Pecola's obsession with blue eyes: born of the psychological conditioning that makes many blacks think white, act white, or desire to *be* white.

Living in her family's museum, where a "floor-to-ceiling mirror retained their faces as the silence did their voices," Selina feels that she is "something vulgar in a holy place" (pp. 5–6). Possessed of more understanding than the Bajan men and women who idolize the brownstones, she realizes that her "heavy silver bangles which had come from 'home'" conflict with the clutter of a white past. She decides that "she did not belong here":

> The room was theirs, she knew, glancing up at the frieze of cherubs and angels on the ceiling; it belonged to the ghost shapes hovering in the shadows. But not to her. (p. 6)

In the description of the family portrait, Marshall symbolically presents the theme of Selina's need to find or create her own place beyond the brownstones that do not belong to her. Selina mutters "contemptuously" that her deceased brother looks "like a girl with all that hair":

> He had been frail and dying with a bad heart while she had been stirring into life. She had lain curled in the mother's stomach, waiting for his dying to be complete, she knew, peering through the pores as the box containing his body was lowered into the ground. Then she had come, strong and well-made, to take his place. *But they had taken no photographs* [italics added]. (p. 8)

The novel is Selina's story of self-discovery, a journey that takes her from Brooklyn to Barbados and that teaches her to reject capital and material things as the ordering principles of her life.

Selina's attitude toward the brownstones is in direct contrast to the attitude of her mother. Silla Boyce is obsessed with owning a brownstone, and she will do anything in this man's country to achieve that goal. The American emphasis on materialism and power has claimed Silla to the extent that she is willing to jettison values that interfere with her ambition:

> If you let a little noise and dirt 'pon your hand keep you from making a dollar you should starve. I tell yuh, to make your way in this world you got to dirty more than yuh hands sometime. . . .

Deighton Boyce, on the other hand, is content with leasing a brownstone. When his friend Seifert advises him to buy—"You might not get the chance again to own such a swell house"—Deighton answers, "Yearwood, what's the rush. I don' owe tiger nothing that I got to break loose my inside buying these old houses" (p. 39). His nonchalance hampers Silla's dream, and Silla,

Selina realizes, is capable of destroying Deighton if owning a brownstone requires his destruction.

Silla and Deighton are two contrasting forces in Selina's life, each adding to her self-discovery. Silla is strong, fearless, and, like the brownstones she idolizes, "formidable." In a park where sunshine lies down with lounging women and runs with laughing children, Silla Boyce brings "the theme of winter . . . with her dark dress amid the summer green":

> Not only that, every line of her strong-made
> body seemed to reprimand the women for their
> idleness and the park for its senseless summer
> display. Her lips, set in a permanent protest
> against life, implied that there was no time for
> gaiety. And the park, the women, the sun even
> gave way to her dark force; the flushed summer
> colors ran together and faded as she passed.
> (p. 16)

Deighton, on the other hand, is warm, and Marshall uses the sun as the controlling image in her pictures of him. When Selina complains about missing a movie, Deighton responds, "I don know what wunna New York children does find in a movie. . . . Sitting up in a dark place when the sun shining bright-bright outside" (p. 9). He was the only one in the family photograph Selina believed:

> For her, he was the one constant in the flux and
> unreality of life. The day was suddenly bright
> with the thought of him upstairs in the sun par-
> lor. . . . (p. 8)

Selina is torn between respect and awe for her mother and sympathy and affection for her father. She understands the truths of the family: Silla works hard to buy a brownstone; Deighton tries one get-rich scheme after another. Silla plans for the future; Deighton dresses in silk shirts and promenades down Fulton Street to the apartment of his concubine. Deighton wishes for the old days when they were lovers in the sun parlor and "could see the sky with its low stars from the bed"; Silla holds herself from him, beating him with guilt for the death of their son and trying to blackmail him into buying a brownstone in exchange for absolution. When Deighton acquires property in Barbados, Silla insists that he sell the land and use the money on the brownstone. His refusal to do so plunges the family into tragedy. Silla plots against Deighton and sells the land, but Deighton, ironically, spends the money on things. Outraged by his betrayal and his continued visits to his concubine, Silla becomes a woman possessed by vengeance.

In fiction, as in real life, the tragic dimensions of black men's reality often obscure the harsh realities of black women. This is the case in *Brown Girl, Brownstones*. It is not easy to admire and respect Silla Boyce, so cruel is her attack on Deighton, whom racism and poverty in Barbados had turned into a broken man. In conversations with Selina he speaks romantically of his childhood in Bimshire, where racism and class oppression created island sport for rich white men:

> We would pick up weself and go seabathing all down Christ Church where the rich white people live. Stay in the water all day shooting the waves, mahn, playing cricket on the sand, playing lick-cork. . . .

> And when a tourist ship come into Carlisle Bay we would swim out to it and the rich white people from America would throw money in the water just to see we dive for it. (p. 10)

But inside, where the wounds have never healed, he remembers "things thrust deep into forgetfulness":

> . . . those white English faces mottled red by the sun in the big stores in Bridgetown and himself as a young man facing them in his first pair of long pants and his coarse hair brushed flat, asking them for a job as a clerk—the incredulity, the

disdain and indignation that flushed their faces
as they said no. . . . (p. 39)

Deighton's attempts to leave his narrow cot in the sun parlor—
first through unrealistic get-rich-quick schemes and finally in a
bona fide job at the factory—sap what little strength he has, but
he was destroyed long before he came to this "mahn's land," long
before the machine crushes his arm, and long before he surren-
ders to a religion where allegiance to "Father" robs him of the
last vestiges of his manhood and his desire to live. Silla's rage is
like a strong wind that topples trees fierce storms have already
uprooted. "It was his wish to suffer that suddenly spurred in her
the need to make that suffering full" (p. 175). She swears out a
warrant for his "arrest and deportation for illegal entry into the
United States" (p. 181). Deighton jumps overboard and commits
suicide before the ship reaches Bimshire. Rage against the
mother consumes Selina:

> "Hitler!" She spat the name in the mother's face
> and brought her small fist down on Silla's shoul-
> der. "Hitler!" she cried and struck again. This
> time her bangles glanced sharply across the
> mother's chin. (p. 184)

Like Selina, we curse Silla Boyce and weep for Deighton. And
yet, like Selina, we are in awe of the formidable beauty of Silla.
The child's reaction to the contrasts of Silla's severity and Deighton's nonchalance are brought together in Marshall's description
of the parents' tales of Barbados. Selina is fascinated by Deighton's stories of his childhood in Carlise Bay, but "thoughts of the
mother intruded."

> What had she and the others who had lived down
> in gullies and up on the hills behind God's back
> done on Saturdays? She could never think of the
> mother alone. It was always the mother and
> others. . . . (p. 10)

The others are the community of black women who share a collective history of oppression in the West Indies and in America. Silla epitomizes the awesome strength of this community of "watchful, wrathful women whose eyes seared and searched and laid bare, whose tongues lashed the world in unremitting distrust" (p. 11). They remind us of the many unnamed black women whose lives provide the data on domestics presented in the historical overview:

> Each morning they took the train to Flatbush and Sheepshead Bay to scrub floors. The lucky ones had their steady madams while the others wandered those neat blocks or waited on the corners—each with her apron and working shoes in a bag under her arm until someone offered her a day's work.

When white children laugh at their blackness and call them "niggers,"

> the Barbadian women sucked their teeth, dismissing them. Their only thought was of the "few raw-mout" pennies' at the end of the day which would eventually "buy house." (p. 11)

These women are not new to hard work or to humiliation, for they were no less devalued in Bimshire than they are in Brooklyn. With a "sardonic laugh," Silla talks about her experiences in "The Third Class":

> . . . a set of little children picking grass in a cane field from the time God sun rise in his heavens till it set. With some woman called a Driver to wash yuh tail in licks if yuh dare look. Yes, working harder than a man at the age of ten. . . . (p. 45)

And when she was not in "The Third Class," Silla "would put a basket of mangoes 'pon muh head and go selling early 'pon a morning when still *only a child* [italics added]" (pp. 45–46). In

Selina's consciousness the contrast between the reality of black
men and the reality of black women is the difference between
Carlise Bay and The Third Class:

> The image of her father swaggering through the
> town as a boy and bounding on the waves in
> some rough game slanted across that of the small
> girl hurrying from the dawn ghosts with the bas-
> ket on her head. (p. 46)

Marshall keeps the victimization of black men in focus throughout the novel as she paints the details of racism and poverty in
the Bajan community. But she makes the women in the community towering figures in the picture, whose caption reads:"

> *Of all things upon the*
> *earth that bleed and grow,*
> *a herb most bruised is woman. (p. 29)*

Bajan women board the train to Flatbush. Bajan women cook the
meals, rear the children, and work like men in factories. Bajan
women carry several burdens on hips stretched wide by bearing
children for Bajan men. Their perseverance, strength, and tenacity of will are the life forces for the children, the men, and other
women.

Miss Thompson is not a Bajan woman, but she is no less strong
and no less admirable. She is a maid, hairdresser, and mother.
Her work day began

> at nine o'clock that night in the office building
> where she worked as a cleaning woman. At dawn
> she had eaten in an all-night diner, dozing over
> her coffee, then as the morning cleared, she had
> come to the beauty parlor (p. 28).

There, for only a stolen moment, she dressed

> the ugly unhealed ulcer, yawning like a small
> crater on the instep of her foot. . . . This done,
> she leaned back and, for the first time in twenty-

> four hours since she had been up, *permitted her-*
> *self to feel tired* [italics added]. (p. 28)

When her long work day ends, she returns to her small tenement
apartment to care for three small girls. Marshall writes with
admiration of Miss Thompson's warm flowing of love and compas-
sionately of "the eyes shrouded with a profound sadness" (p. 41).
She writes with tenderness of the friendship between Selina and
Miss Thompson. Unlike Silla Boyce, whose conversations with
Selina are battles for control, Miss Thompson listens with patience to the young girl's frustrations. Significantly, when Selina
is confronted with the racism of a white woman, she remembers
Miss Thompson's resistance to racial humiliation. In no small way
Miss Thompson's racial pride helps shape Selina's racial consciousness. Perhaps her portrait is a criticism of Bajan dismissal
of black American pride. Surely Miss Thompson in her strength
can keep company with the community of Bajan women.

But no black woman in the novel is equal to Silla Boyce in
strength, fierce tenacity of will, and dogged determination. In
the factory scene, Marshall compares Silla's strength to the pis-
tons of large and formidable machines. The scene is engrossing
and rich in the concrete images that make Marshall's prose so
brilliantly poetic. Selina goes to the factory to "intimidate" Silla,
hoping that the mother's plans to sell her father's land in Barbados will not be realized:

> Timidly she pushed open a heavy metal door and
> almost slammed it back in fright as an enraged
> bellow tore past her. She was suddenly drowned
> in a deluge of noise: belts slapping on giant pul-
> leys, long shafts rearing and plunging, whirling
> parts plying the air, the metal whine of steel
> being cut, steam hissing from a twisting network
> of pipes on the ceilings and walls, the nervous,
> high-strung hum of the smaller machines and
> finally the relentless frightening stamp of the
> larger ones, which made the floor shudder. It
> was a controlled, mechanical hysteria, welling up

like a seething volcano to the point of eruption,
only to veer off at the climax and start again.

Selina sees her mother matching her strength against the force of
the machines:

> She fitted the lump of metal over the lathe center
> and, with a deft motion, secured it into the head-
> stock and moved the tailstock into position. The
> whine of her lathe lifted thinly above the roar as
> the metal whirled into shape. Then she released
> the tailstock and held the shell up for a swift
> scrutinizing glance before placing it with the
> other finished shells (pp. 99–100).

Silla Boyce is the "collective voice of all the Bajan women"
(p. 45). It is a voice of sadness, but never resignation; of pain, but
never despair; of struggle, but never defeat. Selina knows that
she must journey beyond these women to find her own self and
values that will not corrode her humanity, but she realizes that
first she must understand Silla, "that she would never really
understand anything until she did" (p. 145). In spite of her
"theme of winter" and the "lips set in a permanent protest
against life," Silla Boyce is Selina's inspiration, a symbol of the
possibilities for growth, survival, and wholeness.

Brown Girl, Brownstones is the definitive novel about the
search of West Indians (and especially those from Barbados) for a
culture that combines the old and the new in the creation of a
Bajan-American culture. This theme is present in Marshall's second novel, *The Chosen Place, The Timeless People* (1969) and
also in her collection of stories, *Soul Clap Hands and Sing*
(1961), but it is most brilliantly developed in *Brown Girl, Brownstones*. Marshall explained that the story of the Boyce family, in
part autobiographical, deals with

> a fairly commonplace experience on the Ameri-
> can scene: the adjustment of an immigrant peo-
> ple to the American culture. In my case, it was

the experience of the West Indian immigrant in America, especially the Barbadian West Indian who settled largely in Brooklyn and created a somewhat exotic little world of his own there. I wanted to capture the contrast of the familiar and the exotic and to recount, with freshness and insight I hoped, the whole sometimes painful process of two ways of life meeting and merging to create something distinctively new. (p. 319)

This is an experience familiar to all black Americans, as Mary Helen Washington writes, and it had its first significant expression in DuBois' statement on double consciousness: Black Americans must look at the world through two eyes. The questions Paule Marshall asks of her characters, Washington continues, belong to the spiritual and psychological strivings of black people in this country:

How do we remember the past so as to transform it and make it usable? How do we preserve those qualities of survival and endurance that are at the deepest emotional core of one's black identity? How do an oppressed people survive spiritually, and on what grounds can they construct a future in a world in which the "soul-beauty" is despised. (p. 319)

Finding the answers to these questions takes Selina from innocence to knowledge, from adolescence to womanhood. The journey is one of anger, confusion, and dishonesty. She deceives her mother by continuing an affair with Clive, an artist whom the Bajan community does not approve of and whom Selina eventually leaves because of his refusal to take charge of his life. She works devotedly for the Association of Barbadian Homeowners and Businessmen only because she plans to win the annual scholarship and use the money for a trip to the islands for herself and Clive.

Selina is unable to follow through with her plans. She refuses the Association's scholarship check and makes a public apology, which signals her growth into a woman:

> My trouble was maybe that I wanted everything to be simple—the good clearly separated from the bad—the way a child sees things. But it's not that simple or separate and children can't understand it. Now that I'm less of a child I'm beginning to understand. (p. 303)

Silla is outraged:

> Lies! Getting up in front people talking a lot of who-struk-John about how much you like them and then throwing their money back at them. Talking in parables! Using a lot of big words and still not saying why you refuse good money. Disgracing me before the world! (p. 304)

As a young girl, Selina was in awe of such rages. As a woman she faces Silla without fear. She confesses that she has fought Silla with "spitework," blaming her for Deighton's tragedy, but she accepts that which she has not wanted to believe: she is Silla's child: "Remember how you used to talk about how you left home and came here alone as a girl of eighteen and was your own woman? I used to love hearing that. And that's what I want. *I want it!* [italics added]" (p. 304). She no longer fears Silla; she appreciates fully the mother's "awesome beauty" and strength:

> The world would collapse [without Silla], for wasn't the mother, despite all, *its only prop* [italics added]? (p. 46)

Selina books passage on a ship to the island. She will retrace her mother's steps and, like Silla, stand "at the ship's rail, watching the city rise glittering with promise from the sea" (p. 307). But the community to which she will return will be different from the old community of brownstones that "resembled an army massed at attention" (p. 3). At the end of the novel, Selina walks through the park she had known as a child, where Bajan women had once sat gossiping in the summer heat. It now belongs to dope addicts, winos, and hot-blooded young men. She wanders past rows of brownstones from which Bajan music and talk had once emanated. "Now, the roomers' tangled lives spilled out the open windows and the staccato beat of Spanish voices, the frenzied sensuous music joined the warm canorous Negro sounds to glut the air" (p. 309). The Bajan community of her childhood is making way for new immigrants. The brownstones are being razed to make room for housing projects. Selina feels that the "bodies of all the people she had known were broken, the familiar voices . . . shattered." She wants to leave something for them, for the past. She removes one of the two silver bangles all Bajan girls wear and throws it high over her shoulder. "It strikes stone. A frail sound in that utter silence" (p. 310).

In black American culture, grandmothers are sometimes "the only prop" in a child's life. Functioning as surrogate mothers in the black extended family, they are the bridge between the generations, the perpetuators of black culture, the griots (reciters) of family history, the disciplinarians, housekeepers, cooks, and repositories of wisdom and strength. Sociologists and historians alike extol the grandmother's contributions to the survival of black families. But there is no monolithic black grandmother either in real life or in fiction. Like black mothers, they are individuals with their own dreams and aspirations and problems. This is a dominant theme in Toni Morrison's story of Eva Peace in *Sula* (1973), the only grandmother in our gallery of black women. In a small Ohio community singularly impressive for its poverty, Eva Peace struggles alone for the survival of her family. When the youngest of her three children is only five months old, she is deserted by her husband, Boy-Boy, without warning and without explanation. Believing that the survival of her children is contingent on her temporary abandonment of them, Eva leaves them with a neighbor, who expects her to claim them the next day. Her desertion lasts eighteen months. Maternal abandonment is, of course, a cardinal sin in a society that perceives motherhood as a sacred calling, but Morrison shows clearly that Eva's decision represents courage and vision. For in her absence from her children, Eva prepares herself for a lifetime of service to their survival. When she claims them, she has only one leg, and the community rumor is that she sold the leg or put it under a moving train for insurance money—for her children. In this strange story Morrison gives us a black mother's desperate response to destitution.

The rest of the portrait of Eva as mother is less positive, revealing a desire to manipulate her children's lives and the lives of others as well. When she returns from her mysterious trip as a cripple, she begins building a "house of many rooms," of which she is "creator and sovereign." On the second-floor balcony she sits in a wagon—her throne, really—"directing the lives of her children, friends, strays, and a constant stream of boarders" (p. 26). She is "god like," Morrison said of Eva in an interview, seeking to rule the lives of others as would a "king."[41] Especially in her response to her son's wasted life does Eva "play god." Because he is an empty shell, his body emaciated by drug addiction, Eva pours kerosene on him as he sleeps off a "fix," and then sets a match to the mattress. In Mari Evans' "To Mother and Steve" a black mother is criticized for her failure to understand her son's addiction: "all I wanted/was your/love."[42] In *Sula* the mother goes far beyond this failure to understand. She takes her son's life, not because it was "a worthless life," but because "it was too painful to her."[43]

The portrait of Eva as a manipulative woman is important because it is shaped more by sexism than by racial and economic pressures. Eva's character is profoundly the result of her five years of marriage to Boy-Boy. In her marriage she was not the "creator and sovereign" of anyone's life, least of all her own. She was a typical woman, standing in the background as the man used all of life as his playground. Symbolically named, "Boy-Boy" is twice over a boy and not a man, immature and irresponsible. He likes "womanizing best . . . drinking second, and abusing Eva third" (p. 27). Michele Wallace's observation in *Black Macho and the Myth of the Superwoman* (1978) that the macho man believes "his sexuality and the physical fact of his penis were the major evidence of his manhood and the purpose of it"[44] is an apt description of Boy-Boy. When he leaves Eva with three children, without warning or explanation, she is so consumed by poverty that she has little understanding of her dilemma as a woman used and betrayed by a man. Her identity as mother directs both her emotions and her decisions.

Two years later, Boy-Boy returns, unscarred and unafraid, and Eva wonders if she will "cry, cut his throat [or] beg him to make love to her" (p. 30). Morrison here catches woman's need for love and for male attention, as well as her training in passivity and understanding—training that has led to the cultural assumption that woman has an innate propensity for forgiveness. It is inconceivable that Boy-Boy would return, in laughter, to the scene of his sins if the person sinned against were another man, just as it is inconceivable that a wronged man would only "imagine" what he might do to an enemy. For one of the manifestations of sexism, Ashley Montagu explains, is the socialization of men as warriors who have the right, if not the masculine obligation, to take "an eye for an eye and a tooth for a tooth." Women, on the other hand, are socialized "to be nurses who bathe the warrior's wounds," who live to forgive and "preserve others." Man is the "eagle on the wing" and woman is "the cricket on the hearth."[45] It is out of this cultural conditioning that Boy-Boy, unafraid and boastful, returns, and that Eva equivocates between loving and killing him.

She prepares lemonade (a woman's task) and engages in polite conversation with Boy-Boy, observing that he is the "picture of prosperity and good will" in shiny orange shoes, a light-colored suit, a garrish stickpin in his tie, and an ostentatious straw hat. But "underneath all that shine" there is "defeat," for in the big and fast cities of the Midwest Boy-Boy exchanged his soul for a glittering emptiness (p. 31). Morrison does not linger on Boy-Boy's destruction, for the scene is clearly Eva's existential moment, and Morrison's answer to a question that is rarely raised by one-dimensional and traditional images of the self-sacrificing and devoted mother: How does a woman handle deep and devastating hurt? She can turn to religion, as Pauline Breedlove does in *The Bluest Eye;* she can busy her hands making feminine artifacts, as Mrs. Hill does in *Meridian;* or, like Eva Peace, she can descend into a pit of hatred. When Boy-Boy courts the citified woman he brings with him—when he ignores Eva's existence as a *woman*—the descent begins and within seconds Eva has cast her life in a mold of hatred. The woman's laugh, Morrison writes,

> hit [Eva] like a sledge hammer, and it was then she knew what to feel. A liquid trail of hate flooded her chest. Hating Boy-Boy, she could get on with it, and have the safety, the thrill, the consistency of that hatred as long as she wanted or needed it to define and strengthen her from routine vulnerabilities. (p. 31)

The direction of her life from that moment on is traceable to disappointment in love. "Happy or not," Morrison writes, "after Boy-Boy's visit [Eva] began her retreat to her bedroom" (p. 32). She began her existence as a manipulator and as a cold and domineering mother.

Morrison handles the theme of romantic love in a new way that "offers us new perspectives of feminine reality," according to Barbara Lounsberry and Grace Honet. Like other "traditional ordering principles"—the family and the church, to name two—romantic love is a "limited and limiting vision" that promises the constricting view that women become fulfilled individuals only as wives and mothers. Also new in Morrison's treatment of romantic love is her definition of men. She "upturns and jangles our traditional view," so that, "far from heroic and powerful, men are diminished, literally and figuratively, in *Sula*. The male characters' names themselves [Boy-Boy, Tar Baby, Chicken Little, Jude Greene] suggest their immaturity. . . ." Lounsberry and Honet write that "this new perspective of men stunted in growth and development is conveyed most graphically through the Deweys [Eva's boarders] who will never grow taller than four feet and who, in their three-in-oneness, telegraph the horrifying homogeneity of the male experience."[47] This new view of men makes us reexamine the cultural assumption that all women need men and that men are necessarily dominating presences in the reality of women. Further, Eva's decision to keep herself invulnerable to pain impels us to reexamine the vaunted magical powers of motherhood to turn a bitter life into a sweet reality. In her cause-effect treatment of Eva's desertion by Boy-Boy and her maternal stance, Morrison suggests that what women experience in their relationships with the fathers of their children has a major effect on both their maternal postures and their vision of life.

Alice Walker writes brilliantly on the interrelatedness of the roles of wife and mother in *The Third Life of Grange Copeland* (1970). It is, in fact, the thread with which she sews "bits and pieces of used material rescued from oblivion"[48] into a profound and terrifying picture of black suffering in the South. The novel is an appropriate culmination to our discussion of black motherhood because it tells the story of generations of black women within one family; the action of the novel begins with the Grange Copeland family in 1900 and ends with the Grange Copeland family in the 1960s. More than any other work in this chapter, Walker's novel, a reflection of her search for our mother's gardens, shows how tragically the lives of black women can be shaped by racial violence, sexual abuse, and class oppression—problems that are festering sores in the South. The vision is a feminist vision, as Barbara Christian points out:

> Walker describes a legacy from which the creativity of the contemporary black woman can flower. To develop further, the black women of her generation must garner wholeness from the bits and pieces of the past and recreate them in their own image. Walker then uses the un- heralded heritage of black women, the creative sparks as well as the history of restrictions, as the foundation of her artistic vision. A feminist, she explores the relationship between this tradi- tion and societal change as crucial to the search for freedom—not only for woman, but for man, the child, the society, the culture, the land.[49]

The novel is a southern work of art—southern in that it is set in a black rural community in Mississippi, southern in that its characters have not ventured far from the insular environment of this community, and southern in that Alice Walker's artistic vision bears the imprint of the South she knew as a child, a young woman, and a Civil Rights worker. It is not essentially a catalogue of the crimes committed by white people against black people of the soil, though such crimes explode in the foreground and the background of the lives of the characters. Rather, it is Walker's vision of the cruelty that often exists in black male–black female relationships when racism and sexism work together as deterrents to joy and wholeness. More specifically, the novel is about the peculiar burdens of black women in white America. As Walker herself admits, she is "preoccupied with the spiritual survival, the survival whole of black people, and beyond that committed to exploring the oppressions, the insanities, the loyalties, and the triumphs of black women."[50] They are Walker's "revolutionary petunias" growing into beauty in a resistant soil. Such a woman is Mem Copeland.

Young, gentle, and pure, Mem is immunized, it seems, against the pollution of soul and body that claims Josie, an aunt with whom she lives during the summers in a house of prostitution. Josie is a "ruined" woman, a crass and crude prostitute, a slattern who brandishes a razor expertly and hurls at anyone who offends her the low-life language of Poontang Street. Mem is a "walking proper . . . talking proper" lady whose character is reflected in her "cherry brown face and demure slant eyes."[51] Josie "turns tricks" and Mem turns dreams into possibilities by teaching people in the backwoods community to read and write. "Mem put some attention to what she was [teaching], and some warmth from her own self, and . . . concern for the person she was speaking to . . ." (p. 47).

When Brownfield Copeland, who is Josie's "kept man," meets Mem, he experiences a profound sense of shame and, for the first time in his easy life with Josie, wishes for a way out of the sordid entanglement. "Ain't no need for you looking," Josie informs him, "she ain't got no real itch in her pussy" (p. 45). Josie does not understand that a woman can be appreciated for gifts that are not physical or sexual. She has so prostituted herself in every way that she cannot comprehend Brownfield's hunger for something more substantive, more spiritually filling and lasting than the now-monotonous "balling" he engages in with Josie and her daughter. In her "quiet strangeness," Walker writes, Mem awakens in Brownfield these other needs. However, Walker quickly establishes that Brownfield's awakening is not an entry into liberating definitions of male-female relationships. Like all too many men, Walker implies, Brownfield has two missions for a woman in his life. He wants her to be his wife, loving him physically, and his mother, caring for him as if he were a child. Walker writes, "He thought of [Mem] as of another mother" (p. 45).

We do not understand why Mem decides to marry Brownfield, an illiterate man whose character, she knows, has been jeopardized by his sordid affair with Josie, for Walker does not convincingly show the two characters in courtship. In a few brief scenes we see Brownfield awkwardly attempting to win Mem's love, and then we read that Brownfield, out of fear that he was losing Mem to another man, "caught her in his arms [one night] . . . and vowed in words and kisses never to let her go" (p. 48). One could argue that Mem loves Brownfield because he is, like a child, in need of instruction and love. Or one could even argue that Mem's decision to marry Brownfield turns on the myth of women liking to be swept off their feet by men: "he caught her in his arms as she was going up the stairs and vowed . . . never to let her go" (p. 48). Walker's emphasis is not on the *why* of Mem's love for Brownfield; it is, instead, on the *beauty* of their love. For three years they enjoy a relationship of physical joy, surpassing in intensity and passion the lovemaking Brownfield had known with Josie. Mem, like Josie, is a "devouring cat," but she has no claws and no sly intentions. Walker describes the lovemaking of Men and Brownfield lyrically:

> They were passionate and careless . . . making love in the woods after the first leaves fell, making love high in the corncrib to the clucking of hens and the blasting of cocks, making love and babies urgently and with purest fire at the shady ends of cotton rows. . . . (p. 49)

Mem Copeland is a woman of song who completes her woman's work to the rhythm of a joyful melody: "[Mem] sang while she cooked breakfast in the morning and sang when getting ready for bed at night. And sang when she nursed her babies [three in three years], and sang to [Brownfield] when he crawled in weariness and dejection into the warm life-giving circle of her breast" (p. 49). Walker revives her earlier image of woman as mother for her husband when she writes that Brownfield, like the babies, "sucked and nursed at [Mem's] bosom . . . and grew big and grew firm with love, and grew strong" (p. 49).

The love relationship betweeen Mem and Brownfield is equaled in beauty and intensity only by the relationship of Janie and Teacake in Zora Neale Hurston's classic novel, *Their Eyes Were Watching God* (1937). After two unfulfilled marriages, Janie is enveloped by joy in her relationship with Teacake because he treats her as an equal. She is liberated from the curse of black womanhood, which her grandmother preached when Janie was a young girl:

> Honey, de white man is de ruler of everything as fur as Ah been able tuh find out. Maybe it's some place way off in de ocean where de black man is in power, but we don't know nothin' but what we see. So de white man throw down de load and tell de nigger man tuh pick it up. He pick it up because he have to, but he don't tote it. He hand it to his womenfolks. De nigger woman is de mule uh de world so fur as Ah can see.[52]

The load to which the grandmother refers is carried equally by Janie and Teacake, for there is no place for sexual politics in their relationship.

To some extent, the load is also carried equally by Brownfield and Mem early in their marriage, but it is divided according to sexual definitions of labor. He tills the fields. She keeps the house. But their mutual respect for each other's jobs eases the line between "man's duty" and "woman's work," making them communicants in a ritual of love. Walker seems to suggest that when a woman's love for a man is returned in kind and intensity, sexual definitions of work and power pale in significance.

If racism and poverty were not the burdens they are in the black experience, Mem's song as woman fulfilled might have been an unbroken chord in her life. But in the small Georgia town where black men's dreams are shattered in the pernicious institution of sharecropping, Brownfield falls victim to the powerlessness and humiliation of a life of "endless sunup to sundown work on fifty acres of cotton," that brings him nothing more than "two diseased goats for winter meat, some dried potatoes and apples from the boss's cellar, and some cast-off clothes for his children from his boss's family" (p. 53). His manhood is devastated by the sight of his five-year-old daughter "hand-mopping the cotton bushes with arsenic to keep off boll weevils" and by the recurring nightmare that his own life is becoming a repetition of his father's. "He could not save his children from slavery; they did not even belong to him" (pp. 53–54). He is a tragic figure whose emasculation at the hands of a cruel system robs him of his dreams, vitiates his humanity, and leaves in his soul a taste of bitter bile. Walker's sympathy for Brownfield is genuine and deep: "he was never able to do more than exist on air" (p. 55). His destruction as a man becomes, in time, Mem's suffering as a woman: "he determined . . . to treat her like a nigger and a whore" (p. 54).

Conflict between black men and black women is a common theme in black American fiction, and it is more often than not engendered by racism and poverty. In "Father May Bring Home the Bacon, but He Don't Cut No Ice: the Economic Plight of the Father Figure in Black American Literature" (1975), Daryl Dance shows how the system's emasculation of black men often makes them abusive to their wives. The American economic system, she writes, "conspires to make it impossible for the black man to acquire anything more than a mere biscuit, no matter how he plays the economic man. Unable to protect and provide for his family," the black man "is inevitably . . . psychologically castrated." Men who suffer this fate, Dance writes, "yield the reins of power to their wives, abandon their families, or often take out their frustrations [on their wives] and become cruel tyrants in their home."[53] The last response to victimization is Brownfield Copeland's.

Abusive fathers in fiction have their counterparts in real life. Indeed, when black writers, male or female, hold up their artistic mirrors to life, they find reflected therein a history of black male-female conflict. "Historically," writes black activist Ron Karenga, "we black men and black women have been unkind to each other. . . . We have sent each other to hospitals, graves and prison." This has been our history, he continues, because "the systematic destruction of our culture and families threw us into chaos, often confused and misdirected our loyalties and called into question our love."[54]

Another school of thought traces the conflict to the mesmerizing effect the symbol of white feminine beauty and power has had on black men for centuries. This argument was the bone and sinew of the work of Eldridge Cleaver, which captured national attention during the same period that Alice Walker's novel was receiving literary accolades. Confessing that he perfected his rape techniques on black women before he attacked prized white women, Cleaver calls the black man's desire for white women "a sickness [that] must be brought out into the open, dealt with and resolved."[55] Until it is, black men will continue to revere white women and abuse black women, Cleaver believes. Shulamith Firestone expands this thesis and offers another unconvincing and excessively Freudian interpretation of the triangle of black women, black men, and white women. One must recognize, she says, that racism and sexism together have created "an Oedipus/Electra Complex, which is not easily neutralized in the psyches of the three victims."[56]

Walker's vision is not in consonance with Shulamith Firestone's thesis of the "Oedipus/Electra Complex" or with Cleaver's notion of the "sickness" that generates the psyche of black men, for white women are not central to the story Walker tells so brilliantly, and white men are present only because they represent the injustice that cripples Brownfield. Walker's vision of black womanhood, then, belies the assumption that at the root of the black women's problems with her man are the omnipresence and omnipotence of the specter of white female beauty. This is not to suggest that the specter is not present in the small black community; there is no place in this country where it has not made its way into the culture of the people. Indeed, Brownfield attempts to belittle Mem with the reminder that "you ain't white" (p. 58). But Walker quickly explains that Brownfield hates white women and "did not want his wife to imitate [them]." He means that Mem's "color was something she could not change and as his own colored skin annoyed him, he meant for hers to humble her." However, he does not succeed in making Mem "ashamed of being black" because she believes that "color was something the ground did to flowers, and that was an end to it" (p. 58). Her agony lies elsewhere.

Karenga's thesis that the "systematic destruction of our culture" is the cause of black male–female conflict is, to be sure, similar to the explanation Walker gives for Brownfield's abuse of Mem, but it is Calvin Herton's analysis that best shows Walker's imaginative picture of the problem as an unblurred reflection of real life. In *Sex and Racism in America* (1965) Hernton writes that the historical chaos results from the black man's need to blame someone for his failures in a racist society. It is a common saying among black men, Hernton explains, that "when anything goes wrong," the black woman is at fault. A retrenched "depreciatory concept of Negro females" explains why "the black man asserts, half-heartedly, but significantly, that black women are hell to get along with."[57] This attitude becomes, in Walker's portrayal of the Copelands, a disease that is passed down through generations. Destroyed by the same cruel sharecropping system that gnaws at Brownfield's soul, his father, Grange, beat his wife, accused her of sleeping with white men (an egregious sin in the community), abandoned her and the children for weeks on end, and literally drove her to suicide.

While Walker's picture of the relationship of Brownfield and Mem mirrors the facts presented in sociology and history, it does so in a way that makes the imaginative statement more powerful than any scholarly documentation. Walker produces a tour-de-force of black male-female tension. Her characters are powerful; her pictures are worth hundreds of documents. The shadow of eternal bondage in which Brownfield lives is not an abstract concept; it is as real as life and rich in particulars:

> His heart had actually started to hurt him, like
> an ache in the bones, when he watched his five-
> year-old daughter swinging the mop, stumbling
> over the lumps of hard clay, the hot tin bucket

full of arsenic making a bloodied scrape against
her small legs. (p. 53)

The color of the scene is the bright red of fury. The odor is the
stench of arsenic and human vomit. The sound is Brownfield's
heart splintering as he sees his daughter breathing with difficulty
and carrying the "beaten down" look of a "tiny asthmatic old
lady" (p. 54). The power of Walker's images and metaphors
leaves us as moved by Brownfield's tragic decline into self-hatred
as we are angered by his abuse of Mem. Punctuated with italics
and exclamations, Walker's paragraph on the "new" Brownfield
is a eulogy for a dead man:

> His crushed pride, his battered ego, made him
> drag Mem away from school teaching. . . . It was
> his great ignorance that sent her into white
> homes as a domestic, his need to bring her down
> to his level! It was his rage at himself, and his
> life and his world that made him beat her for an
> imaginary attraction she aroused in other men,
> crackers, although she was no party to any of it.
> His rage could and did blame everything, *every-
> thing* on her. (p. 55).

An appropriate analogy for Brownfield's treatment of Mem is
the wife as nigger. She is Brownfield's inferior simply because
she is a woman and he is a man. In her woman's world of servitude there is no need for education, so she must burn her books
or use their pages to stuff large rat holes in their shack. She
saves her earnings to purchase a house; he steals the money and
buys a pig. She saves again; he steals to buy a little red car. He
should have the "things" and the power, even if they come from
her work. Their living conditions are appropriate to her status as
"nigger." Outhouses, rat holes, manure-filled cowsheds turned
into living quarters—all these she should accept in gratitude.
And like a "nigger," she must serve him even as she is abused by
him. Her role is clearly and narrowly defined. She is woman. He
is lord. She must please him. He is free to please only himself. He

succeeds in fulfilling his promise to himself: "he determined . . . to treat her like a nigger" (p. 54).

Mem's identity as a woman means, first, that she cannot adequately defend herself against the beatings Brownfield gives with his plough-heavy hands and his field-large body. After the birth of three children in three years, Mem is truly the "weaker sex." It means, secondly, that she is powerless against a culture locked into the pathology of masculine dominance, which gives Brownfield justification, in his own thinking, for his mistreatment of her. Thirdly, and most tragically, it means that she is vulnerable to physical abuse in intercourse. Brownfield takes her "in his drunkenness," Walker writes, and boasts to his friends of both his sexual power and his fist power. "Give this old black-snake to her," he says, showing his penis and rubbing it suggestively, "and then I beats her ass. Only way to treat a nigger woman" (p. 54). Mem's response to this abuse makes Brownfield's cruelty an egregious crime: she is "a submissive, accepting wife" (p. 59). She is too weak physically to resist his beatings. And she has no refuge to which she can escape. Her mother is dead, her father has disowned her, and Josie does not want her. She is too gentle and too afraid to challenge, even in words, the fierceness of her husband's control. And yet, there are times in her conversations with herself when her woman's rage desires revenge:

> If I was a man, she thought, frowning later, scrubbing the dishes, if I was a man I'd give every man in sight and that I ever met up with a beating, maybe even chop up a few with my knife. . . . (p. 84)

Loneliness is a dominant feature of Walker's portrait of Mem, for she is a woman without a past, without fond memories, without life-giving myths, without self-reinforcing stories related by a grandmother, with ties to a warmly hysterical black church that beckons the disconsolate to its bosom, and without neighbors who give advice and lend support. Mary Helen Washington, writing of black women in real life, captures the loneliness of Mem Copeland. Black women have been alone, she writes, "because the damage done to our men has prevented their closeness and protection; and alone because we have had no one to tell us stories ourselves."[58] But it is Toni Morrison's definition of loneliness that is the most incisive caption for Alice Walker's moving portrait of Mem Copeland: "the loneliest woman in the world is a woman without a woman friend."[59]

In spite of her aloneness and her misery, Mem Copeland functions as a devoted mother. In this role she *is* the superhuman woman of strength, endurance, and compassion to whom a tradition of black American poetry has paid tribute since the nineteenth century. Her every goal, every wish, every struggle, is born of her identity as a mother. She cleans cow manure out of sheds to make them "habitable for her children" (p. 78). She fights Brownfield with words, though never with blows, "always for the children" (p. 95). "She slogged alone, ploddingly, like a cow herself" (p. 99), for the sake of her children. And it is for the sake of her children that she begins to run, to gallop, to race like a stallion bent on freedom.

Risking Brownfield's rage, Mem rents a house in the city and returns to the shack in the country to take control of her life—for the sake of her children. As Brownfield sleeps off his drunkenness, she wakes him by pushing a loaded gun barrel into his "balls," a symbolic statement that her liberation is sexual in nature. She analyzes Brownfield. She understands what the "man" has done to him, but she also understands, more painfully, what Brownfield has done to himself and to his family. Further, she understands, and would have him understand, that a real man should "quit wailing like a seedy jackass" (p. 59). Race cannot be ignored, but neither can it be used as an excuse for all one's weaknesses and sins. This is Mem's message to Brownfield, and one of the major themes of the novel (as well as many of Alice Walker's poems). Walker indicts Brownfield for his failures as a man when she writes that he "did not have the courage to imagine life without the existence of white people as a prop" (p. 47).

Mem invites Brownfield to join her in her new life with the understanding that "it's going to be my house and in my house what the white man expects us to act like ain't going to git no consideration" (p. 96). She lays down nine rules he must follow, all of which can be summed up in one: he will treat her and *her* children with respect and dignity. In "her house" Brownfield finds respect and dignity for himself. There is heat at all times. There is electricity for reading and looking through catalogues. And there is a toilet where Brownfield can "shit . . . without much odor or rain, and much like a gentleman." (p. 96). Walker puts the metamorphosis of Brownfield's life well: he is living "like a white man" (p. 102). But he is a bird of prey that bides its time, circling ominously above those who will be its victims. He plants "a seed . . . that would bring Mem down in weakness and dependence" (p. 103), the seed of procreation. Two pregnancies that do not bear fruit dissipate Mem's energies, rendering her helpless against Brownfield's criminal designs on her destruction. Unable to work, she cannot keep up the payments on the house. Like a vulture, in one fell swoop Brownfield descends on her weakened body and returns her to the manure-filled shack, where she becomes, once again, a "plodding cow."

In spite of her own destruction, Mem holds fast to her sanity and dignity. For the sake of her children, she works as a domestic and returns home to tend house and cook; and she manages, also for the sake of her children, to stretch her face of defeat into a smile. Finally, carrying packages for her children, she faces Brownfield's gun. Seconds later, she lies "faceless in a pool of blood," her still body decorated by a "halo of [the] dozen bright yellow oranges" she had carried in her arms for her children (p. 122). Like the women Walker pays tribute to in "In Search of Our Mothers' Gardens," Mem had worked "for a day when the unknown thing" inside her, pushing her to plant flowers and to dream of different alternatives, "would be made known; but [she] guessed, somehow, in [her] darkness, that on the day of . . . revelation [she] would be long dead."[60]

The story of Mem Copeland carries much of Alice Walker's own rage against black men who abuse black women in real life. In an interview published in *Encore* Walker said that she gets very angry with black women for taking all the stuff they take, "simply because they have a perverted sense of loyalty to black men."[61] However, to suggest that Walker does not respect black men would be far from the truth. Her moving poetry is replete with positive images of black men. To suggest, further, that she sees black men as "the enemy" would be an insult to an artist whose work is rooted in love, understanding, and forgiveness. The largeness of Alice Walker's soul makes her a sensitive and embracing poet. But her largeness of soul does not stand in the way of her artist's search for truth, just as the black woman's belief in what Carrie McCray calls our unquestionable "special set of humanistic values"[62] must not stand in the way of an honest examination of black motherhood. Walker, then, writes of the tragedy, abuse, loneliness, and desperation she finds present in black reality. Like her colleague and friend Barbara Smith, she believes that "sexual politics are as real in black women's lives as racial politics, and are as real as the politics of class."[63] She does not argue, as does Jessie Bernard, that sexism is the greater burden for black women and racism the greater burden for black men.[6] Rather, she argues that the American reality alienates one economic group from another, one race from another, and the male from the female. Copeland's tragedy illustrates, is stark, oppressive, and devastating. And it is in the experience of motherhood, and in wifehood as well, that the sound of the destruction is most profound.

4

"GOING NOWHERE IMMEDIATE"
BLACK WOMEN OF HOPELESSNESS

Edging into life from the back door. Becoming.
Everybody in the world was in a position to give
them orders. White women said, "Do this." White
children said, "Give me that." White men said,
"Come here." Black men said, "Lay down." The
only people they need not take orders from were
black children and each other.

—*Toni Morrison,*The Bluest Eye, *1970*

Poor and unskilled black women have historically been ghettoized in the labor market of white America. They are domestics in white homes, service workers in white-owned hospitals and hotels, field hands on white-owned farms, and operatives in white-owned factories. In large urban areas they are often number runners, prostitutes, and procurers. Of all these categories, that of domestic is the job slot most often associated in the national thinking with black women, and for obvious reasons: black women are disproportionately represented in the labor market in this category.

Jeanne Noble analyzes this labor picture within the context of history; and within that context, she emphasizes race, sex, and class. Explaining that racial and class patterns are stubborn and unyielding in white America, Noble writes that black women have been systematically programmed for the last hundred and twenty years to do that which was essentially theirs to do during slavery: serve as maids and mammies for white Americans:

114

The long shadow of slavery may be fading for some, but over one fourth of all black sisters are still marketing the skills of our ancestors who washed, scrubbed, and hoed in the mansion yards and cotton fields of Southern plantations, and whose daughters entered the census page of the twentieth century with little choice except to do the same.

As late as 1973, "25.5 percent of [black women in the labor market] worked in the service occupations, and among this group 17.9 percent worked exclusively in private households—in other words, as domestics." Of a total of 1.5 million domestics in the nation, 69 percent were black women.[2]

Domestic work is emotionally charged for black women for several reasons. First of all, it has been viewed by the nation, and by black women themselves, as demeaning. "Reflecting the feelings of their society, black women domestics look upon their jobs as requiring little skill, and they believe that nobody would do this work if they could do anything else. . . . They have little sense of their beauty and rarely realize their worth."[3] Second, the job brings home in concrete ways the magnitude of the injustice they suffer because they are poor, black, and female. They leave apartments of poverty to spend the day working in homes of comfort and luxury, and they return to those apartments with meager earnings and injured pride. They see the stark contrast between the world of the have-nots and the world of the haves they labor in to alleviate their families' suffering.

Such work is emotionally charged also because it reinforces for many black women their status in American culture as unattractive women of superior strength. Because they are strong women, they are capable, it is assumed, of performing tasks that white women are not expected to do—such as washing windows, mopping and waxing floors, and carrying large bags of groceries. And because they are unattractive by white America's standards, they are expected to receive pleasure from caring for wardrobes, polishing trays on which cosmetics and fragrances are placed, and keeping clear of streaks and blurs the mirrors that reflect white beauty. In Hollywood movies, black domestics prepared baths for their female employers and even brushed the hundred strokes needed for healthy hair. It was her resentment of these demeaning roles that caused Hattie McDaniel to refuse to be "ghettoized" in the movie industry.[4] In the real world, working as a domestic in white homes has been for some black women like working in the lioness's den. The lioness does not roar; she condescends and humiliates. She does not devour with claws and superior strength; she demeans with expressions of her idealized fragility and beauty.

Added to these problems is the unending list of responsibilities black domestics are required to take on, for the job is never simply a housecleaning job; it includes almost all of the tasks identified by American culture as "woman's work." Black women cook family meals, often preparing favorite dishes for the children and unplanned snacks for the husbands of white women. They launder shirts, polish shoes, and carry and pick up cleaning. And they often serve as the large bosom of humanity on which members of the white family lay their individual burdens of white children, for whom they are surrogate mothers. This last role is emphasized in William Faulkner's portrait of Dilsey in *The Sound and the Fury*. Dilsey "endures" through various crises in the Compson family, and out of her great humanity salves their deepest hurts. She is seen by the nation as the epitome of the black domestic in white America.

The contributions of black domestics to the lives of white women and men are exceeded only by their contributions to the lives of white children. The point being made here is that black domestics throughout history have not been just maids; they have been the great earth mother of this nation.

When we look carefully at all the job of domestic entails, we understand why it is not simply a job. It is an *institution* in American culture. The tragedy is that for all this institution asks of black women and for all it receives from them, it gives little in return. Black domestics understand this imbalance. A character in Douglas Turner Ward's play *"Happy Ending"* describes her life as a domestic with controlled anger:

> ". . . from top to bottom, I cook the food, scrub
> the floor, open the door, serve the tables, answer
> the phones, raise the children, lay out the

> clothes, greet the guests, fix the drinks and
> dump the garbage—all for bad pay. . . . The
> money I git in my envelope ain't worth the time
> 'n' the headache. . . ."[5]

Then there is the condescension of white employers.

Black women understand the polarization of white women and black women into two distinct groups. They know, too, that this polarization is rooted at least as much in race as in class, for black women, regardless of their class, looks, and skills, are never "ladies":

> There are two kinds of females in this country—
> colored women and white ladies. Colored women
> are maids, cooks, taxi drivers, crossing guards,
> schoolteachers, welfare recipients, bar maids
> and the only time they become ladies is when
> they are cleaning ladies.[6]

Denied respect and admiration, "cleaning ladies" in American culture "grow old fast . . . watching white women stay young."[7]

Not all the characters discussed in this chapter are "cleaning ladies," but all are overworked in menial jobs, underpaid, humiliated, used, abused, and ignored. They are sensitive women who understand why they are suffering, and they respond with submission, bitterness, religious rationalizing, clever game playing, or anger. Though they are not always aware of all the factors that affect their lives, they do know that their lives are hostage to forces over which they have little control. Min and Mrs. Hedges in Ann Petry's *The Street* (1946), Josie in Alice Walker's *The Third Life of Grange Copeland* (1970), and Pauline Breedlove in Toni Morrison's *The Bluest Eye*(1970) are on a treadmill, "going nowhere immediate."[8]

The Street was the first protest novel written by a black woman. Set in Harlem during the thirties and forties, the novel is the story of Lutie Johnson's struggle to escape the filth and violence of 116th Street, but it contains the minor women characters who illustrate the position of black womanhood in capitalistic and racist America. The tragedy of black life, Petry writes, is that "the women have to work until they become drudges and the men stand by idle."[9] Young and old, the faces of the women on 116th Street "have a look of resignation, of complete acceptance," which betrays their inability to "protest against anything—even death" (p. 125).

Min epitomizes this complete acceptance in her lifestyle, behavior, and body carriage. She has spent her life as a domestic in white homes, never challenging the racial assumptions her employers make about her and never asking for more than what they consider her due. Though her outward response is one of *total* submission, Min is acutely aware of her exploitation by the white "madams" she works for. When a job is described by the employment agency as "a little cleaning," she knows the white women will add "heavy jobs like washing windows and walls and waxing floors," and "the care of innumerable children whose existence was never indicated on the employment contract." They will ignore her right to "days off" and "increase the work week to include Saturday and often even Sunday" (pp. 82–83).

In sentimental portrayals of the black domestic in white American fiction, praise and affection from white employers serve as palliatives, but for Petry's Min, there are no palliatives. To a one, Min observes, her madams are "openly contemptuous women who laughed at her even as they piled on more work; acting as though she were like a deaf, dumb, blind thing completely devoid of understanding" (p. 82). The sexual identity she shares with them is vitiated by race and by class. Indeed, Min sees white women as more her enemy than white men, because they overwork her one moment and humiliate her the next. The only white women Min knows are her cold and insensitive madams and the beautiful creatures whose faces appear in the conspicuous billboards that decorate the train that carries her from Harlem to suburbia.

Her life experience has destroyed Min's sense of self-worth. All she has ever known, Petry writes, is the polarity of black women as subjects of hard work and abuse and white women as madams of affluence and hostility. Nothing in her experience—or in the experiences of the other blacks she knows in Harlem— suggests that change is even remotely possible. Thus Min is resigned to things as they have always been. She looks closely at her life and sees "years and years like that": working as "a seven-day-a-week domestic serf who must do any job ordered by the white employer," burying herself under "great mounds of dirty clothes . . . getting no extra pay for the extra time involved," and remaining on a job "no matter how much work there was or how badly people treated her." Through it all, she has accepted whatever happened to her without making any effort to avoid a situation or to change one. By her own admission, she has "permitted herself to be used and mistreated" (pp. 82–82).

From the houses of white women, where she is exploited because of her race and class, Min returns to a small basement apartment, where she is exploited because of her sex. This is the point Petry makes as she fits the jagged pieces of Min's relationships with men into a picture of horror. In her experiences with white madams, Min at least receives something in return for her submission to hard work and humiliation; there is, after all, her meager earnings. But from black men, to whose control and hostility she also submits, Min receives nothing. What is worse, she must devise ways to keep what she has earned from being stolen from her. Three husbands always managed to find her money, "as though they could smell it out . . . where it was put in coffee pots, under plates, in the icebox, under mattresses, between the sheets or rugs" (p. 76). And when they were not robbing her, they were physically abusing her. All of them "had taught her" the techniques of brutality:

> First, the grip around the neck that pressed the windpipe out of position, so that the screams were choked off and no sound could emerge from her throat, and then a whole series of blows, and after that, after falling to the ground under the weight of the blows, the most painful part would come—landing with force, sinking deep into the soft, fleshy parts of her body, her stomach, her behind. (p. 221)

Wife beating and rape are sanctioned by the cultural notion that man has the right to dominate woman. Susan Brownmiller writes that a woman is vulnerable to rape because "forcible intercourse" is possible, and she is likewise vulnerable to beatings because she is, in most instances, physically weaker than a man. In Petry's imaginative re-creation of the reality of poor black women in Harlem, we find the suggestion that black women are distinguishable from black men as "victims" by their peculiar vulnerability to "man's basic weapon of force." Force, whether as rape or as a physical beating, is "the ultimate test of [man's] superior strength," or a conscious "act of intimidation by which . . . men keep . . . women in a state of fear."[10]

Petry's depiction of the dynamics of race and sex in Min's life is complex, shifting back and forth in emphasis. She does not pit race against sex, for every observation she makes about sexual oppression is clearly tied to "the street," her compelling metaphor for racial and class oppression. But in the structure of her novel, especially in the chapters dealing with Min, she reflects the ideas of Susan Brownmiller and other contemporary feminist scholars. In that male intimidation is physically and ruthlessly brutal, in that it takes place in the sanctity of Min's "home," in that it is committed by a member of her own race, and in that it is offered in response to a caring that approaches maternal tenderness, it is indisputably the greater personal burden. This is an imaginative statement of the point Abbey Lincoln makes in her essay "Who Will Revere the Black Woman?" In a list of abuses the black woman suffers, Lincoln includes the following observation: "her head is more regularly beaten than any other's woman's, and *by her own man*."[11] By including this suffering in her portrait of Min, Petry debunks the idea of the black woman as emasculator.

Min's self-destructive submission to male abuse is credible and in character. Her powerlessness and humiliation in the world of white madams has convinced her that there can be no comfort, peace, security, or respect for "colored women" and programmed her to accept abuse at the hands of black men. Lacking any awareness of the interplay between sexual oppression and racial oppression, and having no will for a struggle of any kind, Min places her life in the hands of white women and black men, two "others" whose reality is very different from hers.

In her common-law marriage with the superintendent of the apartment, Min is "spineless and . . . limp . . . like a soggy dishrag," a "whispering woman" whose "shrinking withdrawal in her way of sitting" suggests a "profound sense of self-denial" and a desire to take up "the least possible amount of space" (p. 21). When she opens the door to the apartment in the evenings, she seems to question her right to enter: "Min's key was inserted in the lock timidly, with a vague groping movement, and when the lock finally clicked back, she stood there for a second as though overwhelmed by the sound it made" (p. 90). Once inside the damp, narrow basement apartment, Min serves the superintendent as dutifully and unquestionably as she serves her madams: she washes his clothes, darns his socks, cooks his meals. In her own home she is an unpaid maid who keeps the place tidy for his comfort, without any assistance from the superintendent. She does not think or speak or ask questions. She simply moves through her "woman's work" as one who has internalized the most fundamental assumptions about woman's place and man's role. She has told herself repeatedly, and always with conviction, that "a woman by herself didn't stand much chance" (p. 86).

Until the superintendent is distracted by the presence of a new tenant, Lutie Johnson, Min accepts her posture of "shrinking withdrawal from life." However, when she learns that her "home" is threatened by the super's insane and aberrant desire to possess Lutie Johnson, Min makes what she believes is the first "defiant gesture" in her life: she goes to a prophet to have the super "fixed" (p. 82). Beneath the surface, this "defiant gesture" is not a challenge to things as they are, for the "fixing" of the super is meant only to assure that Min's place in the apartment as servant is not disturbed. But the "fixing" achieves the opposite of what Min expected: instead of changing the super, it changes her. She gains confidence from the magic of the bright green powder and the candles that she burns mysteriously for no more than five minutes each day, and she becomes aware of a part of herself that she had hidden under the mask of submission. She puts her key in the door with a thrust of "assurance" and the sound is "decisive and loud" (p. 90). For the first time in her life she has power over someone, though she doesn't realize that this "magic" power is at every moment threatened by her acceptance of assumptions about her basic powerlessness. These have blinded her to a fundamental fact about power that Marilyn French expresses simply and forcefully in *The Woman's Room*

(1977): "power is not something you possess, but is something granted to you by those you have power over."[12]

When Min forgets to observe the rituals suggested by the prophet, she is seized by a profound sense of dread. Every movement of the super

> made her heart jump. . . . Every sound he made was magnified. His muttering to himself was like thunder . . . and . . . set her eyes blinking so that she couldn't stop them. When he beat the dog, it made her sick, because as each blow landed the dog cried out sharply and her stomach would suck in against itself. [And when he was quiet], she felt impelled to locate him . . . for there was no telling what awful thing he might be doing. (p. 225)

This seizure of fear, heightened by her belief that she cannot win in a struggle of any kind, precipitates Min's decision to leave 116th Street. She speaks of "having room to breathe," and realizes at last that "she'd been running, running, running, and hadn't been able to stop long enough to get a nose full of air" (p. 224). She comes close to self-realization, but a lifetime of racial and sexual oppression prevents her from coming close enough. Once out on 116th Street, away from the superintendent, Min searches again for the "security" the presence of a man offers. She speaks coquettishly to a pushcart man, who assists her with her few belongings. Min's life is not likely to change much—the pushcart man, who will be her fourth "husband," carries the table in which her money is hidden.

Petry convincingly demonstrates how racism and poverty have robbed Min of a positive self-image. She is less convincing in showing that the black male's exploitation of the black female is solely the result of race and poverty. To be sure, the superintendent has lived in the darkness of the basement for years and, deprived of light, has become a deviant. Other black men, equally powerless in the white-dominated society, are rendered incapable of forming healthy relationships with women. Indeed, every black man in the novel is depicted as a victim of "the street," too crippled to enjoy the psychic health necessary to allow them to love and support the black women in their lives. While these facts explain the tragic devastation of Petry's black male characters, they do not explain why black women in her book submit to male control and abuse. For that explanation, we must look at Petry's treatment of cultural assumptions about "woman's place."

That these assumptions are present in the novel is evident in Petry's use of the advice of Mrs. Pizzini, an Italian woman whose husband owns a shop on the street: "not good for the woman to work when she's young. No good for the man" (p. 38). This was the sexual ethos that undergirded American culture in the forties. As the historical overview in Chapter 2 made clear, women left their "place" in the home to support the war effort, and at the end of the war, they were advised to return to their "natural" role as wives and mothers in the home. It was during this same period that "the feminine mystique" reached more deeply into the national consciousness. Although Mrs. Pizzini's advice is thoroughly "American," then, it is hardly relevant to black women and Petry's irony is justified: Mrs. Pizzini can subscribe to the notion of woman's "place" in the home because racism has not forced her to leave that "place" for the survival of her family.

From a psychological perspective, however, it does not matter that the advice is irrelevant to black reality, for values that shape the mainstream culture find their way into the consciousness of all members of the society, no matter how far outside the mainstream they may be. While there are polar groups in America— one black, the other white; one male, the other female; and one the haves, the other the have-nots—there is essentially one set of criteria for what is normal and what is deviant. This fact is most apparent in the numerous sociological studies that speak of the "deviance" of the black families that do not conform to America's standards of normality: the woman in the home, the man in the world of work. Such sociological assessments, like Mrs. Pizzini's warning, are examples of what Ryan calls the trick of "blaming the victim."[13] Inadvertently, they help perpetuate myths about the black experience, and in so doing, they validate the status quo.

What is Petry's response to the prevailing notion of the forties that "woman's place" is in the home? She seems to challenge this cultural assumption indirectly by depicting Mrs. Pizzini as a static character who stays in the same place, doing the same things, and even saying the same things. There is money in her life but no sparkle. Again, in her observations on the white Chandler women, who are filthy rich but very traditional women— Petry calls our attention to their empty existence. Though it is difficult to separate Petry's attitude toward race and class oppression from her attitude toward sexual oppression, we can speculate that the negative portraits of white women who remain in their "place" are comments on the sterility of "woman's place." There is no need to speculate on Petry's opinion of the impact the assumption has on black women. She attacks the system for believing in that "place" and denying it to poor black women.

The reality of Min and other black women in the novel bears the imprint of a corollary assumption about woman's place: man should be aggressive, and woman should be passive. Hence Min's "shrinking withdrawal from life."

Thus, racism makes Min subservient to white women, sexism makes her submissive to black men, and economic deprivation makes her, even in her flight from "the street," a black woman who is "going nowhere immediate." It is interesting that this novel of the forties parallels the thinking of black feminists of the seventies in the Combahee River Collective, who write that it is "difficult to separate race from class from sex oppression [in black women's lives] for they are most often experienced simultaneously."[14]

Since victimization of black people in general and black women in particular makes psychic health and economic success difficult, it follows that there can be no winners on "the street." But paradoxically, not all people are losers. Some of the characters in *The Street* manage to use the system for their own self-aggrandizement. Such a woman is Mrs. Hedges, a "very black woman," who ritualistically sits at the open window of her first-floor apartment, watching the coming and goings of black people. Even on cold days, she is there, as if bolted to her place, watching the women passers-by with eyes "as still and as malignant as the eyes of a snake":

They are the lonesome, sad-looking girls just up
from the South, or little girls who were tired of
going to high school and who had seen too many
movies and didn't have all the money to buy all
the things they wanted . . . [and] other little girls
who were only slightly older who woke up one
morning to discover that their husbands had
moved out. With no warning. Suddenly. (p. 159)

Mrs. Hedges studies them carefully and, at the propitious moment, calls out, "Dearie . . . I been seeing you go by. And I was
wondering if you wouldn't like to earn a little extra money sometime" (p. 157). Mrs. Hedges is a "colored madam" who lures black
women into the trap of prostitution. It might be thought that
putting a black character who capitalizes on black powerlessness
in a novel of protest would dilute the protest, but Petry understands that black participation in the victimization of black people
is but a deeper plunge into the same river.

What is most interesting about Petry's presentation of this
problem is her emphasis on Mrs. Hedges' sensitivity to her own
unattractiveness. Cursed by an "enormous size" (p. 151), she is
not considered feminine in a culture that worships slender
frames; nor, with her deep-purple blackness, beautiful in a culture that worships whiteness. She desperately wants a man's
love, which, she believes, will give her a sense of worth in spite of
her physical curses. When she leaves her small Georgia community for Harlem, it is to "find a man who would fall in love with
her" (p. 151). Her migration to the North is prompted by sexual
desire, not by the dream of escaping racial oppression in "the
promised land."

The move is one of several ironies in the novel, for on "the
street" even attractive women must suspend their dreams as
women as they struggle to survive as blacks—and often the suspension lasts forever. Mrs. Hedges learns this soon after she
arrives on 116th Street. In her small black community in Georgia, she was a curiosity. In Harlem, she is a monstrosity. On the
faces of white people in employment agencies she sees "an uncontrollable revulsion. . . . They glanced at each other, tried in vain

to control their faces or didn't bother to try at all" (p. 151). Unable to find work and without the money to return to Georgia, Mrs. Hedges prowls the streets of Harlem, driven by a "gnawing, insatiable hunger." In her abysmal poverty she scavanges in garbage cans for food and clothes herself in discarded rags. A pathetic contrast to her fantasized image of herself, she wears "thin, ragged clothes that exaggerate her size and discarded men's shoes" that cramp her feet "so that she limped slightly" (p. 151).

On one of her nightly prowls for food, she meets Junto, a white man who is as destitute as she, but whose whiteness is a decided advantage in a racist culture. Because he is both white and male, he has been socialized to be both competitive and powerful. Out of this socialization he converts his foraging into a business. With Mrs. Hedges' help, he collects scraps, sells them, and in time amasses a fortune. The relationship between Junto and Mrs. Hedges is a metaphor for the exploitation of black people. Mrs. Hedges tills, but she does not reap bountiful harvests. Although Junto could not have succeeded without her assistance, she is definitely less than a real partner. In fact, she is a janitor in one of his many buildings, and the procurer of his lucrative prostitution business.

Mrs. Hedges solicits women so desperate they see no alternative to prostitution—"good girls" whom the environment has corrupted. Petry's one-dimensional image of prostitutes is common to novels of the literary school of naturalism. With a social worker's attention to details of cause-and-effect, Petry denounces the injustices that force the innocent to prostitute themselves. Three decades later, black women novelists would expand their artistic lens and give us a different image of prostitutes. Morrison, for example, in *The Bluest Eye* (1970) describes a group of black prostitutes—the "merry gargoyles," she calls them—as "whores" who have never been innocent or good and who "hate men, all men, without shame, apology, or discrimination" (pp. 47–48). But Petry's goal as an artist of the forties was to protect the victimization of black people. In her vision therefore, prostitutes must be *victims*.

Petry's analysis of prostitution in America is actually more complex than her one-dimensional image of the "ruined" woman suggests. In some ways, she agrees with Maimie Pinzer, a nineteenth-century Jewish prostitute, who wrote that poor women choose "their means of survival from a position of socially structured powerlessness," and their options are always the same: "prostitution, marriage and unskilled menial jobs."[15] But black women in Petry's vision do not have the option of marriage as an avenue to security, since their men are victimized by the same system that victimizes them. Also, they are ten times more likely to be entrapped in poverty than white women. And finally, their humanity is systematically denied primarily because they are poor black females, and only secondarily because they are prostitutes. So, no matter how similar are the sufferings of poor white women and poor black women, racism makes a crucial difference.

Mrs. Hedges gives little thought to the pernicious life in store for the vulnerable women she is procuring. She is interested only in making money without having to go into the world and confront the laughter and ridicule her appearance produces. This need to protect herself at the expense of other women explains why it is she who suggests to Junto that he begin a business of prostitution with her help. Her rationalization reveals how profoundly she has internalized the cultural assumption that men, but not women, should be cared for. Because black men "hadn't got anything out of life and knew clearly that they never would get it," Mrs. Hedges reasons, they need a way "to escape their hopes and fears" (p. 156). Thoroughly conditioned by sexist assumptions about men's needs and women's obligations to meet those needs, she does not realize that black women, too, need an escape. That they are the vehicles for man's escape is an expression of the profoundness of their oppression.

Once Mrs. Hedges has security as a "partner" in Junto's business, she takes her woman's dream out of suspension. Without money, she had no hope of gaining a man's love; with money, she can buy what her physical appearance has denied her. She does not equivocate about her goal: nothing except the presence of a man in her life can validate her and make her whole. More is involved here than the romantic fantasy of a woman in search of a Prince Charming who will make her a queen. In fact, Mrs. Hedges has no such illusions; she knows that she will not be pampered or even loved. She simply wants a man in her life, and with money "she could pick [one] for herself and he would be glad to have her" (p. 152). For her, therefore, economic success is not a means of survival in a racist society. Rather, it is the prerequisite for her dreams as a woman.

The fickle hand of fate—always operative in naturalistic novels—destroys Mrs. Hedges' woman's dream forever. In Theodore Dreiser's *An American Tragedy* fate is a drowning accident; in Richard Wright's *Native Son* it is an accidental suffocation. In Petry's *The Street* it is a raging fire. Mrs. Hedges pushes herself through a narrow aperture in the burning five story building, feeling her flesh tear and burn. It is significant that even in the midst of this life-and-death situation, her thoughts are on her woman's dream: all she needed "was to get badly burned, and never as long as she lived would any man look at her and want her." Her agony is profound: "No matter how much money she acquired, [men] still wouldn't want her. No sum of money would be big enough to make them pretend to want her" (p. 152).

Miraculously, Mrs. Hedges survives the fire, but she must live the remainder of her life without hair on her head. That Petry chooses baldness as the most damaging scar Mrs. Hedges suffers as a result of the fire underscores the sexual ramifications of the portrait. Hair, of all physical assets, is culturally associated with beauty, softness, and femininity. Many black women, from childhood until death, undergo a painful heat-and-metal-comb process in an effort to make their kinky hair more like the soft straight or curly locks of white women. Mrs. Hedges can wear a wig, of course; she can cover her disfigurement with expensive clothes, or even undergo plastic surgery at Junto's expense. But all these efforts would be useless, for she has lost forever the possibility of obtaining a man. So, in her bandanna she takes up her station at the window of the apartment building on 116th Street in Harlem and holds herself aloof from the horrors of life in that community. Racially and sexually, she is a lost woman.

The sad, lonesome girls in Walker's *The Third Life of Grange Copeland* make their way down rural roads of dust and between vast fields of cotton. Though this masterpiece of southern black literature, as Walker explained in an interview, is "ostensibly about a man and his son," it is "the women and how they are treated that colors everything."[16] The colors are the grays of oppression, the blues of loneliness, and, for Josie, the most colorful woman in the novel, the reds of passion and anger.

Josie was born on the rich clay soil of Georgia and was reared in a small rural community owned by white men who exact from black sharecroppers a pound of their dreams for every ounce of harvest their labor brings. In this community there are only two roles for women—wife/mother and whore. Josie was socialized to believe that power belongs to white men, who own the land, and to black men, who own their women. She is as certain of the latter as she is of the former, for she has been reared in a male-dominated home. Her mother is a woman of silence and fear, "a meek woman" who "rarely agreed with [Josie's] father, but never argued with him."[17] Josie is programmed to believe that this is the way things are for women and the way they must remain. Only when she is humiliated and abused as a woman does Josie begin to dream and to plan a new life for herself, but in the new life she leaves the racial boundaries of her life undisturbed.

Pregnant at sixteen, Josie incurs the wrath of her father and is cast out of the house for the shame she has brought to the family. She attempts to regain her father's love at a party she gives in his honor. He takes her gifts, sits proudly amid his circle of male friends like a patriarch whose right to the throne is god-given and beyond challenge, and refuses to acknowledge the party is Josie's plea for reconciliation. Out of frustration she takes the drinks he refuses to accept from her hands and gulps them down, one by one, until she is intoxicated. She falls "clumsily on her back within the curve of the all-male semi-circle" (p. 40). Judge, jury, and now executioner, Josie's father presses his foot into her shoulder and forbids anyone to touch her: "I hear she can do *tricks* on her back like that" (p. 41). Josie's mother weeps, but she does not challenge her husband's right to hold her daughter under his foot "like a spider deformed and grotesque" (p. 41). Instead, she suppresses her maternal rage and submits to her husband's control.

The cultural assumption that men are women's protectors has no voice in Walker's novel. Perhaps, as Elizabeth Schultz suggests, this assumption figures mainly in fiction written by black men: Frank Yerby's *Health Card*, James Baldwin's *Beale Street*, and John Killens's *Youngblood*, for example. "Black women novelists seem to have less faith [in the black man's role as protector] for they present the black woman as having to protect herself. Her form of resistance is liberating, but it is resistance by reaction, through hatred, anger, and violence."[18] In Petry's portrait of Min in *The Street*, a novel of the forties, and Walker's portrait of Mem in *The Third Life of Grange Copeland*, a novel of the seventies, the black woman struggles alone, and often her adversary is her male "protector." Clearly, this is Josie's tragedy. Receiving no support from her mother as she is crushed under father's foot, she has to struggle out of bondage alone. Like a phoenix who rises from the ashes with unfurled wings, she soars above male control to become the richest and most powerful black person, male or female, in the community. Her damnation has become her salvation, and she achieved it alone.

Salvation from male oppression, however, is not the same as liberation from sexual assumptions about male control and female surrender. Josie decides that she will never again be controlled or humiliated by a man, but she does not see her particular grievances as emblematic of women's reality. Her response to these grievances is to seek vengeance against those who abused her. If women are bodies to be used by men for their pleasure and then discarded, so be it. Josie intends to make the most of what she is supposed to be. She becomes a prostitute.

In a little shack on the aptly named Poontang Street, Josie does "her job with a gusto that denied shame" and "demands her money with an authority that squelched all pity" (p. 41). In time, having saved her earnings, she moves from the little shack to her own establishment, the Dew Drop Inn, the only house of pleasure in the community. As proprietor and prostitute, she vents her rage at men in the community.

> When they became too old to "cut the mustard" any more, she treated them with *jolly* cruelty and a *sadistic* kind of concern. She often did a strip tease in the center of their eagerly constructed semicircle, bumping and grinding,

moaning to herself, charging them the last
pennies of their meager old-age savings to watch
her, but daring them to touch. (p. 41)

Economic power—so rare for women in the small community—
does not liberate Josie. She is respected because she is wealthy,
but she is confined to a role named by men for women. Tragically,
she is able to strike out sadistically against men, but unable to
redeem herself from their image of her as a ruined and worthless
woman. She is a prisoner, then, continually executed by the male
community's assessment of her as a sex object. Like Petry's Mrs.
Hedges in *The Street*, she is a winner who loses.

Elizabeth Schultz has observed that both the black "respectable woman" and the prostitute are forced to view themselves as
sexual objects, removed from the "possibility of growth and freedom."[19] Early in life Josie falls victim to male designs on her
physical vulnerability. Walker writes lyrically, "Josie had never
been young, had never smelled of milk or flowers, but only of a
sweet decay." If someone would "take the trouble to expose inch
after inch of her to one bright consuming fire of blind adoration
and love," Josie might be "made clean" (p. 42). But the smell of
decay lingers, for there is no challenge to sexism in the rural
community; and convinced of her irredeemable worthlessness as
a woman, Josie plays well the role of a "devouring cat, voracious
and sly" (p. 36).

One of the prevailing myths about women is that they are
always vulnerable to the tragedy of having loved and lost. By
sentimental ballads and fairy tales, girls entering puberty are
psychologically prepared for the agony and the ecstasy of romantic love. This myth, like all myths, connects to an extent with
truth, and Walker develops the point in her story of Josie. Having lost her first love, Grange Copeland, Josie envelopes
Grange's son, Brownfield, in unchecked passion. She attempts
"to eat him up, swallow him down alive" (p. 36). She pampers
him, functioning as both mother and lover. She fights her whorish daughter for his affection. She makes him economically dependent on her, the better to effect control over his life. She uses
him for the physical pleasure he gives her. She is, in fact, "masculine" in her relationship with Brownfield: Josie adopts and per-

fects every posture deemed acceptable for men in their relationships with women. Even the male desire to sleep with virgins (a
desire that strokes their egos) is included in Walker's description
of Josie: Josie takes pleasure in "screwing" Brownfield because
he is "a clean young animal" [she and her daughter] had not
finished soiling" (p. 41). This is Josie's game, and while it gives
her pleasure, it does not fulfill her as a woman. For that, she
needs a special love to which "woman gives her all."

But Josie never experiences fulfillment. She "gives her all" to
the Copeland men, Grange and his son Brownfield, without
realizing that their destruction in the narrow space of race can
only deepen her misery in the dark enclosure of sex. As sharecroppers they live in virtual slavery, and they see the world
through eyes jaundiced by self-hatred. Grange strikes out at the
sharecropping system and "Captain Shipley" by abusing his wife,
Margaret, and using Josie as a salve for his pain. His sorrow is
profound, but so, too, is Margaret's. She is weary of endless
hours of woman's work in the house and exhausting physical
labor in the field. After five years of patience and understanding,
she follows Grange's example. She neglects her child; she has
affairs. Because she is female, she is vulnerable to additional and
even justifiable abuse from Grange. After all, even in the face of
her husband's infidelity a woman does not have the right to seek
love away from the marriage. Because she is black, she is vulnerable to the lust of Captain Shipley, all the more vulnerable, Walker implies, since her loyalty to Grange would permit her to
grant Shipley favors in exchange for reductions in Grange's debt.
Predictably, her attempts to steal a little pleasure for her life
give her only encompassing misery. When she gives birth to
Shipley's child, Grange has an excuse to abandon her. Her guilt
and despair lead to her murder of the half-white child and her
suicide.

The economic system that once enslaved the father also en-
slaves the son, for there are few alternatives to sharecropping for
black people in the small Georgia town. Like his father before
him, Brownfield tills land owned by a white man who enjoys the
full harvest of Brownfield's labor. Like his father, Brownfield
strikes out at this cruel system by abusing his gentle wife Mem

and their three children, taking diabolical pleasure in seeing
them grovel in fear before him:

> Instinctively, with his own life as an example, he
> had denied the possibility of a better life for his
> children. He had enslaved his own family, given
> them weakness when they needed strength,
> made them powerless before any enemy that
> stood beyond him. Now when they thought of
> "the enemy" their own father would straddle
> their vision. (p. 86)

Brownfield is beyond salvation because he yields his humanity to
external forces and justifies the monster within by placing all
blame for his failures on white folks. When he moves his family
from a decent house in town, which Mem had rented, to a squalid,
hay-filled shack owned by Mr. J. L., Brownfield embraces his
own damnation.

At this most difficult period in Brownfield's life, Grange returns to do penance for the sins of his first life, the sins which
explain, in part, the tragedy of his son. Unlike Brownfield,
Grange left the South in search of promises of a new life in New
York City, or in search of experiences that could remove his guilt
as a negligent father, abusive husband, and defeated human being. He finds neither. In the cold and impersonal world of New
York, his blackness is no less depised, his manhood no less questioned. He learns this lesson painfully when he sees a pregnant
white woman fall into a pond in Central Park. He attempts to
rescue her, but the woman disdainfully refuses to take his out-
stretched hand. This experience is the beginning of Grange's
discovery of self. On the one hand, he feels responsible for the
woman's death because he had not insisted that she accept his
assistance. On the other hand, he feels that her death was his
liberation. Walker writes:

> The death of the woman was simple murder, he
> thought, and soul condemning; but in a strange
> way, a bizarre way, it liberated him. He felt in

some way repaid for his own unfortunate life. It
was the taking of that white woman's life—and
the denying of the life of her child—the taking of
her life, not the taking of her money, that forced
him to want to try to live again. (p. 153)

It is this desire to "live again" that takes Grange back to the
small Georgia town. He reaches out to Brownfield, to save him
from crippling self-hatred, explaining that he "used to blame the
white folks too. For they *is* the cause of all the dirt we have to
swallow." But this attitude is the real danger, he explains:

"By George, I know the danger of putting all the
blame on somebody else for the mess you make
out of your life. I fell into the trap myself! And
I'm bound to believe that that's the way the
white folks can corrupt you even when you done
held up before. 'Cause when they got you thinking that they're to blame for *every*thing they
have you thinking they's some kind of gods! You
can't do nothing wrong without them being behind it. You gits as weak as water, no feeling of
doing *nothing* yourself. Then you begins to think
up evil and begins to destroy everybody around
you, and you blames it on the crackers. *Shit!*
Nobody's as powerful as we make them out to
be. We got our own *souls* don't we? (p. 223)

His sermons come too late for Brownfield, who in Grange's
absence had begun "to destroy everybody around" him. His efforts to comfort and feed Brownfield's family only widen the gulf
between father and son. His newly discovered humanity only
magnifies Brownfield's loss of his soul. Ironically, Brownfield festers in rage. He strikes out at the father whom he fears as much
as he loathes by aiming the full barrel of a shotgun at Mem's face
and standing without remorse over her lifeless body.

He wouldn't repent. None of what he had done
mattered any more. It was over. What had to

happen happened: the beautiful faded, the pretty
became ugly, the sweetness soured. He had
never believed it could turn out any other way.
But what had *she* thought, his quiet wife, when
he proved to be more cruel to her than any white
man, or twenty? . . . Instead of rage, she had had
an inner sovereignty, a core of self, which, alas,
her husband had not had. She had possessed an
embedded strength that Brownfield could not
match. (p. 245)

Following Mem's death, one daughter becomes a prostitute.
Another goes insane. Ruth, the youngest, becomes Grange's
child, his way to salvation, his "third life." It is this Grange
Copeland to whom Josie gives everything. Out of "love," she sells
her business and shares the money with Grange. With his money
and, mainly, hers, he buys a farm where he "raised *his* own
bread, fermented *his* own wine, cured *his* own meat." Finally *he*
was *his* own boss—"at least *he* was free" (italics added, p. 156).
For Josie, however, there is no freedom. Only with Ruth does
Grange share his intimate feelings and only because of her is he
redeemed and made whole. Josie plots with Brownfield to have
the courts take Ruth from Grange, not realizing that even if Ruth
lives elsewhere the new Grange can no longer love the Josie of his
past. He can be gentle toward her and even feel the pain of her
loneliness, but he cannot love her as she wants to be loved. Nor
does she realize that Grange would sacrifice his life for Ruth's
chances for a full and meaningful existence. Thus, does he murder Brownfield in the courtroom when he loses custody of Ruth.
Having removed the only obstacle to her future, Grange stoically
returns to the farm and waits for the posse. Josie is once again
alone. In her sixties she is bereft of her fortune and aged out of
the "bumping and grinding" that had been her livelihood: "once
again she had been used by a man and discarded when his satisfaction was secured" (p. 156). Her father's judgment of her becomes her own: she was "the biggest curse in her life and it was
her fate to be an everlasting blunderer into misery" (p. 150).

Walker takes the feminist position that in a sexist culture
women are socialized to believe that their lives must be reflectors

of the lives of men. But she seems to reject the notion that socialization is the *only* cause of the differences between women and men. In the images and colors that define women in the novel, there is the implication that the special quality that distinguishes women from men is women's preference for love over power, their delight in giving as opposed to controlling. When black men can be whole in white society and resist "the ostensible psychological necessity to brutalize black women as the only outlet for the hatred, anger, shame and envy resulting from their own brutalization,"[20] black women will thrive because they are so capable of intense love.

In Toni Morrison's *The Bluest Eye* (1970) black women move from light into darkness when they migrate from the rural land of their birth to the industrial Midwest. Set in a small Ohio town in the forties, the novel is the tragic story of eleven-year-old Pecola Breedlove, "who yearns for acceptance into life of pretty dresses and shoes . . . and jewelry, into . . . a Storybook life peopled by a laughing mother and smiling father and friendly playmates." She takes as her ideal, writes critic Joan Bischoff, "the blonde-haired, blue-eyed girl epitomized by Shirley Temple," and reasons that "if she herself were thus given beauty, she would simultaneously fall heir to the rich tangibles and intangibles of the world of her dreams."[21] Imprisoned in both poverty and blackness, she finds her wish fulfilled in insanity. As the earlier discussion of Pauline Breedlove illustrated, it is she who contributes in a major way to Pecola's insanity.

A master at making place function as character development, Morrison begins her chapter on the Breedlove family with a description of the storefront house in which they live. "It is a strange house that does not recede into its background of leaden sky, nor harmonize with the gray frame houses and black telephone poles around it." Rather, it foists itself on the eye of the passerby in a manner that is "both irritating and melancholy" (p. 30). The house is more than a dwelling place; it is the mirror in which the confusion and violence of Pauline Breedlove's life is sharply reflected. In one of the most insightful studies written of *The Bluest Eye*, Joan Bischoff examines not only the symbolic description of the storefront house as a mirror of Pauline's life but also the symbolic heading of the opening chapter. She calls attention to Morrison's clever use of a typical passage from a Dick-and-Jane reader of the forties. In the reader, the passage is a scene of middle-class, suburban white family life:

> Here is the house. It is green and white. It has a
> red door. It is very pretty. Here is the fam-
> ily. . . . They are very happy. . . . See the cat. . . .
> Mother is very nice. . . . Father is smiling. . . .
> (p. 7)

In the novel, the passage is a "distorted run-on . . . one long collection of consonants and vowels seeming to signify nothing:"[22]

> Hereisthehouseitisgreenandwhiteithasareddoorit
> isveryprettyhereisthefamilytheyareveryhappy
> . . . seethecat . . . motherisverynice . . .
> fatherissmiling. (p. 8)

This run-on chapter head introduces the empty, misshapen life of the Breedloves and points up the existence of two separate societies in white America. Even when "mother" is present and "father" is smiling, the black family experience is perforated with chaos and violence.

When Morrison describes the Breedloves in the first chapter, we see Pauline, her two children, Sammy and Pecola, and her husband, Cholly, living bleak and lonely lives. Pauline is convinced that they are irredeemably ugly and that the poverty and chaos of their private lives are directly traceable to race and other physical attributes. With her talent for symmetrical phrasing, Morrison writes that Pauline and her family moved into the house "because they were poor and black," but they remain "there because they believed they were ugly" (p. 34). Pauline wraps her blackness, poverty, and ugliness around her "as a mantle . . . as an actor does a prop: for articulation of character, for the support of a role she frequently imagined was hers—martyrdom" (p. 34).

Morrison also writes of Pauline's frustration as an artist denied an outlet for her creativity. As earlier discussions have shown, the thwarted desires of the black woman artist are focal points in several black women's novels. The dilemma is addressed brilliantly by Alice Walker in her essay "In Search of Our Mothers' Gardens" (1974), where she writes of black women of the past, especially in the South, who "stumbled blindly through their lives . . . yielding . . . to the prophecy that they were unworthy even of hope." Many of them were artists, "driven to the numb and bleeding madness by the springs of creativity in them for which there was no release."[23] Without developing the idea as fully as she does in *Sula*, Morrison alludes to Pauline's artistic yearnings. They are not expressed in clay or paints, for Pauline had access to neither during her poor Alabama youth. Neither are they expressed in writing, for Pauline, as the oldest of eleven children, was forced to quit school to tend house for her working mother. Rather, her artistic yearnings are expressed in her delight in arranging things so that the finished product suggests order and beauty:

> She loved, most of all, to arrange things. To line things up in rows—jars on shelves at canning, peach pits on the step, sticks, stones, leaves. . . . Whatever portable plurality she found, she organized into neat lines, according to their size, shape or gradations of color. . . . (p. 89)

Pauline's dominant characteristic, however, is her overwhelming self-hatred, which precludes struggle of any kind. She is aware of the turning wheels of racial oppression in her life, but she makes no effort to stop the turning. Instead, she oils the axles and polishes the spokes so that the wheels turn more smoothly, more rapidly, and without interruption. She wears her maid's uniform with pride and bows low to the racist demands of the white Fisher family. She does not bemoan her lot in the house of whiteness and plenty. Rather, she smiles as she plays the role of surrogate mother for the Fishers' young daughter, Polly. She struts as she surveys the results of her handiwork—an immaculate house filled with enticing aromas of homemade pies and other dishes the Fishers enjoy. In her storefront house, "irritating and melancholy" in appearance, she is irredeemably ugly. In the Fisher home, she is beautiful and important, made so by the magic of service to white people.

The unmistakable resemblance between Morrison's Pauline Breedlove and the traditional image of the black mammy is surely intentional. As we have seen, the black mammy is a pervasive character in white American fiction. She appears as Dilsey in *The Sound and the Fury*, Calpurnia in Carson McCuller's *A Member of the Wedding*, Berenice in Harper Lee's *To Kill a Mockingbird*, and simply "Mammy" in Margaret Mitchell's *Gone with the Wind*. Whatever her name, and whatever the artistic merit of the book that contains her, she is always a dutiful black female servant who attempts to keep white families from cutting their souls on the shattered pieces of their morally bankrupt lives, while able to place only a thin and soiled bandage on the open wounds of her own family. Morrison uses the image, but she distinguishes between Pauline's reasons for being a mammy and the reasons that inform the myth. Pauline cleans the Fisher home so that its affluence and power are dazzling, and she neglects her own storefront house, letting the dust collect around the frayed furniture in the tiny and dreary narrow rooms. Affectionately she gives baths to the Fishers' daughter, Polly, dries her in thick white towels, and brushes the yellow hair as it slips like strands of gold between her fingers. To her own daughter, Pecola, she gives the back of her hand and cutting words of disgust, displeasure, and disapproval.

In one of the most poignant scenes in the novel, Pauline the mammy confronts Pauline the mother. Unexpectedly, Pecola appears at the Fisher home in need of maternal comfort and some whiskey, which she and her friends superstitiously believe will keep them from being "ruined" like the prostitutes in the community. When she accidentally knocks a freshly baked pie off the stove, she incurs the wrath of her mother:

> In one gallop she was on Pecola, and with the
> back of her hand knocked her to the floor. Pecola
> slid in the pie juice, one leg folding under her.

> Mrs. Breedlove yanked her up by the arm,
> slapped her again, and in a voice thin with anger
> called her "a crazy fool." (pp. 86–87)

The scene is a powerful statement on racial self-hatred and self-denial: Pauline rejects her own daughter because she has erased from her psyche the line separating reality from illusion, mammyhood from motherhood.

And yet, Pauline Breedlove is *not* a typical black mammy, for Morrison takes the image and turns it upside down and inside out so that one sees the image of the mammy as it is reflected in the psyche of Pauline Breedlove. Without denying Pauline's dutiful service to the white family, Morrison renders Pauline's understanding of what she does as mammy, and more importantly, why. She serves the Fishers not out of blind loyalty to white people, but because she believes that *she* deserves some power and peace in life, and it is only in their world of plenty that she can get them. In her mind, then, she is not yielding to powerlessness; she is acquiring power. She is convinced that "power, praise and luxury were hers in this household" (p. 101).

The sexual dimensions of Pauline's life are equally complex and equally tragic. As a woman, she knew bliss in the red-clay, all black community of the small Alabama town of her birth, where all the colors of spring were in her soul. Her love for Cholly and their relationship of warmth and trust were "like all the bits of color from . . . down home" (p. 91). In Alabama they "loved each other" and Cholly "seemed to relish her company" (p. 92). When they leave the South, the colors of spring disappear from Pauline's life, replaced by a smoke-laden sky and streets paved with concrete.

The negative impact of the North on black families from the South is a common theme in history and sociological studies. John Hope Franklin writes that "family disorganization and disintegration were a logical consequence of all the social ills associated with the maladjustment in urban life."[24] In *The Negro Family in the United States* (1939), the first serious study of the black family, E. Franklin Frazier develops the same thesis, offering data on broken homes, juvenile delinquency, and "fathers on leave."[25]

Since the publication of Frazier's study, sociological analyses have continued to document the detrimental effect of the northern experience on the black family, and they have been reflected in black fiction's "mirror of reality"—dramatically in Paul Laurence Dunbar's *Sport of the Gods* (1906) and John Oliver Killens' *Sissie* (1966). Morrison's portrait of the Breedloves is, therefore, part of a tradition in black literature.

Where Morrison's novel is different is in its treatment of Pauline's response to the changes the migration has made in her life as a woman. In the South, she had been happy to wait passively on a country road for the magic of love. In the North, Cholly comes and goes as he pleases, gorging himself on the ephemeral pleasures of city life, while Pauline remains confined at home, exhausting herself with the unending tasks of woman's work. She has no economic power, for Cholly decides how the family's money is spent and when. Even when Pauline goes out to work as a domestic to add to their income, Cholly retains the power of the purse. The particulars of her life are familiar details in sociological studies of poor black families in which the man— contrary to the myth of the black matriarchy and contrary to the belief that employment brings power—holds unchallenged the reins of power. Racism denies Cholly power in the larger society; sexism gives him power in the privacy of his home.

Another dimension of Morrison's depiction of the Breedloves' alienation in the North is the extent to which Pauline sympathizes with Cholly as he metamorphoses from a gentle man to a drunken wife beater. When her white employer advises her to leave Cholly, Pauline analyzes her plight not just as a woman abused by a man but, significantly, as a black woman whose man is being psychologically diminished. Pauline's identity as a *poor* woman produces sympathy for Cholly: "What he gone give me alimony on?" And her allegiance as a *black* woman causes her to soften her rage: "It didn't seem none too bright for a black woman to leave a black man for a white woman" (p. 95). What is there in life for a black woman, Pauline asks, if not union with a black man? White people simply don't understand what "good a man is." They think he's "good for paying bills" because white men work and white women stay home. For Pauline, who is capable of supporting herself, Cholly is "good for" adding meaning to her life as a woman. He validates her because he is a man, and also because he shares with her a history of racial outrage.

Pauline Breedlove knows only one joy in life, and that joy is associated with her sexuality. In the early days, she recalls, lovemaking with Cholly gave her a sense of power and wholeness she could not otherwise experience:

> When Cholly let go of all he has, and give it to me. To *me*. To *me*. . . . I feel a power. I be strong, I be pretty, I be young. . . . And it be a rainbow all inside. (pp. 103–104)

When her sexual life with Cholly diminishes, Pauline retreats into religious rationalizing, which convinces her that the sorrow of her life "don't make no difference . . . it is sure to be a glory" (p. 100). But she wistfully longs for the one experience that once gave her "glory" here on earth, an experience associated with her reality as a woman. Sadly she says that the "only thing I miss sometime is that rainbow" of sexual pleasure (p. 104).

From a feminist perspective, Morrison's novel is a study of the various degrees of fulfillment women experience as women. Pauline is at one end of the spectrum. Other women characters are less obviously deprived—at least economically. Some are "comfortable" completely immersed in motherhood and find peace in resignation to the limitations on their lives. Mrs. McTeer, whose daughters befriend Pecola, is such a woman. She rears her family in rooms "peopled by roaches and mice" (p. 12) and open around windows and doors to the cold wind. She makes ends meet by taking in boarders and by "watching every possibility of excess" (p. 17). Like other women in the community, she dreads the "real terror of life," being put "outdoors," and "having no place to go." Claudia McTeer explains the reality of her mother and other women in the community:

> Being a minority in both caste and class we moved about . . . on the hem of life, struggling to consolidate our weaknesses and hang on, or to

creep singly up into the major folds of the garment. (p. 18)

The second group of women, whom Morrison calls the "sugarbrown Mobile girls," (p. 69) lives in better neighborhoods where everyone is employed and where there are nice houses with porch swings and sunflowers and pots of bleeding hearts. These women are poor imitations of what they believe whiteness to be. They have smooth hands and slim ankles. They wash with "orange-colored Lifebuoy soap, dust themselves with Cashmere Bouquet and soften their skin with Jergen's Lotion" (p. 68). Though they marry and have children, they find sex repulsive. At land-grant colleges and normal schools where they are educated, they learn "how to do the white man's work with refinement . . . how to instruct black children in obedience" and how to develop "thrift, patience, high morals, and good manners" (p. 68). They are fake and frigid women who deny their blackness and their sexuality, who try to get "rid of the funkiness."

> The dreadful funkiness of passion, the funkiness of nature, the funkiness of the wide range of human emotions.

> Wherever it erupts, this Funk they wipe it away; where it crusts, they dissolve it; whever it drips, flowers, or clings, they find it and fight it until it dies. They fight this battle all the way to the grave. (p. 68)

The third category of women Morrison depicts in *The Bluest Eye* have no desire for prosperity or rootedness of any kind. These women are prostitutes, embittered and frigid in lovemaking because they choose to be. And they choose to be because they "hate men . . . without shame, apology, or discrimination." Puerto Ricans, Mexicans, Poles, Jews, white men, black men— all men come under "their jaundiced eye" (p. 47).

Regardless of the category in which her women characters exist, Morrison makes an unchanging observation about them:

they are removed from the possibility of self-knowledge, self-expression, and freedom. The measure of their lives is the extent to which, in old age, they will be able to look back with satisfaction on their younger years. Walker assesses Josie's life from this same perspective, for she writes of Josie at sixty without economic security and, worse, with no memories of a joyous past. Ann Petry draws Mrs. Hedges and Min as women with burdens so acute that they grow old too fast. All of the women characters discussed in this chapter—those in a novel of the forties, those in two novels of the seventies, those in an urban environment, and those rooted in the dust and clay of the rural South—edge "into life from the back door." It is only in old age that they experience freedom and security. Morrison writes:

> Then they were old. . . . With relief they wrapped their heads in rags, and their breasts in flannel; eased their feet into felt. They were through with lust and lactation, beyond tears and terror. . . . They were old enough to be irritable when and where they chose, tired enough to look forward to death, disinterested enough to accept the idea of pain while ignoring the presence of pain. *They were in fact and at last free* [italics added]. (p. 110)

5

"JOURNEYING FROM CAN'T TO CAN" AND SOMETIMES BACK TO "CAN'T"

BLACK WOMEN OF CHALLENGE AND CONTRADICTION

What about the colored woman? What about her?

> —Mariah Upshur in Sarah Wright,
> This Child's Gonna Live, *1969*

we are lonely
. . . .
knowing that we must
walk back-wards nonchalantly on our tip-toessss
> *into*
happiness
> *if only for stingy moments*

we know too much
we learn to understand everything,
to make too much sense out
of the world
of pain
> *of lonely. . . .*

> —Carolyn Rodgers, "A Poem for Some Black
> Women," *1969*

From the nineteenth century, when Sojourner Truth asked, "Ar'nt I a Woman?" to the 1970s, when Shirley Chisholm spoke boldly of the two burdens against which black women must struggle simultaneously, many black women in white America have challenged in various ways the impact that racism and sexism have had on their reality. During slavery their resistance was often subtle—they put glass in the master's food, poisoned animals, broke tools, and feigned illness and ignorance to avoid work; but sometimes it was overt and violent—they ran away from plantations, they killed overseers and masters, and they killed themselves.

In the post–World War II period with which this book is concerned, black women were not unlike their ancestors in bondage: they resisted oppression both covertly and overtly. Many pretended to be ignorant, played clever games of submission, and wore a mask that concealed their true selves when doing so was an advantage. Other women, however, removed the mask and overtly challenged the restrictions placed on their lives. They journeyed from the South to the North in search of the "promised land." In the South and in the North, many of them fought oppression in violent ways. Not all black women incarcerated in the prisons of this nation are there for black-on-black crimes. Some are there because they struck out against whites who overstepped the safe limits of oppression. To this picture should be added the sustained involvement of many black women in the Civil Rights Movement of the sixties and the Black Power Movement of the sixties and seventies, as well as in smaller, but no less important, movements that sought change in their realities.

Throughout this history of challenge and resistance many black women have tended to give up the struggle for change before their goals are realized. They rarely live for themselves alone, so they rarely struggle without thinking of others. Therefore, if their resistance to oppression puts their husbands, children, and communities in jeopardy, they yield. Thus they journey from "can't to can" and then painfully back to "can't."[1]

It is fairly easy to document a tradition of challenge and resistance in the history of black women when we consider racial and class oppression. It is not so easy, however, to document such a tradition when we consider sexual oppression, for in scholarly works, black women are treated mainly as blacks and not as women. Nevertheless, we can make several assumptions, the most obvious of which is that black women who resist control of their lives by one group of "others" will not easily yield to control by another group of "others." A second assumption is that the sensitivity of many black women to sexual oppression early in the history of black America—even during the antebellum period—did not die with the passing of years, for sexism certainly did not fade away in the culture of this nation. Indeed, the challenges to sexism and racism made by black women in the seventies were perhaps explosions of many years of suppressed resentment. One black woman says that "inside all of us is a volcano on the verge of erupting."[2]

We can further assume that the pattern of resisting and then yielding evident in the racial history of black women has been present in their sexual history. Indeed, it could be argued that the pattern is even stronger there, for the challenge to sexual limitations raises fundamental questions that affect the women's personal lives, and the persons they challenge are often the men they love and whose children they have borne. Moreover, while they can easily find support among other black women for challenges to racial and class oppression, they often find themselves alone when they challenge sexual oppression. In fact, myths about women are so basic to our culture that women who attempt to reject them totally must reject a part of who they are. For these reasons, we can assume that many black women journey from "can't to can" and sometimes back to "can't" not only as blacks but also as women.

The women characters analyzed in this chapter make that journey in the contexts of race, class, and sex. They are, therefore, unlike the characters analyzed in the previous chapter, "Going Nowhere Immediate," who lead lives of submission and despair. Nor are they like the characters who will be analyzed in the following chapter, "Giving Birth to Self," who sustain challenges to limitations of any kind on their realities. Rather, their response to their anomalous position in white America lies somewhere between the two ends of the spectrum of consciousness. They are lonely women forced by external factors to "walk backwards nonchalantly on tiptoes into happiness if only for stingy moments," and as they resist and yield, they seek "to make . . . sense out of the world/of pain/of lonely."[3] We hear them as they speak for themselves. Their names are Lutie Johnson in Ann Petry's *The Street* (1946), Cleo Judson in Dorothy West's *The Living Is Easy* (1946), Mariah Upshur in Sarah Wright's *This Child's Gonna Live* (1969), Ursula Corregidora in Gayl Jones's *Corregidora* (1975), and Eva Medina in Jones's *Eva's Man* (1976).

Lutie Johnson was the first female protagonist in black American fiction to commit murder as an expression of her rage, and the novel in which she appears, *The Street*, was the first novel by a black woman in this country to receive significant literary attention beyond the decade in which it was published. It has not, however, received literary applause. Robert Bone considers it worthy of comment in *The Negro Novel in America* (1958), but he calls it a *"roman à thèse* . . . which offers a superficial analysis of life in a northern ghetto."[4] Noel Schraufnagel, in *From Apology to Protest: The Black American Novel* (1973), praises *The Street*'s realistic illustration of "the effects of environment and oppression on an individual," but considers "the melodramatic conclusion" more appropriate for "popular pulp fiction [than for] a fine novel."[5] Addison Gayle, who rates many black proletariat novels highly for their theme and craft, writes that Petry's work, though "provocative and powerful," is weakened by her failure to develop a "denouement [and] to revarnish her work, add color to her painting." Common to all these critical assessments is a comparison of *The Street* with Richard Wright's *Native Son*. "Change the characters," Addison Gayle writes, and *The Street* becomes "little more than a carbon copy" of *Native Son*. "Both Wright and Petry wrote in the naturalistic idiom; both were interested in the effects of the environment upon psychological make-up of characters; both were aware of the images handed down from the past";[6] and both created antiheroes driven to murder by the exigencies of black life in white America.

In reciting the similarities between *Native Son* and *The Street*, critics ignore the significance of a major dissimilarity: the sexual identities of the protagonists of the two novels. Wright's protagonist, Bigger Thomas, is male. Petry's protagonist, Lutie Johnson, is female. By definition, then, their realities are different, just as Wright's vision as a male artist is, by definition, different from Petry's vision. Moreover, Bigger Thomas is a young male in his late teens who has not functioned in the sexual roles of husband and father. Lutie Johnson, on the other hand, is a mature woman in her early thirties who has functioned in the role of wife and is the mother of an eight-year-old son. Critics who see Petry's vision as but a "carbon copy" of Wright's ignore the extent to which a character's age, sexual identity, and sexual roles affect his or her reality. Critics do recognize that Petry's aim is to show that a black woman, like a black man, struggles against forces in the environment that would circumscribe her life. However, writing from a male perspective, they ignore the added burdens that being a woman places on her. They do not understand that Petry's decision to place a black woman in an environment that is a "carbon copy" of the environment in which Bigger Thomas is victimized suggests that Petry intended to document not only the impact of racial oppression on the psychological makeup of her character, but the impact of sexual oppression as well. They fail to understand the thesis that Beatrice Royster develops with skill and sensitivity in her work: "*The Street* is the ambience of tragedy for the black female of the twentieth century"[7] in that it documents the brutal attacks made upon her because she is black and because she is female.

When the novel begins, Lutie Johnson, estranged from her husband, is alone with her eight-year-old son in a world of violence and corruption. Lutie looks for a reasonable apartment on 116th Street, in the very heart of Harlem. This will be but a temporary residence because she intends to fight her way out of poverty and into prosperity. The opening scene of the novel, considered by some critics a masterpiece of symbolism and imagery, introduces Petry's "dismal view of human nature" and her belief that "tragic disharmony" characterizes both the universe and human nature. A cold November wind "announces . . . the discord between man and nature"[8] and foreshadows Lutie's struggles in the ghetto. Like a monster with a mind of its own and an indomitable will to destroy, the wind

> did everything it could to discourage the people
> walking along the street. It found all the dirt and
> dust and grime on the sidewalk and lifted it up so

that the dirt got into their noses, making it
difficult to breathe; the dust got into their eyes
and blinded them; and the grit stung their skins.[9]

The people on "the street" quickly submit to the wind's on-
slaught, for they have learned the futility of struggle. Theirs is a
conditioned response that sends them "stooping" or rushing for
cover. Lutie has no such conditioned response, for she is a new-
comer to this environment of poverty, violence, and helplessness.
She has lived amid opulence and power as a maid for a "filthy
rich" white family in suburban Connecticut and, from their mat-
ter-of-fact discussions of stocks and bonds, has come to believe in
the American capitalist dream. Into her very soul she has ab-
sorbed the philosophy that "anybody could be rich if he wanted to
and worked hard enough and figured it out carefully enough"
(p. 32).

Petry draws heavily on her experiences as a newspaper reporter in the bowels of Harlem and, enraged by what she saw
firsthand, she attempts to "show why the Negro has a high crime
rate, a high death rate, and little or no chance of keeping his
family intact in northern cities." In fact, she succeeds, as Richard
Wright does not, in giving us the concrete particulars of this
reality. She explains that "there are no statistics in the book . . .
not as columns of figures," but they are "present in the background," in the hardships of people "who live in overcrowded
tenements."[10] "The street" is a wasteland of human suffering,
"bordered by garbage cans" that symbolize how life here is discarded with impunity by a system that "sucked the humanity out
of people—slowly, surely, inevitably" (p. 144). On "the street"
the women work as domestics, hand pressers, or prostitutes; the
men work in menial, low-paying jobs, or not at all. The children,
left unattended because of chronic family breakdown, begin in
their preteens to prepare for a lifetime of taking drugs, pimping,
or anything that short-circuits their sordid reality. All the people
on "the street" are confined to narrow and suffocating roles pre-
scribed by white America, and too many have "lost the ability to
protest against anything" (p. 125).

Lutie Johnson protests against everything that hinders her
because she is black. In fact, in attitude and behavior she is a

forerunner of the black militant of the sixties, refusing to "scrape and bow" to white people. Her pride will not let her wear the expensive clothes Mrs. Chandler gives her after a few wearings. Her pride will not permit her to laugh and jest with white butchers who, rumor has it, use embalming fluid on the meats sold in Harlem. And her pride will not let her accept change from the hands of a white grocer, "because he was white and forcing him to make the small extra effort of putting the change on the counter gave her a feeling of power" (p. 44). The central point of Petry's racial portrait of Lutie is the character's desire for wider options than those synonymous with the black experience.

Petry foreshadows Lutie's tragedy at the very beginning of the novel with an image of walls that move gradually and persistently to narrow the already small space in which she is trapped: the walls in the apartment "were reaching out for her—bending and swaying toward her in an effort to envelop her" (p. 13). After each new wave of self-confidence—always without cause—Lutie pushes harder against the "bending and swaying" walls. Every time she returns to the apartment after being on "the street," she finds that the "walls seemed to come in toward her, to push against her with more force and persistence" (p. 53). On the night that she emerges from her self-imposed isolation to enjoy a evening of forgetfulness in Junto's Bar and Grill, the walls seem to "walk at" her (p. 56). When she learns that she has no chance of making money singing at Junto's, when she senses intuitively that her relationship with her son is being threatened by their poverty and by her growing impatience, and when her funds are depleted and she can no longer believe in her lofty goals, she realizes that "from the time she was born, she had been hemmed into an ever-narrowing space, until now she was very clearly walled in" (p. 201). The stage is set for Lutie's initiation into a world of violence.

From well-articulated plans for success that would be easy to carry out if she "worked hard enough," she moves to a sense of urgency about the need to fight against the doors that "have been slammed in her face" because she is "poor and black." She would "shove [them] open; she would beat and bang on [them] and push against [them] and use a chisel in order to get [them] open" (p. 118). Lutie is "both a conscious and unconscious fighter and rebel," writes Vernon Lattin, "a rebel, ironically, in the American tradition."[11] The irony to which Lattin refers is present in every scene of the novel and saturates every effort Lutie makes to "fight her way out." She fights for lofty alternatives to the suffocating exigencies of black life, but she does not understand the omnipresent force of "the street" and its various "traps," so she fails to choose the proper weapons for her battle. She does not recognize that, in spite of all of her plans and hard work, she will always be the offspring of black people who are systematically programmed into powerlessness.

The story progresses swiftly to tragedy. Her son, Bub, attempts to earn money decently to contribute to their living expenses, but he falls innocently into a trap the super set for him and ends up in juvenile detention. From this moment on, Lutie's blinding naivete is presented as a tragic flaw in her character. She goes, naively, to an attorney on "the street" for assistance with her son's case, not realizing that neither bond nor legal service is required to get her son out of detention. Naively, she seeks a loan from Boots Smith, a seasoned veteran of "the street," who cannot enter into a contract of dignity, for, as Lutie herself sees, he is a man who has "no softness, nothing to indicate that he would ever bother to lift a finger to help anyone but himself" (p. 98). When he attempts to rape Lutie in exchange for the money, the walls close in on her. Consumed by rage, Lutie strikes Boots Smith again and again, venting her rage against all the forces that have relentlessly conspired to destroy her. In the end, a murderer, she has no dreams, no plans, and no future. She has learned in the most tragic way, writes Vernon Lattin, that the American Dream that shaped her ambitions was always "itself . . . the spring that operated the trap."[12]

In interviews Ann Petry has emphasized that race stands at the center of her artistic vision. I have already quoted her intention to demonstrate the crippling effects of racism and capitalism on the lives of the people who live in ghettoes across America—and this literary goal she achieves brilliantly. The fact that Petry does not speak of sexual oppression in interviews about her novel does not mean that she fails to include it in her artistic vision. It is no accident that she opens her novel with a scene juxtaposing racial oppression and sexual violence, suggesting the forces that will victimize Lutie Johnson. The scene introduces the reader to the filth and poverty of "the street," but its drama is the sexual violence of the superintendent. It is significant that Lutie can tolerate the filth of the apartment, but she is "drunk with fear" (p. 12) of the superintendent's sexual desires. She sees him "eating her up with his eyes" and knows, even when her back is turned, that he was "sniffing on my trail, slathering, slobbering after me like some dark hound of hell seeking out, tonguing along the back of me" (p. 21).

Critics do not overlook the role the superintendent plays in Petry's protest against the environment, but they often see only half of that role. They understand that he symbolizes the ultimate in victimization, for he "has come to represent the underground forces symbolized by the street itself . . . and survives mainly on sexual fantasies," writes Addison Gayle.[13] But critics do not understand that the superintendent's perversity is but an exaggeration of the sexual exploitation that runs rampant in the ghetto, unchallenged and institutionally supported. Consequently, they fail to see that Lutie, as a *woman*, responds to the first appearance of the superintendent with *"instinctive, immediate fear"* (p. 18).

This fear is obviously the result of the socialization that teaches black women about their physical vulnerability. Lutie remembers marrying at the young age of seventeen because her grandmother believed marriage would save her from men like the super. And she has always known that as a black woman she is hated by white women and sought after by white men. In the home of the white family in Connecticut, she is suspect not because she is black and therefore must be dishonest and lazy (purely racial stereotypes), but because she is presumed to be promiscuous and whorish (racial and sexual stereotypes). White women assume that "all colored girls [are] whores" (p. 31), and white men "ain't never willing to let a black woman alone. Seems like they all got a itch and urge to sleep with 'em" (p. 33).

This image of the black woman as whore is not confined to white people. It festers in the minds of black men and creates a code of sexual behavior that sometimes results in the abuse of black women. Wright alludes to the problems of black women in his moving portrait of Bessie, who drowns her despair in drink and expresses her self-denial in sex that is at best an abusive, pleasurable way for Bigger to assert his manhood. That Wright understands the plight of such women is demonstrated in Bessie's tragic plea for her life:

> All my life's been full of hard trouble. If I wasn't hungry, I was sick. And if I wasn't sick, I was in trouble. I ain't never bothered nobody. I just worked hard every day as long as I can remember, till I was tired enough to drop.[14]

But Wright's emphasis is on the forces that thwart Bigger's manhood, not on those that thwart Bessie's womanhood. Ann Petry, on the other hand, reaches into the souls of black women for their peculiar agony. *The Street* is an explosion of the sounds of racial and sexual agony. The sounds from the run-down apartment buildings are the sounds of men beating their wives or abusing their mistresses. They are heard in the super's treatment of Min. They are heard crashing through broken windows as nameless men scream their obscenities at nameless women: "you black bitch, I oughta' killed you long ago" (p. 136). And they are heard in Boots Smith's announcement that he will teach Lutie a lesson. As a man, he does not "take that kind of talk from dames. . . . Not even good-looking ones like you. Maybe after I beat the hell out of you a couple times, you'll begin to like the idea of sleeping with me and with Junto" (p. 265).

The central point of Petry's novel is that poor black women are beaten spiritually and economically by "the street," and because they are women, they are beaten physically by black men. All of the violence on "the street," writes Beatrice Royster, "grows out of, or is precipitated by, sexual encounters between men and women."[15] This fact does not mean black men are "the enemy." They are not. They are the "other" victims of "the street." Like Brownfield in Alice Walker's *The Third Life of Grange Copeland*, they have been programmed into sexism and destroyed by racism, and the two experiences are inextricable in America. While they elicit Petry's rage, they are within reach of her sympathy.

Petry repeatedly describes women who work and men who do not work, painting a picture of inequality in the thirties and forties that is not far from Sojourner Truth's observation in the nineteenth century that "colored women go out washing, which is about as high as a colored woman gets, and their men go about idle, strutting up and down."[16] But she immediately explains that the men are idle because white people enslave black women in white homes and crush the manhood of black men by keeping them unemployed. This history explains why Lutie's rage is heavily commingled with a sense of guilt. Because she chose to work and function in a role society assigns to men, Lutie believes she was partly responsible for the failure of her marriage.

Lutie's attitude toward "woman's place" is shaped by her middle-class aspirations. Indeed, Petry suggests that Lutie is partly responsible for her own failures by calling into question her strivings for upward mobility. Lutie believes that she and her son, Bub, are better than other blacks in Harlem because she has seen inside the workings of white America and therefore knows how to dream the right dreams. The world of stocks and bonds, of luxury and waste, of things and treasures, is the world to which she aspires. She wants Bub to sleep in rooms that are decorated with carpets, curtains, and fine mahogany furniture. She wants him to wear knickerbockers and attend the best of prep schools, as the Chandler boy does. And for herself, in her hidden fantasies, she wants to be like the white middle-class women whose lives are glorified in subway ads, magazines, and movies.

She believes that women should stay in the home because that is what middle-class white women do. Class, then, causes Lutie to internalize cultural assumptions about both her race and her sex, and it prevents her from seeing the direction from which the light in the tunnel of her darkness might possibly come.

Making it possible for black women to stay in "their place" as women is one of the solutions Petry proposed to the problems of family disorganization and teenage crime she wrote about as a journalist. She believed that if women could stay home and tend the hearth, the family unit would be stronger; and if the family unit were stronger, black youths would be sheltered from the pervasive violence in Harlem. In the novel she implies that if all things were in place for blacks in white America, Lutie would be home and her husband, Jim, would be gainfully employed. Petry's response to "woman's place," then, like Lutie's, is unquestionably tied to the problems of racism and poverty. However, by documenting the double jeopardy of women in white America, Petry was a harbinger of the sexual consciousness that broke through in the late sixties and seventies, allowing black women to question the assumption that race is the only deterrent to their self-actualization. No matter how deeply she felt about the victimization of black men, Petry did not conceal from the reader her observation that black men are yet another force with which black women must contend.

Implicit in every sympathetic portrait Petry draws of victimized men is her conviction that they in turn victimize black women. They use women as buffers against the cold wind of "the street," as givers of pleasure, as money-making objects if they are pimps, and as credentials of their masculinity. Lutie's father, "Pop," for example, brings "a procession of buxom lady friends" home, exposing Lutie at a young age to the sordid in life and going against "Granny's unconcealed disapproval," because "using women was a way of demonstrating his manhood" (p. 55). The same point is made about Jim, who attempts to regain his lost manhood by bringing in another women as cook, housekeeper, and lover. All the men in the novel partake of woman's emotional nourishment, woman's body, and sometimes woman's earnings to keep themselves on their feet.

Lutie Johnson's struggle to maintain her dignity as a woman is as difficult as her struggle to achieve the American Dream. In her life they are inseparable struggles, though failure in the one need not preclude success in the other for the black woman. The point critics often miss in their analysis of Lutie Johnson is that she never compromises her woman's pride for her black aspirations. When all the signs indicate that Lutie could, in fact, make her way out of the filth and violence of "the street," she holds fast to her image of herself as a woman of dignity and hopelessly confronts Boots Smith. Surely this fact alone makes the novel more than a "carbon copy" of *Native Son*. As Beatrice Roysters claims, *The Street* is one of the most powerful "mandate[s] for black women to dismantle the cloak of blind innocence, to recognize the falsity of the American Dream . . . [and most significantly] to resist exploitation of their bodies by men of all races."[17]

In 1948, two years after Ann Petry wrote *The Street*, Dorothy West published *The Living Is Easy*. Both novels are significant works in black American literary history. Both writers were major participants in the political, social, and literary movements that made the forties such a dynamic period in American history. Petry flirted with Marxism, writing political pieces for *The Amsterdam News* and *The People's Voice;* and West, serving as editor of *Challenge* and *New Challenge*, worked closely with black and white writers who challenged the mainstream philosophy of American politics. Interestingly, both writers come from middle-class New England backgrounds (Petry from Connecticut and West from Massachusetts), and both women left New England to live and work in Harlem during the twenties and thirties (Petry as a reporter and West as a social investigator). There the similarities end, however, for while Petry used Harlem experiences to draw a convincing portrait of a black woman in revolt, West in her novel made no mention of Harlem.

The setting of *The Living Is Easy*, is Boston at the turn of the century, and the protagonist is Cleo Judson, a southern-born black woman who marries the wealthiest black man in Boston. Like Lutie Johnson's, Cleo Judson's struggles are class-oriented, born out of her desire to be accepted into the black "counterfeit Brahmin"[18] society of Boston.

The setting and theme of the novel are considered by some critics to be welcome departures from what they see as the dominance of sociology in black American fiction. In *The Negro Novel in America* Robert Bone praises West's craft in producing a "bitingly ironic novel—of the ruthless success drive of the Negro middle class" that does not subordinate "psychological interest to social criticism."[19] It is a welcome departure also because it does not examine traditional "Negro" locales such as Philadelphia, Chicago, or—the cultural capital of Black America—Harlem. Instead it describes "the psychological, social and material lives of the small but important Negro populations that have always been scattered throughout New England."[20]

None of the laudatory assessments of the novel mentions its vision of womanhood. Robert Bone alludes to the rule of sex in the novel when he calls Cleo Judson a "castrating female" and a woman of "masculine protest,"[21] but he does not explain the source of her protest convincingly. He calls attention to the novel's "touch of primitivism" and to West's "Freudian approaches to personality."[22] In fact, he seems so impressed by West's ability to avoid excessive "social criticism" that he fails to recognize that Cleo Judson, whom he calls the "most fascinating women in recent Negro fiction,"[23] is one of the most sexually hostile women in black American fiction. While it is true that she struggles ruthlessly to become a black Brahmin, a point Bone emphasizes, it is also true that she struggles to control her life and destiny in the same way that she believes men are permitted to control theirs. Unable to do so because she is a woman, she is resentful of what she sees as male power and female passivity. West writes that Cleo Judson "felt the spleen spread to the pit of her stomach. *Men were her enemies because they were male*" (p. 68).

The novel begins after Cleo has left the South of her birth and moved to Boston, where she marries Bart Judson, the wealthiest black man in the city, and gives birth to one child, a daughter named Judy. In the opening scene of the novel Cleo is on one of her many trips to her husband's banana business to cheat and lie for money to meet her extravagant needs. Immediately, Dorothy West introduces the theme of racial denial: Cleo is planning her strategy for the rental of an impressive house as far away from "niggers" as Bart's money and their race would allow, for she disavows any identity with the black people in Boston unless they are Brahmin blacks. She has trained "her tongue to the northern twist, [learned] to laugh with a minimum show of teeth, and [memorized] a new word in the dictionary every day" (p. 25). She has prepared herself to be a member of the black elite of Boston.

In the role of mother, her major goal is to ensure Judy a place "behind the tea tables of Boston," the "impeccable mold" of class and refinement that women of breeding "inherit" (p. 92). Since inheritance is out of the question for Judy, Cleo subjects the child to a rigid program in refinement. She hires a private teacher to give Judy genteel manners and the proper accent; she sends the child to a private school in Brookline, an upper-class suburb of Boston; she teaches the child exercises that will make her Negroid nose more aquiline; and she insists that Judy understand that a "proper Bostonian never showed any emotion but hauteur"

(p. 40). Undergirding this program is a lesson in racial denial: Judy must never identify or associate with "knotty-head niggers" who are nothing but "midget comedians" (p. 5).

These maternal goals and Cleo's own obsessive desire to "belong" precipitate her ruthless deception of Bart, for they require more than the allowance she receives for household and family needs. Her goals do not, however, precipitate Cleo's biting and unchecked hostility toward her husband. That facet of her personality—the most dominant in the portrait—derives from her frustration as a female who rejects the assumption that women should stay at home as contented mothers and wives. The dichotomy of man's world and woman's place burns anger into Cleo's soul each time she visits Bart at the market: "Here in the market place was all the maleness of men." Everything in this world represented male strength, male power, and male freedom:

> This was their world in which they moved without the command of women. The air hung heavy with their male smell and the pungent odor of their sweat. Their rolled up sleeves showed the ripples of their hard muscles. (p. 70)

Cleo Judson chafes at the unalterable fact that her "sphere was one untroublesome child who gave insufficient scope for her tremendous vitality" (p. 69).

Realizing that she is bound by tradition and culture to roles that do not name her as she wishes to be named, Cleo attempts to make the best of a necessary evil: she functions in the role of wife, but she uses that role to chart her own destiny and the destiny of her daughter. Though she trains Judy to take the place "behind the tea tables of Boston," at every stage of the training she teaches the girl, in "belittling descriptions of men," that marriage should not be the major goal of her life. It had not been Cleo's goal, but she had none of the alternatives to "woman's place" that she plans for Judy. At the age of fourteen she had been "discovered" by a wealthy white woman from New England who was convalescing in South Carolina. When the woman offered to take Cleo to Springfield, Massachusetts, for proper training and education because she hated "to see this sultry loveliness ripen in the amoral atmosphere of the South" (p. 24), Cleo's life took a turn she had not anticipated or desired. When the benefactress became gravely ill, Cleo moved to Boston, where she lived with another white benefactress. There her duties were similar to those she had had in Springfield. She functioned "like a servant, but she was considered a ward. She was fed and clothed, and given a place at table and a chair in the parlor, except when there was company. At such times she put on an apron, held her proud head above the level of everybody's eyes, and wished they would all drop dead" (p. 29). As an eighteen-year-old arriving in Boston, she had had two goals: first, to run away from her benefactress and then to go on the stage. She imagined herself singing and "kicking her heels on a stage in a swirl of lace petticoats," but she was emphatic about having the stage to *herself*. "She wasn't going to sing an old love-song with any greasy-haired coon. She wasn't going to dance any cakewalk with him either, and let his sweaty hand ruin her fancy costumes." (p. 29).

Cleo's sensuous image of herself on stage is not unlike the way she is seen by the nephew of her benefactress. He had heard about Negroes, especially about voluptuous and passionate Negro women, "and the information was correct." Living in the house with Cleo, he is unable to control his desire. It grew "in his loins and there was nothing he could do to stop it. All he could do was try to keep it from spreading to his heart" (p. 29). Young and naive, Cleo does not understand the young man's pining, but Bart Judson, whom Cleo met by accident in the market place, cautions her against remaining as ward in the home: "She was not safe and never would be safe, as long as she stayed within the reach of his clutches. She was too young to be alone in Boston. She had no mother to guide her. She needed a good man's protection. She needed a husband" (p. 34). It is in this context that Cleo becomes a wife. She marries Bart only because "she wanted to get away" (p. 34). It is at first a loveless marriage and a strange one in that Cleo refuses sexual intercourse for two years. When she finally gives in to what she saw as Bart's "superior strength," she "found a weapon that would cut him down quickly and clearly. She was ice. Neither her mouth nor her body moved to meet his and with her eyes opened wide Cleo mocked the busyness below (p. 35)."

Open contempt for men is not an unusual emotion for women who are prostitutes, but Cleo is not a prostitute. From the perspective of some feminists, however, she might be considered a "respectable prostitute" in that she sleeps with Bart not because she is interested in the lovemaking, but because it is a necessary service rendered in exchange for her "woman's" allowance. What makes her unusual is her refusal to pretend. Her sexual disinterest is overt—a display of power—and she makes no excuses or apologies for it. "Men are all stomach," she says with disdain, "and the *other thing*. It would be a happy day for women if both could be cut out" (p. 222).

Robert Bone posits that Cleo's contempt for men grows out of her family experiences in the South.[24] She witnesses her father's devotion to his wife and, most especially, her mother's joy in wrapping her life around her husband. In the kitchen Cleo sees her mother bleach corn in lye water made from fireplace ashes, and as her father spits his tobacco juice in the ashes, the mother, carefully and even tenderly, takes ashes from the center of the pile. Cleo comments that "Mama thought everything about Pa was wonderful, even his spit" (p. 16). West's Freudian approach to personality, to which Bone refers, is demonstrated in the suggestion that Cleo envies Mama's love for her husband. Only at night when her woman's chores are done and the children are asleep is the woman truly happy. Cleo knows "by Mama's silver laughter that she was finding time for Pa," and she is certain that "Mama loved Pa better than anyone. And what was left over from loving him was divided among her daughters" (p. 17).

It is evident that Cleo worships Mama and regrets that of the four daughters only she "looked like Pa." Charity has Mama's softness, Lily the doe eyes and Serena the cherry-red mouth, the dimpled cheeks, and Cleo "looked like Pa." She had not been blessed to be Mama's child, and yet she was the only daughter who knew that Pa was not the head of the house. The house was "run by the beat of Mama's heart" (p. 22). She is rebellious, calling Mama's attention to her, and grinning when the strap is "laid on hard and heavy." She is wild and unharnessed, and yet contemplative. She is burdened by the impermanence of life and the "terror of the future"—the knowledge that nothing lasts, "that sisters turn into wives, that men take their women and ride way, that childhood is no longer than a summer day" (p. 22). She is burdened especially by the terror of Mama's mortality. When Mama is gone, she tells herself, there would be "the look of her and the silver laughter in the daughters whom she had blessed with her resemblance." Cleo promises to keep her sisters with her always. "So long as they were within sight and sound, they were the mirrors in which she would see Mama" (p. 22).

Bone's theory of "the dethroned child" has validity, but it does not and cannot fully explain Cleo's resistance to traditional woman's roles, and for a novel that is as rich in irony and psychological insight as Bone contends, a one-dimensional picture of the basic personality makeup of the protagonist would be unacceptable. Bone studiously ignores West's allusions to Cleo's sensitivity to the two worlds in society—one designed for men and the other designed for women—that make the flashbacks to Cleo's southern childhood extremely important. West describes Cleo's interest in climbing trees and hanging from her hands, in fighting boys and in riding a wild stallion. She is a problem child for her parents because they do not know exactly what to do with a girl who is wild, uncontrollable, and bent on mischief. Bone calls Cleo's liveliness "neurotic behavior"[25]—a term steeped in sexism when it is used to describe female behavior that is out of line with cultural expectations. The more usual term for those who exact different standards of behavior from girls than from boys is "tomboy." In a study of "tomboyism" in American culture, psychologist Janet Hyde writes that "Tomboyism . . . is considered a stage to be outgrown because girls must learn to replace active 'masculine' behaviors with passive 'feminine' behaviors." In the absence of wider options for girls whose interests lie in the world outside of dolls that neither move nor speak, "tomboyism" is perceived as "a confusion of gender identity."[26]

West writes of Cleo's sensitivity to the existence of two worlds: the "at home" world, where there is "nothing to do," and the world "away from home," where there is action, life, and freedom (p. 12). She depicts Cleo as a girl who has no time "for counting out," figuratively speaking, even when the rules of a child's game call for patient counting. "The wildness was in her, the unrestrained joy, the desire to run to the edge of the world and fling her arms around the sun, and rise with it, through time and space, to the center of everywhere" (p. 13). Whether intentional or unintentional, images of Cleo's behavior in the outside world allude to the character's early resistance to sexual modes that tranquillize her vitality. One such image brings to the reader's mind Candace Compson in *The Sound and the Fury*. Faulkner foreshadows Candace's loss of her virginity—and indeed, her break with southern expectations for women—when he writes of her "soiled panties." West uses a similar image to foreshadow Cleo's later aversion to imprisonment in woman's sphere. After her bold ride on a wild stallion Cleo observes that her injury was "a minor one. She had split the seat of her drawers" (p. 14). The injury is so minor that it does not deter her from climbing a tree and hanging from its limb, with her "drawers" exposed. When a boy laughs at Cleo's behavior ("to him a girl carrying on so crazy cut a funny figure"), a fight ensues and, determined to win, "no matter how," Cleo butts the boy in the groin, "where the weakness of boys was—the contradictory delicacy" (p. 20). These images, unmistakable in their allusions to Cleo's sexual consciousness even as a young girl, foreshadow Cleo's unconventional behavior as an adult and her determination to control Bart Judson, "no matter how." They are the implicit manifestations of Cleo's explicit belittlement of men and pride in women:

> What is there to being a boy? What was there to being a man? Men just worked. That was easier than what women did. It was women who did the lying awake, the planning, the sorrowing, the scheming to stretch a dollar. That was the hard part, the head part. A woman had to think all the time. A woman had to be smart. (p. 21)

These details put Dorothy West in the company of women writers of the seventies who seek to descend into the psyche of women where there might be a volcano waiting to explode. But West was not a feminist, and consequently she enlarges her portrait of Cleo Judson to include ambiguities that avowed feminists might not acknowledge in the psyche of a woman who is the most antimale character in all fiction written by black women. The ambiguities make for a penetrating psychological study of Cleo Judson. She schemes her husband out of his earnings and robs her daughter of her childhood to become one with a group of people she intensely dislikes. She disavows any interest in the South and any identity with southern blacks, and yet she longs for "the salt flavor of lusty laughter." When she thinks of Bostonians and their inability to respond spontaneously to anything, she feels like "cutting the fool for the hell of it" (p. 44). She subdues Bart Judson with her scorn, yet there are moments when her "ice" comes dangerously close to melting in the heat of the passions she keeps under control. "Her need for love was as urgent as her aliveness," West writes, but Cleo would not face the knowledge that she "was incomplete in herself." As the years of marriage with Bart go on, she begins to listen for his key in the door, and in his absence her life becomes "suspended" (p. 36).

Ironically, the "no matter how" approach Cleo takes to achieve her goals leads to her downfall. Her psychological castration of Bart, her destruction of her sisters' happy marriages, and her theft of Judy's childhood are the sins for which Cleo must suffer. One by one those people who had loved her and whose lives were fractured by her cold, manipulative personality desert her—first her sisters, then her daughter, and finally her husband. But her nemesis is most especially that sin that stands at the center of West's novel: Cleo turns her back on the Negro struggle in the South, a struggle that takes the life of the husband of one of her sisters, for the sake of Cleo's own advancement. The punishment she incurs is what she fears most. When Bart's banana business is destroyed by World War I, she loses her status and ends up in a boarding house in a poor section of Boston.

Since West's main purpose in the novel is to satirize middle-class blacks whose obsession with class blinds them to the urgency of the racial struggle in the South, she does not use Cleo Judson as her voice in the novel: Cleo's views on class and race are obviously not West's views. Nor are Cleo's attitudes toward men West's attitudes: Cleo's contempt for men is contrasted to Bart Judson's tenderness as a man and to Cleo's sisters' need for their husbands. And yet, for all West's displeasure with Cleo's manipulation of human beings, there is an interesting subtheme that grows—perhaps beyond the writer's intentions—into a fascinating and intriguing picture of a woman who challenges the existence of a "world" for men and only a "sphere" for woman.

Mariah Upshur in Sarah Wright's *This Child's Gonna Live* (1969) also sees two contrasting worlds in black culture—man's world and woman's place—but unlike Cleo Judson, she recognizes that each one is a small and narrow space in the cosmic world of white power. She has no interest in belonging to a social set, for in Tangierneck, Maryland, all black people are in one set, and all struggle to keep their heads above destitution in a "godforsaken"[27] place. And as the mother of four children and the wife of a "going-nowhere man" (p. 20), Mariah has no obsession except that of freeing her children from Tangierneck's ignorance and poverty. She is acutely sensitive to the racism that holds the black community in fear, but she is equally sensitive to the narrowmindedness that denies women positions of power. She is tired of hearing Jacob and other men in the community talk "about the colored *man's* problems," and boldly she asks, "but what about the colored *woman? What about her?*" (pp. 11–12).

In an interview Sarah Wright defined herself as a "housekeeper" and added that "housekeepers and homemakers are workers." Her artistic vision, she explained, "reflect[s] this concern,"[28] this interest in dignifying "woman's work" at the same time that it suggests the need to redefine woman's role in our culture. Like Wright, Mariah Upshur is a "housekeeper and a homemaker," and throughout the novel she is seen doing "woman's work." Sarah Wright devotes two full pages to a list of chores Mariah does in the course of a day. From sunup, Mariah tries

> to fling her whole self into the chores of morning.
> *Had* to wash up, put on her everyday clothes.
> *Had* to mix pan of bread, sift a-many maggout
> out of the flour first. *Had* to find an onion and
> sprinkle some sugar on it over it, set it out in the
> yard in good hopes that the sun would come up

strong and draw the syrup out of it to ease up
Skeeter's chest. *Had* to get those washtubs
down from the house. . . .

And the rhythm of unending work continues till sundown:

[Had to] pump enough water for that bunch of
dirty clothes. [Had to go] up and down, up and
down, up and down over that scrubbing
board. . . . Had to feed those two or three Bantam hens she was saving for a Sunday dinner. . . . Had to look over [the children's]
homework. . . . Had to figure out what in the
name of God she was gonna feed that bunch for
supper. . . . (pp. 24–25)

This is Mariah's life, not Jacob's. As a man, he works in the
fields and devotes the rest of his life to winning back the Upshur
land stolen by Miss Bannie, a white woman who owns Tangierneck. Mariah is enraged by the assumption that she should ex-
haust herself with never-ending work in the house while Jacob,
because he has worked in the fields during the day, sits by idle.
He comes home, Mariah tells herself, "to sit with his feet propped
up by that stove and see [her] fall right over on her feet with the
work in a way of speaking and not do another thing else" (p. 25).
This is the pattern of their lives throughout the novel, for Jacob
has been socialized to believe that a good man cares for his family
and a real man leaves work in the home to his wife. Wright
repeatedly shows the tension this division of labor creates. When
she is pregnant with her fifth child, Mariah calls out for assistance from Jacob in carrying large tubs of water to the stove. His
answer is a telling comment on his sexist posture:

"Mariah, ain't you got no sense? I done told you
a-many a time to set these tubs on the stove and
then you tote in the water, in a bucket."

Enraged and hurt by Jacob's lack of sensitivity to her physical
condition and the chores she has to do daily, Mariah tries to get

Jacob to understand she needs his help with the jobs she has to do, not his advice on the way she should do them:

> "How many steps you want me to make, Jacob,
> 'fore I topple over and die? How many steps? It
> takes a-many a trip to fill this tub, bucket by
> bucket, when I set the thing on the stove first. I
> do it that way when you ain't home, but how
> come you want me to do it when I ain't able?
> How come you want me to do it when you're
> right around here doing nothing?" (p. 35)

Sarah Wright adds a dimension to her treatment of sexism that is not present in the other novels examined in this book. That dimension is the role of the church in limiting women's lives. In fact, the church is the very seat of sexism and narrow-mindedness in the community. It reinforces the submissiveness of southern blacks by teaching that the Lord will make a way for them somehow and, most especially, by insisting on the necessity for proving to white people that blacks are moral and decent people who uphold the law and abide by the Scriptures. Women are expected to be the most moral of all, because the Bible teaches, and the community believes, that

> a woman is a mighty unclean person unless they
> learn how to respect their menfolks. Menfolks
> just have to put up with them. . . . Women sup-
> posed to take to the keeping of the house and not
> to the keeping of business outside the house.
> Suppose to obey their man! (p. 168)

Wright's indictment of the church is seen less in the men's interpretation of the Scriptures than in the churchwomen's role as judge, jury, and executioner of any woman who steps outside her God-decreed role. Mariah is such a woman. She conceives a child out of wedlock and must go before "the Committee" of churchwomen, who are dressed in white and self-righteousness and who pass judgment on "hot-behinded" (p. 181) whores. When Mariah explains that her lovemaking with Jacob in the fields one spring was an expression of her sexuality, the women remind her that men have a right to their sexuality, but women must deny what they feel: the Lord forgives the passion of men, but he does not forgive that of women.

Sarah Wright's treatment of sexism and religious narrowmindedness is inseparable from her treatment of racism, the dominant theme in the novel. The novel catalogues the crimes committed by whites against blacks. Miss Bannie steals the Upshur land and controls the lives of those who work it. Indeed, in her long black car, she is the power who controls the whole community. Worse than her control, however, is the violence of hooded white men who come in the night to burn and to frighten and, in some cases, to kill blacks, both men and women. Neither this control nor this violence is more devastating than the poverty of the community. Tangierneck is cut off from other communities—isolated, backward, and poor. Poverty is manifested in the diet of salt pork, molasses, and bread Mariah's children receive daily. Poverty is manifested in the worms that crawl from the nose and behind of one child and in the consumption that racks the small frames of two other children. It is this narrow, racist, and dismally poor community from which Mariah will journey from "can't to can" for herself and for her children.

In several ways Mariah Upshur is a misfit in this community. Racially, she is a misfit because she does not fear Miss Bannie and advises the men to confront the white woman with the sin of her past—her child by a black man. She wants the community to take an aggressive position on the need for a new school for their children. In general, she would take on the system to make it clear that she is not a "nigger." As Jacob tells his sons, a "nigger is someone who can't do no better" (p. 89). Mariah insists on doing better by journeying from the "god-forsaken" place to the "promised land."

She is a misfit also because she sees the community's religion for what it is—self-righteousness, hypocrisy, and narrowmindedness. The Committee women make pretty things for the church, prepare food for church gatherings, and sit on the mothers' bench attempting to direct the lives of children and other women. After her indictment by the Committee, Mariah refuses to attend church, and in response to comments on her back-sliding, she catalogues in her own mind the various sins of men in the community and the deliberate blindness of women to those sins. Wright establishes that Mariah is doing penance for her past sins, and that she is actually far more religious than the women on the Committee. Throughout the novel she prays to God for forgiveness and prepares herself psychologically for the day of judgment before his throne.

Finally, Mariah is a misfit because she will not take a back seat to men. When male leaders in the community, including her father, talk about the problems of men, she risks the back of her father's hand and the anger of the other men by reminding them, again and again, that "colored women" have their own set of problems in Tangierneck and that those problems are as severe as any black men face. During her marriage to Jacob she speaks her piece. He orders her not to seek welfare because it offends his male pride, but she rushes to join the wagonload of women traveling to the city welfare office. He orders her not to work in the fields, but she works anyway because she is saving pennies for her departure from Tangierneck. She is a strong woman whose courage and dream of possibilities for her life make her one of the most magnificent women in the group of characters analyzed in this book. She struggles against nature, against white power, against community women, and against community men—all alone. She never has "time to sew for myself" (p. 94) and she feels that her life "ain't been nothing but wind" (p. 113). But by challenging various segments of the black community and the white system, she attempts to journey from "can't to can."

Her journey is thwarted by her obligations as the mother of five children and the wife of a "going nowhere" (p. 64) man whose history of oppression is her history. She resembles in many ways Helga Crane in Nella Larsen's *Quicksand* (1928), a novel about the racial and cultural identity crisis of an upper-class black woman. Helga Crane escapes the stultifying culture of upper-class blacks by marrying an uneducated preacher who speaks to her intense sexuality. He takes her, and she releases without fear her "long-hidden, half-understood desire."[29] She is a willing prisoner of her passions, for

> night came at the end of every day. Emotional,
> palpitating, amorous, all that was living in her
> sprang like rank weeds at the tingling thought of
> night, with a vitality so strong that it devoured
> all shoots of reason. (p. 202)

Helga gives birth to four children in succession and discovers how tragic has been her devotion to lovemaking with this man who is outside her experiences and her dreams. She is, in fact, "used . . . up" by the children (p. 203). She looks

> in helpless dismay and . . . disgust at the disor-
> der around her, the permanent assembly of
> partly emptied medicine bottles on the clock
> shelf, the perpetual array of drying baby clothes
> on the chair back, the unceasing litter of half-
> dead flowers on the table . . . and she was thank-
> ful, whenever possible, to be relieved from the
> ordeal of cooking. (p. 205)

Having had "more than enough" of the "quagmire in which she had engulfed herself" (p. 218), Helga decides to take control of her life and journey "from can't to can." Tragically, as she plans the journey, she discovers that she is once again pregnant. The novel ends with Larsen's succinct and compelling statement on the "quagmire":

> And hardly had she left her bed and become able
> to walk without pain, hardly had the children
> returned from the homes of the neighbors, when
> she began to have her fifth child. (p. 222)

Like Helga Crane, Mariah Upshur must give up her journey toward brighter horizons because she is burdened by the responsibilities associated with motherhood. She has five children of her own, and the deaths of two women in the community leave her with three more. Overwhelmed by the realization that she cannot leave Tangierneck, Mariah decides that the only journey she is ever going to be able to make is the journey from life to death.

Death is calling her, she tells herself, beckoning her to come so that she can face judgment for the sins of her past. Her attempted suicide by drowning was foreshadowed early in the novel when Wright wrote of Mariah's respect for water as "a bossy thing. Fit anywhere it wants to. Sometimes it goes quiet. Sometimes it goes noisy. But any way it goes, it takes over" (p. 36). As Mariah wades into the cold waters of the sound, she repeats the prayer that has been like a refrain to every scene and conversation in the novel: "Let my children live." Ironically, it is this passion for her children's welfare that pulls her back from death into life.

At last this woman of courage, strength, and tenacity makes peace with her soul. She decides she will no longer contemplate death or grieve over her past sins. She will find redemption in serving and dignity in the roles of mother and wife. From a feminist perspective, however, Mariah has journeyed from contemplating "can" to accepting "can't." Wright does not suggest that there will be changes in Jacob's understanding of Mariah as a woman or his definition of himself as the man in the family. Mariah will struggle with Jacob as she has always struggled, and she will challenge the women of the community as she has always challenged them. With the death of Vyry, a woman whom the community respects, Mariah will probably emerge as a leader, but the dimensions of her personal life will remain the same. This is clearly implied in the closing lines of the novel. As Jacob, in his way of showing love, reprimands Mariah for being a "fool woman" going out into the cold waters, knowing that she can't swim, she answers:

> "Jacob, I forgot to put the dough to bake in the
> oven so you and the children could have some
> nice hot bread for your dinner." (p. 253)

In *This Child's Gonna Live* we see Mariah, a woman of dignity and compassion, in the home and in the fields, and in both places she sings hymns to the Lord. In Gayl Jones's *Corregidora* (1975) we see Ursa Corregidora in a nightclub or in seedy restaurants, where she sings the blues. Whereas Mariah is religious, rural, and southern, Ursa is worldly, urban, and northern. In addition to these differences, there is the stark difference between the history of oppression that Wright examines and the history of oppression that Jones recounts. For Mariah, white people in Tangierneck steal the Upshur land and hold an entire community in the grips of poverty and powerlessness. For Ursa, who functions in a black community that has virtually no contact with whites, the history of oppression is the tragedy of her maternal ancestors, the Corregidora women. The story of the women is told in the late 1940s, but the tragedy began during slavery and lasted through three generations. Corregidora, a Portuguese seaman turned plantation owner, turned rapist, turned breeder of mulatto women, enslaved and exploited the Corregidora women.

The story comes out in monologues that "seep from Ursa's consciousness in moments of psychological stress."[30] Corregidora was a slavemonger who slept with his slaves, sired children by them, and then slept with the children. He was a breeder who sent his women out to sleep with other men so that he would have mulatto children for the market. As the story is told throughout the novel in Ursa's subconsciousness, it is a bizarre and horrifying tale of perversity and abuse, a commentary on the sickness of the slave culture. Corregidora slept with his own children, and his wife slept with them as well:

> And you know sometimes the mistresses was doing it too so they could have little pocket money that their husbands didn't know about. And getting their brothers and their brothers' friends and other mens they know, you know, and then they make theyselves right smart money for their purse. Naw, Corregidora's wife didn't do that. She slept with you herself.[31]

From the age of eight, Ursa hears the story of the Corregidora women, from "Great Gram" first and then from her mother, until it becomes an abiding part of her consciousness. Their past becomes her past and, in a terrifying way, controls her present. For her, Corregidora is "the symbolic progenitor of all evil . . . much like the serpent in the mythical Garden of Eden."[32] Most especially, he is a symbol of the evil that is peculiar to the reality of black women: they are bodies to be used and abused. Because of this history of oppression, Ursa is taught that she has a special mission in life: she must "make generations. They can burn the papers but they can't burn conscious. . . . And that['s] what makes the evidence. And that's what makes the verdict" (p. 24).

In a nightclub in Kentucky Ursa's singing is soul-piercing, entrancing, sensuous, and entertaining. She sings the blues because it is her way of turning pain into pleasure and of freeing herself psychologically from "the tyranny of historical oppression,"[33] which, Jones establishes, is peculiar to black women. She fears that the tragedy of her maternal ancestors might find its way out of her subconscious into the center of her life. To the question, "Who are you?" Ursa answers, "I am the daughter of the daughter of the daughter of Ursa of currents, steel wool and electric wire for hair" (p. 75).

Claudia Tate discerns two dramas in the novel: the "internal drama," which deals essentially with the Corregidora legend, and "the external drama," which deals with Ursa's problems with her husband, Mutt Thomas. Mutt is a macho man, insisting on his right to own Ursa. He neither realizes nor cares that her singing of the blues is an expression of her creativity and her way of fingering the scars on her psyche made by the Corregidora tragedy. She is his wife and must therefore obey his orders. When he insists that she stop singing, an argument ensues. He pushes Ursa down the back steps of the nightclub, and the fall results in her having to have a hysterectomy. As "the daughter of the daughter" who must "make generations," Ursa cannot keep her promise to her maternal ancestors. She divorces Mutt and "seems to be left with no alternative but to live out her life alone like all the Corregidora women before her."[34]

Claudia Tate posits that Ursa would have been content to remain alone had she not been "frightened by a lesbian encounter while convalescing at the home of a friend." She worries, Tate writes, whether men will still desire her or whether she will "succumb to homosexual embraces."[35] Jones's vision does not easily support Tate's comment on Ursa's fear of homosexuality. It does, however, support the interpretation that Ursa worries about not being desired by men. This point is clear in Ursa's lovemaking with Tadpole, the man who befriends her after the operation. As he takes her, she demonstrates in the sexual act that she still knows how to lie with a man.

Ursa marries Tadpole, but within a short period of time she returns to Mutt, who has never given up sending her pleas for forgiveness and messages of love and need. There is some vagueness in Jones's handling of the relationship between Mutt and Ursa. We feel that Ursa does indeed love Mutt Thomas. The emotional and physical bond between them is obviously strong, for Ursa forgives Mutt for making it impossible for her to keep her mission as a Corregidora woman. We also sense, and Jones develops this point explicitly at times, that Ursa feels the need to hurt Mutt. This point raises a fundamental question about the novel's vision of black male-female relationships. What is the relationship of the Corregidora legend to Ursa's reality as a black woman if not that it is an extreme statement of the exploitation that black women experience beyond slavery with their own men?

Several arguments can be made for this interpretation. One is that Jones weaves the story of white male exploitation of black women throughout the novel, but in her vision of Ursa's life in the 1940s she makes no references to white men and no references to white exploitation. Interestingly, however, sexual exploitation continues into the present. Corregidora forced black women to make generations because he profited from this exploitation. Mutt Thomas accidentally prevents Ursa from making generations because he believes he has the right to control her. His limiting view of women is similar to Corregidora's. Jones writes that Mutt sees Ursa's "pussy . . . as the center of her . . . being," and she adds that Mutt believes it belongs to him and only to him.

Past and present seem to come together as Ursa engages in an oral sex act with Mutt. She gives him, as Great Gram had given Corregidora, "a moment of pleasure and excruciating pain at the same time, a moment of broken skin but not sexlessness . . . a moment that stops before it breaks the skin." This is Ursa's power as a woman—and Jones implies, perhaps without intending to, that it is Ursa's only power. In the act that defines the center of her reality according to Mutt, she has the power to kill him: "I could kill you" (p. 212). Clearly, Ursa loves Mutt and wants to be loved by him. Clearly, she desires him physically. But Jones seems to say that because of the lessons she has learned about the historical oppression of black women, Ursa hates Mutt as much as she loves him.

Although these arguments support the interpretation that Jones extends the legend of sexual exploitation during slavery to apply to black women out of slavery, there are perhaps as many arguments to the contrary, for the novel, powerful though it is, often moves in and out of focus. It raises many provocative questions to which it does not give easy answers. In fact, Tate's interpretation of Ursa's fear of embracing homosexuality is precipitated by this shift in focus. Jones treats two lesbian characters with sensitivity, but she steps back from developing them of making clear use of them in the novel. Our failure to get a handle on the novel that does justice to Jones's vision demonstrates the need for clearly defined and tested approaches to lesbian criticism. With such approaches, we might find that *Corregidora* belongs to the tradition of lesbian or latent lesbian fiction that J. R. Roberts and Barbara Smith celebrate in *Black Lesbians: An Annotated Bibliography* (1981).

Jones's vision of black womanhood is more fully developed in her second work, *Eva's Man*. In fact, in some ways, *Eva's Man* is a companion work. The theme of hate and desire is repeated, as are the themes of sexual exploitation and of oral sex as a reflection of a woman's hostility and her power to kill. The vision remains one of horror. Toni Morrison is therefore correct in saying that Jones's writing is "an exception to black women's writing" in that it is "never . . . about joy."[36] But it is not just the absence of joy that places Jones's second novel in a category all its own. There is also its preoccupation with raw and crude sexual lust, sexual profanity, and sexual perversion. Jones's artistic mirror is broad enough to reflect everything that happens in the netherworld of sex. Like many female erotic novels published in the sixties and seventies, *Eva's Man* reads at times like the script of an X-rated movie.

The novel is an exception to black women's writing also because it emphasizes sexual victimization almost to the exclusion of any interest in racial oppression. The other black women writers examined in this book allude to sexual victimization, but they do so within the contexts of racism, sexism, and poverty, and they extend genuine sympathy to the black man as a victim turned victimizer. Ann Petry, for example, writing three decades before Gayl Jones, indicts Boots Smith for his attempt to rape Lutie Johnson, but even while doing so, she keeps before the reader's mind Smith's victimization and sense of helplessness. This same posture is present in the fiction of Alice Walker, a contemporary of Gayl Jones. In her first novel, *The Third Life of Grange Copeland*, Walker writes movingly of the tragedy of Brownfield in the corrupt and unjust sharecropping system of a small Georgia town.

Gayl Jones departs radically from this tradition of holding the system at least partly responsible for the black man's victimization of the black woman, and in so doing she adds a dimension to imaginary black womanhood that is decidedly new. The black man's brutal victimization of the black woman is the major chord in her work. Some consideration should be given to Jones's opinion that the particulars of the victimization of the black man, which might explain his treatment of the black woman, need not be presented in fiction. "For the black man," Jones says, "his very life is a criticism of the society in which he lives."[37] This same attitude could have been taken by other black women writers who, like Jones, chose to examine the black man's sexual cruelty, but those writers wisely understood that a careful writer never assumes that his reader already knows the particulars that forge a certain kind of personality. The verdict on *Eva's Man* is that its author's neglect of particulars about the black man's victimization results in his appearing to be innately a victimizer rather than a victim turned victimizer unwittingly.

In an interview published in *The Massachusetts Review* Gayl Jones described her novel as "a horror story" that starts with "the telling and sometimes the answers come out of the telling."[38] This is an accurate description of the technique she uses in *Eva's Man*—the story is told in disconnected dialogue, in dreams and fantasies, in fractured time sequences and "hereabout-whereabout" places, in memory and myth, in flashbacks that take the reader into Eva's past, wherein the explanation of her act lies. Jones further explains that in "using memory and fantasy as well as storytelling," she reclaims Eva Medina's "whole past, and reveals all the things that lead up to . . . her relationship with her lover."[39] The skillfully handled first-person point of view facilitates this reclaiming and, most importantly, humanizes a strange woman.

Eva is forty-three when the novel begins. Her crime took place when she was thirty-seven. For five years she has been in the psychiatric ward of an upstate New York hospital, presenting to all the "Dr. Frauds" who examine her a face frozen in nonchalance, exhibiting neither guilt about the act for which she was committed nor concern for her welfare. As the flashbacks begin, Eva is resurrected from a comatose state into clarity, and the *who* of her identity and the *why* of her act unfold metaphorically and clearly. Dispassionately, she explains, "I opened his trousers and played with his penis. My mouth, my teeth, my tongue went inside his trousers. I raised blood. . . . I squeezed his dick in my teeth. I bit down hard."[50]

The flashbacks, Gayl Jones explains, make a "connection" with Eva's act of sexual violence because all of them are metaphors of the sexual victimization of black women Eva has witnessed since she was a child of four. Indeed, the statement that best explains Eva's past and Jones's vision of black male–black female relationships is repeated frequently in disconnected dialogue and fantasy throughout the novel: "all [men] think about is where they going to get their next piece" (p. 154). Jones attempts to dispel the notion that Eva and her lover represent a statement on male-female relationships in the black community: they "stand for themselves, really,"[41] she says. But this disclaimer is hardly convincing in light of the heavy emphasis on sexual abuse that characterizes all the flashbacks and all the dreams. The recurring theme of the novel, Jones's disclaimer notwithstanding, is that black men see black women as sexual objects, "bitches," and "whores" who like to be laid and who will accept abuse.

The first flashback that informs the reader of Eva's exposure to sexual victimization relates to Eva's childhood in a small New York apartment building where she lives with her mother and father. What she remembers most about those years is her mother's preoccupation with the subject of sex, an interest avidly shared by her mother's friend, Miss Billie. In Eva's memory and fantasy the two women talk freely and graphically about sexual perversion, aggression, and violence; about Old Man Logan, who masturbates in the presence of women; and about the day-in and day-out sexual brutality of men that scars the psyches and bodies of women in the community. She is instructed not to let Old Man Logan "mess with you . . . cause he ain't nothing but a shit" (p. 12). Eva begins to see all men as "shit" because in all encounters they seek only "to mess" with women.

The theme of men "messing" with women undergirds all of Eva's experiences as a young girl. When she was only eight, young Freddy Smoot "messed" with her with "a dirty popsicle stick" (p. 13), having learned from his environment that the relationship between men and women is characterized exclusively by sexual encounters in which the man aggressively demands service and the woman, upon pain of a beating, delivers. He takes a dirty popsicle stick and moves it around under Eva's pants as she, following his orders, "squeezed him like a milkweed" (p. 13). Jones uses double entendre here: "dirty" symbolizes the baseness of sexual encounters in the community; and the "popsicle stick," something one finds in a filthy gutter, stands throughout the novel for man's erection, and in this instance for the pervasiveness of sexual abuse that is even part of the consciousness of the very young.

The popsicle experience, one of several incidents of sexual victimization, is followed by others in which Eva is pursued, cornered, fondled by young boys or by older men who are acting out the culturally defined behavior of their sex. From all these encounters (and there are many) Eva develops a fear of men. As she recalls her experiences with her "man" in a cheap hotel room, she realizes at age forty-three that "fearing is a better word" for her emotional response to men. All of them are "old shits" who want only "to mess" with women.

In her discussion of black female adolescence Joyce Ladner writes that by the age of eight, a black girl in the ghetto has "a good chance of being exposed to rape and violence,"[42] and this experience plays a decisive role in the girl's definition of womanhood. Jones's fictive world mirrors the real world Ladner and other sociologists have studied. In the sanctity of her home

Eva sees sexual encounters as very natural occurrences in the life of her mother. She recalls in the psychiatric ward that her mother took a lover who was ten years her junior, a musician who possessed the sexual prowess associated with that profession. Only in her memory and fantasy does Eva understand what she could not understand as a young girl: her mother's interest in Tyrone was entirely sexual. The relationship had nothing to do with her mother's need for companionship, for tenderness, or for a broader definition of self. It was rooted purely in sexual desire. Tyrone came into their private lives to "mess" with her mother at her mother's invitation. The trauma of the relationship is that it makes Eva available to Tyrone: He begins in small ways to teach Eva about her sexuality, and eventually attempts to rape her.

Since "all men think about is where they going to get their next piece" (p. 151), Eva is taught to avoid them. And yet, she hears her mother and Miss Billie express concern about Miss Billie's daughter, who, at twenty-seven, has not slept with a man. Whereas early promiscuity is frowned upon, validation of self in sexual encounters with a man is expected. In the cultural ethos of the community, a woman without a man is either insane or lesbian. These fears for Eva are created by her propensity for staying at home. At seventeen, she should have had "the meat and the gravy too," and Mrs. Medina encourages her daughter to go out into the world of womanhood.

The sexual mother is certainly unusual in black fiction. And in black American poetry mothers are so devoted to their responsibilities—making those great sacrifices for their families—that they often repress or conceal their sexuality. But many sociological studies of black women as mothers give a different picture. Joyce Ladner, Camille Jeffers, Carol Stack, and others write of the exposure of young girls to the sounds of lovemaking, an exposure that is often created by the exigencies of poverty that deprive women and men of privacy. In the novels examined in this study—and in all other novels written by black women from 1853 to the present—the only mothers whose sexuality is central to their lives are Jones's Mrs. Medina and Toni Morrison's Hannah Peace (to be discussed in the following chapter).

Two images of women dominate *Eva's Man*. One—hardly new to black literature—is the image of the "whore." The word is used loosely throughout the novel to refer to all women, but, significantly, it is used by men only. Men don't cajole women; they coerce them. Men don't "jive talk" women; they humiliate them. Men don't "make love" to women; they "fuck" them. This damaging picture of male-female relationships precludes any saving graces that might move those relationships to a level in which the women's personhoods are respected and their physical services appreciated and revered. Whether they are wives or mothers, "good" women or "bad," all women in the eyes of men in the novel are "whores" and "bitches."

Again, it is significant that Eva hears the words "whore" and "bitch" in the sanctity of her own home. She often heard her parents making love, but there is one experience she remembers vividly and with horror. "He had her arm and he was undoing her blouse," she recalls. "Then it was like I could hear her clothes ripping . . . now he was tearing that blouse off and those underthings. I didn't hear nothing from her the whole time. I didn't hear a thing from her." What she hears is her father saying, again and again, "Act like a whore, I'm gonna fuck you like a whore. You act like a whore, I'm gonna fuck you like a whore" (p. 37). Her mother's silence is sufficient evidence either of guilt or submission to masculine strength.

When she becomes a woman, Eva searches for something that challenges "whoredom" as an unavoidable reality for women and "fucking" as the unalterable posture men have toward lovemaking. But she cannot escape the image, for it is in the ethos and culture. Wherever she goes, she is labeled a "whore and a bitch" simply because she is a black woman. She explains to the psychiatrist that her lover, Davis, simply assumed that she was "that kind of a woman." All men, she continues, saw her that way. "Always . . . Always. No matter what I . . . They all would" (p. 171). She is uncertain of what she can do to relieve herself of this burden, to exorcise the curse from her life. Simply by walking, talking, breathing—simply because she *is*—she is a "whore" or a "bitch" in the eyes of black men.

The second image that dominates *Eva's Man* is that of "the queen bee." The "queen bee" is the alternative to the oppressive forces that push women into whoredom. In the eyes of the community the "queen bee" represents a posture toward men no

normal woman would want to adopt. Eva is told by her mother
that the "queen bee" is a woman "sucked hollow by a man"
(p. 73). She stings them out of anger or out of her desire for
something more than the abuse they offer. She is a "queen bee
because every man she had ended up dying." Miss Billie explains,
"I don't mean natural dying, I mean something happen to them.
Other men know it too, but they still come" (p. 30). They have to
"be stung by the bee before they can see" that women are more
than whores. They believe that all women need "the fork" between their legs, but the "queen bee" teaches them that the
breasts they suck contain blood. She is a "Medusa," really, whose
strange eyes invite them to a world of pleasure and then turn
them to stone.

Myths and fantasies, dreams and memories, come together in
Eva's mind to paint a horror picture of male-female relationships
that reflects the institutionalized devaluation of black women begun in slavery. Then "every black woman was, by definition, a
slut according to the racist mythology; therefore, to assault her
and exploit her sexually was not reprehensible and carried with it
none of the normal communal sanctions against such behavior."[43]
Bell Hooks writes that most people, even a highly respected
scholar such as Susan Brownmiller, "tend to see devaluation of
black womanhood as occurring only in the context of slavery. In
actuality, sexual exploitation of black women continued long
after slavery ended and was institutionalized by other oppressive
practices,"[44] which are so integral a part of American culture that
they cause black women to doubt their own morality. Gayl Jones
weaves this history of devaluation into her story of Eva Medina,
who learns to doubt her morality in a black community where
sexual exploitation of black women is commonplace. In an interview with Claudia Tate Jones explained that the images in the
novel show "how myths or the ways in which men perceive
women actually define their characters."[45]

Eva's response to these myths is her encounter with Davis in a
cheap hotel room where every word, movement, color, and odor
suggest horror, perversity, destruction, and death. It has all the
makings of a gothic scene, but instead of ghosts and unsolved
mysteries and forebodings, there are sexual victimization and
sexual violence. All her life Eva had heard about and seen the

dangers of men and sex. Finally, she finds herself confronting both. Driven by forces she cannot control, Eva walks into the pits of whoredom. Davis makes love to her when she is bleeding. He "fucks" her and calls her "bitch" repeatedly. He refuses to let her comb her hair, refuses to let her leave. She is like an animal he rides again and again, beating her with a whip of verbal abuse, demanding that she not whinny or slow down. He keeps her in the cheap hotel room as an animal is kept in a cage, and brings her dinners in a greasy bag from the restaurant. The dinners symbolize the coarseness of the encounter, for they are always cabbage, sausage, and horseradish that look "like Baby's doodoo" and that fill Eva with gas. Impressed with his own sexual prowess and convinced that all women want to be "had" by men, Davis believes he is doing Eva a favor. After all, he tells her, "she ain't been getting it" (p. 7). And when he takes her, he goes in "like he was tearing something besides her flesh" (p. 51). Sonia Sonchez' "Poem No. 7" comes to mind:

> . . . he poured me on
> the bed and slid
> into me like glass
> and there was
> the sound of splinters[46]

At Eva's trial, those who will decide her fate are men who do not understand her strange past. Those who will decide whether she is sane or insane are also men who do not understand the woman's rage within her soul. Theirs is a very simple explanation of her actions. She killed Davis because he was "cheating" on her or because he was sexually cold toward her: "hers was a crime of passion, and his was a crime of coldness" (p. 82). As her past is reclaimed, Eva understands that she castrated Davis and poisoned him because "he came to represent all the men she had known" (p. 81). Her act of violence is an extreme expression of the rage of which Anaïs Nin writes. When women are engulfed by "angers that have come from damage that has been festering, from anger that hasn't been expressed, or anger that is not understood," the result is "an explosion."[47]

Elvira, the lesbian who shares the prison cell with Eva, understands Eva's rage and her silence following Davis' murder more than the trained experts who are supposed to explain human behavior. Their common identity as black women is more of a bond than their sexual preferences are barriers. Elvira calls Eva "honey" and gives her the first taste of unqualified love. She taunts Eva with her open legs, and Eva remembers her mother's teaching that "once a woman opens her legs, she can't close them" (p. 142). Elvira turns the statement a different way: "once a woman closes them, do they stay closed?" (p. 142). She offers Eva an alternative to sexual victimization, and in embracing Elvira, Eva moves from "can't to can" in sexual fulfillment. Only when Eva embraces lesbianism does she hear and speak sweet words: Jones ends the novel:

> "Tell me when it feels sweet, Eva. Tell me when
> it feels sweet, honey." I leaned back, squeezing
> her face between my legs, and told her, "Now!"
> (p. 177)

6

GIVING BIRTH TO SELF

THE QUESTS FOR WHOLENESS OF SULA MAE PEACE AND MERIDIAN HILL

"I don't want to make somebody else. I want to make myself."

—*Sula Mae Peace in Toni Morrison*, Sula, *1973*

"You are free to be whichever way you like, to be with whoever, of whatever color or sex you like— and what you risk in being truly yourself, the way you want to be, is not the loss of me. You are *not* free, however, to think I am a fool."

—*Meridian Hill in Alice Walker*, Meridian, *1973*

The emerging sexual consciousness of black women in the nation is reflected in the work of Alice Walker and Toni Morrison. Walker, a gifted and prolific writer, became "within a relatively short space of time . . . a touchstone in black literature, especially that created by female writers."[1] In 1968, still in her twenties, she published her first book of poetry, *Once*. In 1970, not yet thirty, she published her first novel, *The Third Life of Grange Copeland*. Since then, she has written a collection of short stories, *In Love and Trouble* (1973); two volumes of poetry, *Revolutionary Petunias* (1973) and *Goodnight, Willie Lee* (1980); a second novel, *Meridian* (1976); and *The Color Purple* (1982), which won a Pulitzer Prize. Mary Helen Washington writes that "from whatever vantage point one investigates the work of Alice Walker—poet, novelist, short story writer, critic, essayist, and apologist for black women—it is clear that the special identifying mark of her writing is her concern for the lives of black women."[2] Like Langston Hughes in the twenties and thirties, Alice Walker in the sixties and seventies displayed her talents in various genres and, also like Hughes, became admired by colleagues and respected by critics:

> Hardly any conference or seminar on Black American literature can be called viable without proper attention being paid to Walker's visionary plots, her laconic style impacted with a premature wisdom, her fervent regard for history . . . or her perceptive and fertile analysis of continuing social dramas.[3]

Toni Morrison is the empress of black women's fiction, a master of her craft, and the creator of some of the most complex and intriguing women in American literature. In the space of twelve years, she wrote four major novels. *The Bluest Eye*, was published in the same year as Walker's first novel, *The Third Life of Grange Copeland*. That was 1970, the beginning of the decade in which black women would follow the advice Shirley Chisholm gave in the sixties on the need to speak truthfully and courageously about their plight as women.

If Walker explores "the oppressions, the insanities, the loyalties, and the triumphs of black women,"[4] Morrison illuminates in the lives of imaginary women the presence of "beauty, love" or, more often, "the absence of [love]."[5] Before her debut as a novelist, Morrison was a senior editor at Random House, where she was instrumental in publishing a number of significant works by black writers such as Henry Dumas, John McClusky, and two literary powerhouses, Toni Cade Bambara and Gayl Jones. She was a major black thinker and doer in this position, but it is as a novelist that she has made distinctive contributions to a deeper understanding of the black experience, most especially that which shapes the lives of black women. In 1973, her second novel, *Sula*, was published; in 1978, her third, *Song of Solomon;* and in 1981, her fourth, *Tar Baby*. Morrison was the first novelist in America since Richard Wright to have her work chosen as the main selection of the Book-of-the-Month Club.

Morrison is hailed as the creator of three complex women—Eva Peace, Sula Mae Peace, and Hannah Peace—affectionately called "the Peace women." Walker is hailed as the creator of Mem Copeland, Josie, and Meridian, women of the soil whose individual and collective uniqueness is unsurpassed in American literary history. Morrison is a northern writer; Walker is a southern writer. Their literary visions are shaped by these different perspectives, and yet, out of their collective consciousness, Walker and Morrison speak a similar truth and create women who are spiritual sisters.

Meridian is a young, pure, saintly woman of the South who has functioned in the roles of wife and mother. Sula is an "evil" and defiant woman of the Midwest who has been neither wife nor mother. What they have in common is intense desire to give birth to themselves as persons. Their individual quests for selfhood are precipitated by different personal needs and reflect different attitudes toward the human condition. The stages of their journeys toward selfhood and the people they love and leave along the way are, therefore, decidedly different. But the goals of their quests are the same—a clearer understanding of self and expanded room in which to hum their own melodies and sing their own lyrics.

Set in a small semirural community in Medallion, Ohio, and covering a time span of five decades (1920 to 1965), *Sula* is the intriguing story of Sula Mae Peace, an acutely sensitive, enigmatic, and defiant woman whose nonconformity is a "living criticism . . . of the dreadful lives of resignation other women live."[6] Joan Bischoff compares Morrison's protagonist to Henry James's Maisie of *What Maisie Knew*. She is "the modern preternaturally sensitive but rudely thwarted black girl in today's society."[7] As a young girl she so startles the community with her extreme emotional impulses that her growth into a "strange, strong and independent woman" is all but predictable. She rejects "behavioral standards of all kinds" and attempts to "rely solely on herself."[8] It is to herself and only herself that Sula wishes to be good, for early in life she adopted the philosophy that "being good to somebody is just like being mean to somebody. Risky. You don't get nothing for it" (p. 35).

Sula challenges the limitations on her individuality and, to the consternation of the community, openly and hostilely disregards

time-honored conventions and traditions. She becomes an outsider with "a quality of abandon."[9] At twenty-seven, she takes
pride in being a single woman and says, with strong conviction,
no man "ain't worth more than me" (p. 124). Instead of actively
seeking lovers and stroking them into matrimony, or letting
them stroke her into matrimony, she sleeps with men as if she
were "trying them out and discarding them without any excuse
the men could swallow" (p. 99). She uncategorically rejects the
standards "others" use to measure her life, insisting on the right
to create a "version of herself she could reach out to and touch
with an ungloved hand" (p. 104). This version of herself is decidedly not the traditional view of a woman as wife and mother.
Both roles, in her opinion, are coffins in which a woman's self is
buried and never exhumed.

Before Sula is introduced to the reader, Morrison gives a life-
throbbing picture of the community in which her drama of
defiance takes place. It stands "in the hills above the valley town
of Medallion and spread[s] all the way to the river" (p. 63). It is
connected to the valley by one road only, which is shaded by
beeches, oaks, and chestnuts. Strangely, this community "in the
hills" is called "the Bottom." "It all started," Morrison writes, as
"a joke," a "nigger joke" about a white farmer who convinced his
ignorant and unsuspecting slave, to whom property had been
promised with freedom, that the land in the hills was not only
"the fertile valley," but also, from God's vantage point, "the bottom of heaven." With its rows of shacks and "its hilly land, where
planting is backbreaking, where the soil slides down and washes
away the seed all through the winter" (p. 5), the Bottom is closer
to hell than to heaven. But the name remains unchanged, and
from generation to generation the people repeat the "nigger
joke" with "wet-eyed laughter," concealing "the cruelty of their
fate" (p. 4).

A community that is the opposite of what its name suggests,
that yields to "the cruelty of its fate," that accepts what is,
though its "wet-eyed laughter" betrays its understanding that a
challenge is needed—such a community casts Sula's challenge to
convention and tradition in sharp relief. For in this culture of
sameness and boredom, defiance is neither understood nor tolerated. The profoundness of Sula's defiance is a reflection of the

sharp contrast between who she is and what the Bottom decrees for its women. Place in *Sula*, therefore, plays a significant part in the credibility of the character and the realism of the plot. The same point should be made about the function of time in the novel. Although a woman like Sula would be startling in any era, she is fascinatingly unique in a semirural town during the thirties, forties, and fifties when the nation's conscience did not bear the imprint of women's struggles for wider options in their lives.

Sula is presented in various stages as she grows from childhood to adulthood. As Morrison analyzes Sula in this growth process, she analyzes as well the three individuals who shape her personality, values, and defiant posture toward life. Significantly, all three characters are women, and each offers Sula different responses to womanhood. The most influential and intriguing of the three women is Sula's grandmother, Eva Peace, who was discussed in Chapter 3. When Sula is introduced in the novel, she is a child of three who has moved with her widowed mother into the home of her grandmother. The move is a decisive point in Sula's life in that it introduces her to various kinds of strangeness. The grandmother's house itself is a strange structure, with "many rooms that had been built over a period of five years to the specifications of its owner, who kept on adding things: more stairways . . . more rooms, doors and stoops" (p. 26). No one asks questions about the strange house, just as no one asks questions above Eva Mae Peace, "the creator and sovereign of this enormous house," who sits in a wagon on the second floor, "directing the lives of her children, friends, strays, and a constant stream of boarders" (p. 26). Fewer than nine people in the town can remember when Eva had two legs, but no one ever asks how she lost her leg. There is something about Eva's ability to control, to dominate, to command attention that makes her disability glamorous. In a "rocking chair top fitted into a large child's wagon," she is enthroned as the sovereign of the house and the community (p. 26).

It is in this strange house of strange boarders lorded over by a strange and domineering woman that Sula Mae Peace grows into a woman. She grows without the sustaining love that is essential for healthy socialization, for Eva Mae Peace, despite all her gestures of magnanimity toward "strays," is unable to embrace her granddaughter with warmth and affection. Sula's life, like the lives of Eva's boarders, is an arrangement that requires control, not love, and Sula is lost in the noise and numbers of the strange house. Hannah, Sula's mother, is guilty of indifference: her "relationship to [her daughter]," Morrison explains in an interview, "is almost one of uninterest. She would do things for [Sula], but she's not particularly interested in her."[10] She tells a friend, "I love Sula, but I just don't like her" (p. 49). Sula overhears her mother's pronouncement and runs "flying up the stairs. In bewilderment, she stands at the window fingering the curtain edge, aware of a sting in her eye" (p. 49). Months later, when Hannah burns to death, Sula watches, not because she is paralyzed, but because she is "interested" (p. 67).

Never knowing the security of love or the warmth of a home environment that identifies her as central to that environment, Sula understandably becomes estranged and impulsive. She cuts off the tip of her finger to deter an attack by a group of tough boys, she watches as a boy from the community drowns in a lake after he slips from her hands, and she witnesses the burning death of her mother with curiosity and detachment. She grows into a "strong, strange and independent woman" because, as a young girl, she had already begun a journey of defiance.

In the "house of many rooms" Sula learns about women's roles and women's sexuality. By Eva, who engages in a good deal of coquettish play with men in spite of her age (she is well into her eighties), Sula is taught that a woman's role is to attend to the needs of men.

> [Eva] fussed interminably with the brides of the newly wed couples for not getting their men's supper ready on time; about how to launder shirts, press them, etc. "Yo' man be here direc-'lin. Ain't it 'bout time you got busy?" (p. 36)

Though Eva's disappointment in romantic love years ago made her the shaper of her own reality, it has not diminished her belief in the institution of marriage and the service of women. She hates only one man, her former husband, Boy-Boy. Her relationship with other men, Morrison explains, is characterized by "a concentration of manlove" (p. 36).

From Hannah, Sula learns about the sexuality of women. Young, voluptuous, and, in her sexual appetite, insatiable, Hannah "would fuck practically anything" (p. 37). Her interest in men is purely physical, however, for Hannah is "a daylight lover," making love "behind the coal bin, in the pantry, up against the shelves . . . or on the flour sack just under the rows of tiny green peppers." As soon as the lovemaking is over, Hannah wants her lover to depart. What Sula remembers most about Hannah's relationships with men is that Hannah emerged from the lovemaking as if nothing had happened. For her, "sex was pleasant and frequent, but otherwise unremarkable" (p. 38).

Two versions of womanhood, then, inform Sula's adolescence. One, the posture of her grandmother, pays deference to men as persons of importance in the home who should be pampered the way a woman pampers a child. The other image shows a woman attending to her sexuality, wrapping herself around the bodies of men, demanding and giving nothing except pleasure. Both images, Morrison writes, illustrate that "the Peace Women simply loved maleness, for its own sake" (p. 35). As an adolescent, Sula rejects both images—the caterer to men and the whore—and begins a journey toward self-exploration that will widen her options as a woman.

At the age of twelve, Sula begins an intense friendship with Nel, the third woman in her life. Each girl receives from the other the security, love, and identity painfully denied them in their homes. "They found relief in each other's personality," Morrison writes, as "solitary little girls of profound loneliness. Daughters of distant mothers and incomprehensible fathers (Sula's because he was dead; Nel's because he wasn't), they found in each other's eyes the intimacy they were looking for" (p. 45). In a provocative essay entitled "Toward a Black Feminist Criticism," Barbara Smith writes that the friendship between Nel and Sula is an example of "the necessary bonding that has always taken place between Black women for the barest survival. Together the two girls can find the courage to create themselves."[11] For Sula, in particular, the friendship fills the vacant spaces in her life and gives her a kindred soul with whom she can share the fantasies she enjoys "in the attic behind a roll of linoleum" (p. 44).

Together Sula and Nel enter puberty. Together they discover boys. Together they become aware of their own sexuality. Their young bodies throb with excitement as they walk invitingly past groups of men who "draped themselves" in front of the Elmira Theatre, Irene's Palace of Cosmetics, the pool hall, the grill, and other sagging business enterprises whose descriptions make Morrison's sense of place so strong and effective in the novel. Together the girls listen eagerly for the profane phrase "pig meat," which, when uttered by one man in particular, Ajax, suggests "a nastiness impossible to imitate" (p. 43). In this environment Sula learns that to be female is to be wanted in this way, and that to be complimented is also to be insulted. Her budding sexuality makes her study "the cream colored trousers . . . where the mystery curled," for she is certain that in "those smooth vanilla crotches . . . lay the thing that clotted [her] dreams" (p. 43).

In seven years this "new theme of men" for Nel matures into a proposal from Jude, a hard-working hotel waiter who presses Nel into settling down. It is not difficult for Nel to fill the traditional role for women in the community, for, unlike Sula, she has "no aggression" (p. 72). In spite of her closeness to Sula, she has never liberated herself from the cultural assumptions about woman's place and is therefore unable to see the strongly limited role Jude intends to assign her in his life. Morrison makes her most explicit and sarcastic statement on the sexism of some black men when she writes that Jude "needs some of his appetites filled, some posture of adulthood recognized, but mostly someone to care about his hurt, to care very deeply." He wants Nel to enlarge his life, even if it means diminishing her own. "The more attractive [marriage] becomes, the more seriously he pursues Nel"; and the more he pursues her, the tighter the net of submission in which she will be caught. Morrison writes:

> Whatever his fortune, whatever the cut of his garment, there would always be the hem—the tuck and fold that hid his raveling edges; a someone sweet, industrious and loyal to show him

up. . . . The two of them would make *one Jude*.
(p. 71)

Sula slips away mysteriously from their wedding reception and is not seen in Medallion for ten years. Her departure completes the first layer of Morrison's multidimensional portrait of Sula Mae Peace.

This phase of Sula's life encompasses her experiences from age three to age nineteen, and it focuses on her relationships with the three women in her life—Eva, Hannah, and Nel. There are clear signs in this phase that Sula will grow beyond the confines and definitions of conventional womanhood, and one is the symbolic birthmark, which "spread from the middle of [Sula's eyelid] toward the eyebrow." Resembling "a stemmed rose, the mark gave Sula's otherwise plain face a broken excitement and blue-blade treat like the keloid scar of the razored man" (p. 45). On the one hand, the mark is a traditional symbol for womanhood—a rose, suggesting softness, fragrance, fragility. On the other hand, its "keloid" appearance suggests toughness, resistance, and struggle, all "masculine" qualities. Morrison writes, foreshadowing Sula's strangeness, that the mark "will grow darker" as the years pass (p. 45).

Ten years after her abrupt departure from Medallion, Sula returns, and with her comes a plague of robins. Puddles of their "pearly shit" (p. 78) cover every inch of the Bottom. Nature images are skillfully used by Morrison to set the tone of different scenes in the novel and to underscore certain qualities in her characters. The image of "pearly shit" works well toward the latter end: the defiant Sula brings with her chaos and confusion. The nature of her strange personality cannot be ignored by the people in the Bottom or explained as a youthful phase that will pass, for Sula is now a mature woman. The fact of her abiding strangeness is emphasized by the change in Sula's birthmark: it has deepened in color.

Sula immediately begins to shock the community with her profound disdain for all their institutions and traditions, and she takes sadistic delight in the agony and discomfort she produces in them. Women go to church in their finest clothes, carrying platters of steaming food. Sula goes "without underwear" and picks at the food they have prepared. They believe she is "laughing at their god" when in fact she is laughing at the emptiness of their lives. She seduces their husbands and then discards them like well-used toys that are not worth being handled again. The men come to hate her because it is rumored that she sleeps with white men, an egregious sin in the black community. And the women hate her because her very presence is a critical commentary on their reality. At twenty-nine, "she has lost no teeth, suffered no bruises, developed no ring of fat at the waist or pocket at the back of her neck" (p. 99). She seems untouched by the "vulnerability" that has allowed them to be scarred.

All that Sula and Nel shared as friends who were bent on creating "something else to be" has disappeared in the waste of Nel's submission to her vulnerability as a woman. "Talking to Sula had always been a conversation with herself," Nel remembers of those old days, but in maturity Nel is shackled by woman's work while Sula is still in possession of the dream of "something else to be." As Nel talks to Sula in the kitchen of her home, she listens "to the crunch of sugar underfoot that the children had spilled" or busies her hands with ironing clothes, folding diapers, or cooking. Just as Jude planned, she has become, "the tuck and hem of his garment." When Sula seduces Jude and Nel discovers them naked on all fours in the bedroom, Nel is devastated, not only because Sula has betrayed her, but also, and more acutely, because she recognizes she has had "no place to be" (p. 92).

Sula has little sensitivity to the problems black men face in a racist society. Indeed, she rejects the assumption that they have a difficult time because they are black. When Jude capitalizes on this assumption, making it an excuse for his demands on Nel's sympathy ("white man running it—nothing good"), Sula ridicules Jude's pansylike posture and says that black men are far better off than black women. In fact, the only speech Sula delivers in the novel reveals her disgust with black men's exploitation of black women. The speech is so powerful that it is worth quoting at length:

> "I don't know what the fuss is about. I mean, everything in the world loves you. White men

> love you. They spend so much time worrying
> about your penis they forget their own. . . . Now
> ain't that love? . . . Colored women worry them-
> selves into bad health just trying to hang on to
> your cuffs. Even little children—white and
> black, boys and girls—spend all their childhood
> eating their hearts out 'cause they think you
> don't love them. And if that ain't enough, you
> love yourselves. Nothing in this world loves a
> black man more than another black man. . . . So,
> it looks to me like you the envy of the world."
> (p. 89)

Because they surrender themselves to men who know only
their own names and not the names of their women, black women
incur Sula's disgust and disdain. They are pitiful creatures who
refuse to see "the slant of life that made it possible to stretch it to
its limits." They are "spiders . . . whose only thought was the
next rung of the web, who dangled in dark dry places suspended
by their own spittle." They are "merely victims," she says, who
know "how to behave in that role" (pp. 103–104). In no sexual role
are they women of dignity and wholeness. Women "with husbands had folded themselves into starched coffins, their sides
bursting with other people's skinned dreams and bony regrets."
Women without husbands are equally pathetic, for having internalized the assumption that a woman without a man is incomplete, they are "like sour-tipped needles featuring one constant
empty eye." And those with children are "like distant but exposed wounds whose aches were no less intimate." Motherhood's
only contribution to women, Sula believes, is that it keeps them
from committing suicide: "they had looked at their children . . .
and one clear young eye was all that kept the knife from the
throat's curve" (p. 105).

If her racial assessment of black men indicts their immaturity
and dependency, her sexual assessment indicts their inability to
translate "the nastiness" of "pig meat," which had fascinated Sula
in her puberty, into excitement and satisfaction for her. Men
foolishly believe they are giving Sula something she wants, and,
most unforgivable of all, they believe they must be in control.

They want to be above her, determining the rhythm of her pleasure and the moment of the orgasm, which never comes. She
resents that they see her as a sexual object, not as a person who
has ideas and dreams. In Sula's eyes, they merge

> into one large personality: the same language of
> love, the same cooing of love. Whenever she in-
> troduced her private thoughts into their rub-
> bings or goings, they hooded their eyes. They
> taught her nothing but love tricks, shared noth-
> ing but worry, gave nothing but money. (p. 104)

Barbara Smith interprets Sula's attitude toward men and her
rejection of traditional sexual roles as expressions of latent lesbianism. If one takes several poignant quotes about Sula's hostility toward men out of the novel, Smith's thesis seems to be
supportable. The most conspicuous of such quotes is Sula's realization that "a lover was not a comrade and could never be—for a
woman" (p. 104). Referring to this quote, and to Morrison's "consistently critical stance" toward men in the novel, Smith writes,
"Sula's presence in her community functions much like the presence of lesbians everywhere to expose the contradictions of sup-
posedly normal life. . . ."[12] She continues, "the novel is exceedingly lesbian in the emotions expressed, in the definitions of
female character and in the way the politics of heterosexuality
are portrayed."[13] Smith's argument is interesting and, on occa-
sion, comes close to striking a convincing note, but it is con-
tradicted by Morrison's own explanation of the forces that drive
Sula into strangeness and rebellion. Rather than latent lesbianism, Sula's problem is her frustration as an artist who has no
channels for her creativity. In one of the most frequently quoted
passages in the novel, Morrison develops this point and adds a
powerful footnote to Alice Walker's "In Search of Our Mothers'
Gardens":

> Had [Sula] paints, or clay, or knew the discipline
> of the dance, or strings; had she anything to en-
> gage her tremendous curiosity and her gift for
> metaphor, she might have exchanged the rest-

lessness and preoccupation with whim for an activity that provided her with all she yearned for.
And like any artist with no art form, she became
dangerous. (p. 105)

Morrison's use of "artist" deserves some explanation here.
Clearly, there are two levels of interpretations of the word. On
one level, Morrison uses "artist" to mean a person who is gifted
with creativity, and requires a medium in which to express that
creativity. If Sula had had meaningful outlets for her creativity,
Morrison suggests, she could have been a painter, a dancer, a
musician—that is, "an artist" in the usual sense of the word.
Sula's latent creativity is a thematic thread in the novel, since the
absence of an "art form" is the cause of her "restlessness and
preoccupation with whim." On another level, Morrison uses "artist" loosely to suggest a vision of life that is uncluttered by
things, time-honored assumptions, other people, place, time, and
circumstance. As this kind of artist, Sula does not depend on
others but moves in a sphere of feeling and thinking that is con-
tinuously expanding toward the birth of self. Sula, then, is frustrated because she is a creative woman in the usual sense and
also because she is a free-spirited soul. As Morrison takes us into
the psyche of Sula, she blurs the line of distinction between these
two interpretations of "artist" so that her portrait of Sula comments poignantly on Sula's need to actualize herself as a person.
Morrison is convincing in her treatment of Sula's frustrations
as an artist without art form, for Sula is indeed "dangerous." She
watches with interest as her mother burns to death, she commits
her grandmother to a nursing home (a cardinal sin in the black
community), and she breaks all the rules that reflect the community's traditional values. But Morrison is less convincing in her
depiction of the impact that racism and sexism together have on
Sula's defiance. She writes of Sula's discovery that being "neither
white nor male" means denial of "freedom and triumph" (p. 106),
but a careful reading of the novel shows that Morrison's emphasis
is on sexual restrictions, not racial restrictions. To be sure, racism is woven into the fabric of the novel, for it is racism that
creates the "nigger joke" that in turn creates "the Bottom."
However, it is sexism that counts the most in Morrison's portrait
of Sula.

When Sula speaks despairingly of black women's self-denial, she means their willing submission to black men. When she chafes at the notion of "full surrender" and speaks of the irony and outrage of "lying *under* someone" (italics added, p. 106), she means sexual surrender. When she demonstrates the "self" she has created, she does so in a black environment in relationships with black men and black women. And when she reneges on her promise to create "something else to be," she does so in surrender to a black man. This surrender—the third phase of Morrison's richly layered portrait of Sula—is the most conclusive argument against Barbara Smith's thesis of latent lesbianism.

When Sula tires of the boredom of the Bottom and longs for some way out of her own dissatisfaction, she becomes fascinated with Ajax, the symbol of male sexuality in her adolescence. She remembers him as a man who pronounced "pig meat" with nastiness unsurpassed. She was fascinated with him when she was twelve and he was twenty-one because "his vanilla crotch" seemed to conceal the most perfect manifestation of the mystery. When he visits her, unexpectedly and out of curiosity about the strange woman in the Bottom, she takes him immediately into the pantry, as she had seen Hannah do with so many men, and stands "wide-legged against the wall and [pulls] from his track-lean hips all the pleasure her thighs [can] hold" (p. 108).

Sula has seduced men before, but the experience of lying with Ajax is different. With him she is free to be a woman with thoughts, plans, and desires that are not wedded to sex. He loves her passionately and expertly and he courts her with presents that are not the traditional "woman's gifts" of money and perfume. He senses the artist in her and showers her with gifts that reflect his sensitivity to her free-spirited soul. He gives her a "jar of butterflies . . . and let[s] them loose in the bedroom" (p. 109). He does not talk "the same language of love" that has so consistently made men one large personality of dullness for Sula. He respects Sula's mind, and "thinking she was possibly brilliant . . . he seemed to expect brilliance from her, and she delivered" (p. 110). The sexist approach to women confers upon men the obligation to protect women because they are frail, or to pamper them because they are like children in their inability to plan their own lives. This is the opposite of Ajax's attitude toward Sula. He assumes "that she was both tough and wise" (p. 119). With joy, he meets her insistence on protecting herself and expressing her wholeness. He likes her "to mount him so he could see her towering above him" (p. 111). And thus is Sula, for the first time in her life, released from the ritual of masturbation. In every coitus with Ajax she experiences "the high silence of orgasm" (p. 112).

Ironically, Sula's surrender to Ajax places her inside the circle of women whom she had rejected and humiliated. She begins to discover what those women discovered years ago—possessiveness. Morrison writes that "Sula was astounded by so new and alien a feeling." Like the women she once dismissed as "spiders," Sula begins to prance for Ajax and to decorate herself in a way that emphasizes her body and not her mind. Her typicality is tragic. She stands before her mirror—the symbol literature has long used for women's mindless devotion to their own attractiveness—and traces with her finger how "the laugh lingers around her mouth" (p. 113). She becomes so obsessed with being "feminine" that she joins community women who sit for two hours in beauty shops preparing themselves for sacrifice, having forgotten that she had once been a threat to these same women. The extent to which Sula gives her mind over to puerile "woman's concerns" is symbolized by the green ribbon she ties neatly in her hair and by the pleasure she receives from doing "woman's work." On one visit, Ajax finds the bathroom gleaming, the bed made, and the table set for two.

In an interview Morrison explains that "the very thing that would attract a man to a woman in the first place might be the one thing she would give over" once she falls in love.[14] In Sula's case, she gives up her independence, her toughness, and her wholeness to become Ajax's woman. The metamorphosis is a large, threatening cloud on the horizon for Ajax. In low tones of desire, Sula murmurs, "Lean on me," having forgotten that a whole man in search of a whole woman does not desire "a hem and a tuck and fold" in his life. And finally, Sula makes the fatal error of asking Ajax where he has been. She has finally internalized the assumptions about woman's role and behavior in relationships with men, and she has ended her journey toward selfhood. She must now surrender to Ajax physically as she has surrendered in other ways: Ajax "dragged Sula under him and made love to her with the steadiness and intensity of a man about to leave" (p. 115). Having forgotten that she has the right to "create something else to be," Sula is left alone. She has "loved and lost" (p. 122).

After Ajax's departure, Sula is a woman of the blues, but she is not typical even in this regard. When a woman sings the blues, she moans and groans in loneliness, singing the low notes of regret and the high notes of another time with another man. This is Sula's song only temporarily. She sings all the songs there are, and in the final days of her life, she sings the song of both death and freedom that only a broken woman still bent on wholeness can sing. She dies slowly of cancer, as proud in death as she was in life. When Nel visits her, she hears the old Sula of their childhood speaking of triumph: "my lonely is mine" (p. 124).

Devotion and sacrifice rather than alienation and hostility are the themes of Walker's story of Meridian Hill. Meridian is a woman who embraces her community and on its behalf begins a strange "pilgrimage" of sacrifice. She is not a Sula. There are no strange marks on her face. There are no puddles of "pearly shit" made by robins that accompany her on her "pilgrimage." There are no church fairs she disrupts and there are no women who can say that Meridian lay with their husbands and discarded them. Meridian is a child of the soil—pure, innocent, and loving. Like Sula, however, she is forced into "premature adulthood by the donnée of her life" and grows into a strong and independent woman. She begins her journey under circumstances that are antithetical to Sula's.

Sula grows up in a family of relative hardships. Meridian grows up in an intact family of the lower middle class. Sula's mother is an uneducated woman of insatiable sexuality. Meridian's mother is an "educated woman," but "willing know-nothing" (p. 88), a woman of ignorance and frigidity. Sula never knew her father, his death having taken place when she was three. Meridian knows and adores her father. He, too, is educated—a history teacher in the local school—and he is a "dreamy ambitious person . . . who walked over the earth unhurriedly as if conscious of every step and the print his footsteps would leave in the dirt" (p. 40).

Walker reverses the traditional images of the father as the

harsh and distant parent and the mother as the all-embracing friend. Mr. Hill is concerned about people and devoted to causes. Mrs. Hill is concerned about herself and the theft of her life by marriage and especially by motherhood. He sings, she moans. He embraces, she rejects. He loves, she hurts. He stretches himself toward the sun. She imprisons her soul in a dark cave of sour memories. As a child, she ran from her father's beatings. As a teenager, she ran from the sexual desires of white men. She was determined to become a schoolteacher, but her father was determined that she would learn to do only that which women are meant to do: "cook collard greens, shortbread and fried okra" so that "some man might have her" (p. 122). As an adult, she feels compelled to marry and become a mother, only to discover that the agonies of her present equal the agony of her past. When Meridian hears her mother's memories, she "weeps and wishes that she had not been born to this already overburdened woman" (p. 122).

As a young girl, Sula is exposed to her mother's trips into the coal bin and the pantry, where she pulls from the bodies of men all the pleasure they can give. Meridian has no such experiences. The prudish Mrs. Hill never uses the word *sex* in Meridian's presence. Instead, she impresses on her daughter the necessity of being "sweet," not realizing that Meridian has no understanding of the caution against sex that the expression intends. Meridian's early exposure to sex, however, is more complete than Sula's. As a young girl Sula only *imagines* what happens between men and women, whereas Meridian *sees*.

The lascivious Dexter, the local funeral parlor director, pursues Meridian when she is only twelve. Meridian goes to the funeral home and lets Dexter suck her breast and touch "the bottom of her panties. She could sit, holding his head against her breasts—while he busily and noisily sucked—and feel the hot throbbing of his passion almost enter her." She is excited, for her sexuality has already been awakened, but "in the end his obesity . . . is distasteful to her" (p. 59). He is insistent on conquering Meridian, for his pride as a "lover" of skill has been damaged by her rejection. When a man "fucks" a woman well, he believes, he owns her forever. To convince Meridian of the desirability of sex, he arranges for her to witness his assistant's seduction of another schoolgirl. The scene, vividly and graphically described, is at once humorous and resoundingly critical of man's attitude toward woman. The assistant uses his voice and his body to ride the young girl with supercilious vanity, and then coldly pushes her aside when his performance ends. Meridian is unimpressed, even repulsed by the scene. What she remembers most is "the greedy, obscene and ugly" face of the man and the young girl's ignored need for tenderness afterward (p. 60).

Being a spectator is one thing; being a participant is quite another. As both, Meridian is naive, unaware of her physical vulnerability and essentially disinterested. No one in her family has taught her "what to expect from men, from sex." As a result, when she acquires a young boyfriend, Meridian has sex as often as "her lover" wants it, "sometimes every single night."

> And, since she *had* been told by someone one's hips become broader after sex, she looked carefully in her mirror each morning before she caught the bus to school. Her pregnancy came as a total shock. (p. 53)

Meridian drops out of school, marries her lover, and awaits the birth of her son. Her whole life has been changed—and by an experience she did not enjoy.

In those chapters that deal with Meridian before she calls herself whole, Walker questions the relative importance of sex in a woman's life, suggesting that the notion that a woman lives for sexual pleasure is a sexist myth, celebrating the power of man's potency. She alludes to this myth in the scene in which the funeral director's assistant seduces the schoolgirl. Having taken the girl and given what he considers an expert performance, the assistant is convinced that the girl is his forever. For Meridian, the delivery of her body and soul requires more "gifts" than those the assistant can offer women. In fact, Meridian sees sex as a "sanctuary." Only when she is sexually active with one boy, becoming his girl in the eyes of the community, can she get over her fear of men. Only in this "sanctuary," Walker explains, can Meridian "look out at the male world with something approaching equanimity, even charity; even friendship" (p. 53).

At sixteen, Meridian is married, pregnant, and singularly bored by her life. Pregnancy is as negative an experience for her as it was for her mother. It changes her physical appearance, making her once velvety skin "bloated, tight" (p. 56). Marriage is also a negative experience—a long, unbroken moment of emptiness and sameness. Her husband, because he is a male, remains in school in spite of his new roles as husband and father. Meridian, because of the swollen stomach that she carries as innocently as she had engaged in the experience that changed the direction of her life, remains at home, and there she receives a different kind of education. She learns that a wife is forever turning in the small confines of home, doing for others. She is an inept wife and, in time, her ineptitude at tasks she should naturally perform well displeases her young husband. He is bothered by Meridan's

> ironing of his clothes, and even her own, which
> she did not do nearly as well as his mother; the
> cooking, which she was too queasy to do at all;
> and the sex, which she did not seem interested
> in. (p. 57)

When she becomes a mother, Meridian is a younger version of Mrs. Hill. The "creative pain"[15] lasts for a "day and a half," and it creates anger, not love. She is exhausted by caring for the baby, who gasps, screams, twists, and turns, robbing Meridian of her rest:

> It took everything she had to tend to the child,
> and she had to do it, her body prompted not by
> her own desires, but by her son's cries. So this,
> she mumbles, . . . is what *slavery* is like.
> Rebelling, she began to dream each night, just
> before her baby sent out cries, of ways to *murder him.* (p. 63).

She wants out of her servitude: "It seemed to her that the peace of the dead was truly blessed, and each day she planned a new way of approaching it"; it is only out of her "reliance on suicide" that she maintains her sanity (pp. 63–64). This is the true condition of womanhood trapped in the institution of mother-hood—though sexist interpretations of the desires of women bury it in a litany of tributes to feminine selflessness. Adrienne Rich's observation that the institution of motherhood lies when it insists that "maternal instinct" supersedes intelligence has strong support in Walker's portrait of Meridian. And if Rich does not make clear that women themselves often believe in that "truth," Walker does.

Meridian's mother and other women in the community attempt to dissuade Meridian from leaving her husband and child. They explain that Eddie is a "good" man. He does not beat her or "cheat" on her—implying that, as a man, he has the right to do both, and that she, as a woman, has the obligation to adjust her needs to providing for his rights. They do not understand, and Meridian cannot explain, that her need for something else in life is not contingent on what Eddie does or does not do. He cannot measure the width of her dreams or chart the course of her journey toward their realization. A woman is not always neces-sarily frustrated because her man is "bad" or fulfilled because he is "good." Rather, she can be frustrated because the culture gives women few alternatives to the suffocation and sacrifice of traditional wifehood and motherhood. Meridian cannot be a wife because the role demands submergence of her self in perfunctory expressions of love and togetherness. And there is no man in her backward town whose intelligence and vision of possibilities for growth complement her own need to "ask impossible questions" and courage "to pursue seemingly absurd paths."[16]

More important than Meridian's lack of interest in being a wife is her inability to be a mother. She is plagued by her mother's question, "Have you stolen anything?" and sensitive to the "paradox of life-giving death" in the history of black motherhood. "In giving life to children who were both unwanted and unap-preciated by society," black women in Walker's vision have also had to give up much of their own lives to sustain those children. "The children know they survive only because their parents com-mitted acts of extraordinary suffering."[17] Meridian's guilt for causing her own mother's suffering and the emptiness she be-lieves will always be hers in marriage, precipitate her departure from the small Mississippi town. She commits the cardinal sin of giving up her child for her own dreams. When she leaves to attend college in Atlanta, Meridian Hill begins the first stage of her journey toward wholeness.

As its name suggests, Saxon College is a metaphor for white Anglo-Saxon values that have seeped into the thinking of middle-class blacks. The school emphasizes self-aggrandizement in a capitalist economy and ladyhood in a sexist society. Walker is sternly critical of Saxon, which represents, of course, the histori-cally black southern colleges in the sixties. In her vignettes of campus life, Walker portrays the school's stress on the acquisi-tion of things and status, and its insistence that its female stu-dents play neat roles. Indeed, the school was a training ground for capitalists and for "ladies": "The emphasis at Saxon was on form, and the preferred 'form' was that of the finishing school girl whose goal . . . was to be *accepted* as an equal because she knew and practiced all the proper social rules" (p. 91). The real life that Meridian witnesses in the streets of Atlanta is ignored by the curriculum at Saxon, and new definitions of the role of women are anathema to Saxon's program for "ladies." The school condones anything as long as it is done "with white gloves" (p. 91). Meri-dian and other like-minded students decide that they have two enemies: "Saxon, which wanted them to become something— ladies—that was already obsolete, and the larger, more deadly enemy, white racist society" (p. 91).

It is at Saxon that Meridian becomes friends with Anne-Marion, a character who is central to Meridian's development. The friendship between the two girls is very different from the friendship between Nel and Sula. As Eva Peace observes, Sula and Nel merge into one personality. Anne-Marion is not the other side of Meridian, or vice versa. They are two distinctly different individuals, as evidenced most clearly in their response to the Civil Rights Movement, in which both are involved during their years at Saxon. Anne-Marion says she is able to "kill" for the revolution and chides Meridian for her inability to "kill." By jux-taposing the two women, Walker is able to distinguish between the noise of faddish militancy and the silence of genuine devotion to the struggle. Actually, Anne-Marion is lying about her ability to "kill": Meridian "knew [Anne-Marion's] tenderness, a vegetar-ian because she loved the eyes of cows" (p. 14). She lies, Walker explains, because she takes her posture toward the revolution from the rhetoric of group thinking rather than from a deep well of concern for her people. Unlike Anne-Marion, Meridian struggles for the hard answers to perplexing questions about the past, the present, and the future. Whereas

> Meridian is always groping for answers even to the point of illness, Anne-Marion is confident, practical, unquestioning. Meridian is compelled to seek the answer to the dilemma of human beings' injustice to each other, but Anne-Marion is content with being the victor rather than the victim.[18]

A true revolutionary, Meridian is held by something that rejects violence as the approach to change. That something is the music of her people, the music of a culture that has been rooted in love. Walker's poetic evocation of black culture is worth quoting in full:

> Meridian alone was holding on to something the others had let go. If not completely, then partially—by their words today, their deeds tomorrow. But what none of them seemed to understand was that she felt herself to be, not holding on to something from the past, but *held* by something in the past: by the memory of old black men in the South who, caught by surprise in the eye of a camera, never shifted their position but looked directly back; by the sight of young girls singing in a country choir, their hair shining with brushings and grease, their voices the voices of angels. When she was transformed in church it was always by the purity of the singers' souls, which she could actually *hear*, the purity that lifted their songs like a flight of doves above her music-drunken head. If they committed murder—and to her even revolutionary murder was *murder—what would the music be like?* (pp. 14–15)

When Meridian makes a commitment to revolution by joining the Civil Rights Movement while she is a student at Saxon College, she is introduced to both the ecstasy and the agony of love. In the Movement, she meets Truman Held, a Che Guevara type of revolutionary who speaks French and sings the praises of "sisters" who are African queens. Meridian is a black queen who will ascend to her deserved throne when, together, they build the black nation. The beauty of his rhetoric is belied by his desertion of Meridian; after impregnating her, he falls in love with a white exchange student named Lynn Rabinowitz. The relationship between Meridian and Truman is the focal point of Walker's analysis of sexism and racism as both work to create the black woman-black man-white woman triangle. The relationship illustrates the "prone" position of all woman in the Student Nonviolent Coordinating Committee (SNCC) during the Civil Rights Movement, but it is a tragic statement on the vulnerability of black women to deep racial and sexual pain.

In the novel the conflict between black women and white women is not in any way similar to the problem black women have with their "madams." In *Meridian*—at least on the surface—class is not a factor, for black women in the Civil Rights Movement are essentially the white women's equals. The conflict is a reflection of the "sickness" to which Eldridge Cleaver refers and the dilemma Firestone Shulamith discusses. Simply stated, black men—some, many, or a few, it does not matter—want white women because they are the closest thing to power black men can get in white America. Black women understand what white women represent in the lives of black men, but they also have their own understanding of what white women are and are not in white America. They see white women as "spoiled" females who have never had to be responsible for their own lives and who do not want to be. From her grandmother and mother, Meridian learns that white women are frivolous, helpless creatures, lazy and without ingenuity" (p. 104). This same assessment is made in June Jordan's poem, "What Would I Do White?"

> *I would do nothing*
> *That would be enough.*[19]

Meridian has her own assessments, based on what she observed in her home town:

Who would want to kiss [white girls]? What
were they good for? What did they do? They only
seemed to hang about laughing, after school, until when they were sixteen or seventeen they got
married. Their pictures appeared in the society
column, you saw them pregnant a couple of
times. Then . . . they sank into a permanent
oblivion. (p. 105)

This view of white women is presented satirically in an incident
involving Meridian and black children in a small southern town
where Meridian lives as a saint, as a remnant of the Civil Rights
Movement, which had once sent hundreds of volunteers into oppressed black communities. The children are anxious to see
"Marilene O'Shay, One of the Twelve Human Wonders of the
World: Dead for Twenty-five Years Preserved in Life-like Condition." She is "A Goddess," "Obedient," "Pure," "Beautiful." She
is dead because her husband killed her when she betrayed him
with another man. It is he who takes her body from small town to
small town to exhibit at money-making shows. Only on Thursday
can she be seen by blacks. Marilene O'Shay is a symbol of "the
white woman protected, indeed mummified, by the sanctimoni-
ous rhetoric of her society, but losing even these questionable
privileges when she exercises her sexual freedom."[20]
   In her portrait of Lynn Rabinowitz, Walker reaches beyond
this sort of stereotype into the complexity of white guilt, showing
a woman who in the final analysis is perhaps the most tragic
woman in the novel. Lynn gives of herself to Truman, has his
child, and walks beside him in the Civil Rights Movement, only to
be discarded when the Movement changes its song from "We
Shall Overcome" to "Power to the People," and becomes the
Black Power Movement. She sacrifices herself on an altar of
guilt, giving in to Truman's abuse and even to rape by one of his
friends, who had lost an arm in the racial struggle. After the
rape, Lynn kisses the stub of her victimizer. Walker is sympathetic toward Lynn, who represents white women driven by
racial guilt to be what black women are supposed to be: "prone"
in relationships with men.
   Black women are not guilty; they provoke guilt because they
have fought against racial oppression throughout this nation's

history. Their posture as soldiers, however, does not save them from sexual exploitation: black men play racial games to exploit black women sexually. Mr. Raymond is a case in point. A black nationalist of the 1920s, he is hardly distinguishable from the Truman Helds of the sixties. A teacher at the college, he calls Meridian into his office and preaches about the "Race as if it were a lump of homogenized matter that could be placed this way or that way, at will, to effect change" (p. 108). He talks emotionally about protecting the virtue of black women from white men, and recites for Meridian the number of "black women who had reported rape at the hands of white men in the years between 1896 and 1963" (p. 108). He is a scholar on the subject, and yet, he sees Meridian, who earns money by performing small tasks for him, as little more than a body he has the right to fondle and exploit: "each day when she rose to go . . ., he clasped her in his arms, dragging her away from the door, the long bones of his thighs forcing her legs apart, attempting to force her to the floor" (pp. 109–110).

Truman's sexism is more sophisticated than Mr. Raymond's crass attempts, in his old age, to make his "limp" penis once again express his manhood, for Truman speaks French, is well read, and is a revolutionary of the sixties. He does not attempt to rape Meridian by using his superior strength. He rapes her devotion to the struggle so that he can rape her body. His sexism is expressed also in his concept of the ideal woman—a virgin—though he himself has deflowered many women and moved on. (So "Where was the virgin to come from? Heaven?" [p. 140].) Truman wants a virgin because he will accept nothing less than what the culture says he deserves. He wants this virgin to be "a woman to rest in, as a ship must have a port. As a train must have a shed" (p. 139). His definition of the role of woman is Jude's definition in *Sula*. Only the metaphors are different.

Like many black feminists of the seventies, Walker refuses the obligation to hold her woman's rage in check until the black man's rights to manhood—total manhood—are ensured. She conveys this attitude in the story of Mem Copeland when she gives Mem the courage to refuse to walk forever in the crevices of Brownfield's self-destruction. The abuse of black women at the hands of black men is, of course, one of the central themes of *The*

Third Life of Grange Copeland. It is not the central theme in *Meridian*, but it is there, directing the course of Meridian's life and the profoundity of her pain. The abuse is not physically violent, for class is a major determinant of the way in which sexism is expressed. Truman is not destroyed, as is Brownfield, by a vicious sharecropping system. Instead, he is confused and spiritually broken by everything in white America that makes all black people suffer from the problem of "double consciousness" of which W. E. B. DuBois wrote in 1898.[21] Truman is black, but his psyche is white-directed. Meridian suggests as much when she observes that "from a distance both Truman and Lynn looked white" (p. 112). Ironically, she makes this observation as she keeps her appointment with an abortionist, who promises to tie her tubes free of charge if he can get "in" on the "extracurricular activity." The abortion is a metaphor for the injury black women suffer because they are physically vulnerable and not respected in a sexist culture. As Truman tosses his head in the wind, riding free-spirited in Lynn's car, Meridian's pain flows in buckets of blood. "It enrages her that she could be made to endure such pain, and that Truman was oblivious to it" (p. 112).

After this ignominious experience, Meridian makes the second of three moves in her life. She leaves Atlanta and settles in a small Mississippi town distinct only for its backwardness and blatant racism. Here she does penance for stealing her mother's serenity. Here she struggles with the bitterness she feels as a woman used and discarded by a man. Her she searches for answers to the "dilemma of human beings' injustice to one another."[22]

When Meridian takes up her life in Mississippi, the Civil Rights Movement is over, but its ideals and the dream it inspired, and the dreams from which it was born, remain a part of her consciousness. She is a revolutionary—a remnant of the Movement—whose courage is all the more remarkable because she believes she is slowly dying. She has strange dizzy spells, painful headaches, and violent seizures. Frequently she is carried motionless on the shoulders of community people to be placed in the narrowness of her cluttered shack. Walker connects Meridian's past to her present in her analysis of Meridian's illness. She first mentions the severe headaches when Meridian is confronted with the question, "Can you kill for the Revolution?" She writes of Meridian's thinning hair when Meridian speaks of her deep love for Truman in a conversation with Mrs. Hill. And early in Meridian's relationship with Truman, Walker alludes to Meridian's psychological distraction, for no matter what was being said, Meridian always "seemed to be thinking of something else." There was about her

> something dark . . . a shadow that seemed to
> swing, like the pendulum of a clock, or like a
> blade, behind her open, candid eyes. . . . (p. 139)

All signs of Meridian's illness reflect the guilt created by the collective history of black women. Through what Barbara Christian calls "a mind-voice which directs the flow of thought and action,"[23] we move back in time and forward and back again, so that the past and the present come together to explain Meridian's vision of the future.

In the final section, titled "Ending," we see the beginning of Meridian's journey from illness to health. Her health returns in stages. At a memorial service for a Civil Rights leader, Meridian finds herself answering affirmatively the question that has been a refrain in the novel: "Can you kill for the Revolution?" She is moved by the beauty of the black church, the only place left where black people can

> congregate, where the problems of life were not
> discussed fraudulently and the approach to the
> future was considered communally, and moral
> questions were taken seriously. (p. 203)

She is also moved by the presence of the father of the slain leader, whom she calls, symbolically, the "son's father," suggesting a parallel between the slain Christ and the death of the leader. And she is moved by the father's words, which come "from a throat that seemed stoppered with anxiety, memory, grief and hope" (p. 202). His words are these three: "my son died" (p. 202). As she listens to the songs of the people, the sermons,

and the sincerity of "brothers and sisters," she is converted to a
new approach to the revolution:

> The people in the church were saying to the red-
> eyed man that his son had not died for nothing,
> and that if his son should come again they would
> protect his life with their own. "Look," they
> were saying, "we are slow to awaken to the no-
> tion that we are only as other women and men,
> and even slower to move into anger, but we are
> gathering ourselves to fight for and protect what
> your son fought for on behalf of us. If you will let
> us weave your story and your son's life and death
> in what we already know—into the songs, ser-
> mons . . . we will soon be angry, so angry we can-
> not help but move." (p. 240)

The conversion lifts a weight from Meridian's soul. She feels a
"breaking in her chest," Walker writes, "as if a tight string bind-
ing her lungs had given way, allowing her to breathe freely." She
finally understands that she must respect her life and "not . . .
give up any particle of it without a fight to the death, preferably
not her own" (p. 204). In making a promise to kill for the revolution, she takes her first step toward health.

The promise to kill brings Meridian to a fuller understanding of
her role in the revolution, and a deeper understanding of the
cause of her illness. She has not wanted to face that she does not
belong to the future, but is "left, listening to the old music beside
the highway." What she will give to the revolution will be the
strength of "memory songs." It is significant that Walker does
not use "sorrow songs"—she is emphasizing hope. Meridian's
contribution to the Movement will be the singing of that music
that holds

> the people together, and if any part of it is lost
> and the people suffer and are without soul. If I
> can only do that, my role will not have been a
> useless one after all. (pp. 205–206)

When Meridian resolves the conflict regarding her role in the revolution, she finds a way to repay the debt she owes her maternal ancestors for their collective history of sacrifice. But there remains the cure for her suffering as a black woman abused and used by Truman. He seeks her out in the small Mississippi town as a man ravaged by guilt. He deserts Lynn and their child, Camara. Even when Camara is brutally murdered, Truman is unable to speak the truth to himself: he loves Lynn and only the antiwhite rhetoric of the Black Power Movement keeps him from expressing his love. He turns to Meridian because she comes from a long line of Harriet Tubmans—strong, understanding, and self-sacrificing women. She is "a woman to rest in, as a ship must have a port. As a train must have a shed" (p. 139). Unlike the Truman of yesterday, who spoke French and in his Che Guevara clothes talked in macho language of the "African woman" he could sexually satisfy, the Truman who searches out Meridian is devastated by confusion and guilt. He leans on Meridian so that she can "help [him] through this shit" (p. 123).

Meridian's response to Truman's plea shows how definite Walker is about the black woman's need to distinguish between what she must do for the race and what she cannot do, as a person, for black men. The two needs, though created by the same culture, do not have equal weight in Walker's vision. Meridian feels sorry for Truman, but like Mem Copeland in *The Third Life of Grange Copeland*, she does not explain away Truman's weaknesses as a man. "Of all the savage nibblings of racism," Walker suggests, "the most poisonous bite is the abnegation of responsibility for one's own soul."[24] By refusing to be a "port" or a "shed" in his life, Meridian forces Truman to realize

> that the most effective way to control anyone is by confusing his or her sex definitions according to the norms of society. The masculine thrust in this society manifests itself in forms of power and acquisition, [while] the feminine thrust manifests itself in passivity, chastity and demure beauty.[25]

Truman must understand the extent to which he has permitted

his name for himself to come from a society that is both racist and sexist. He has believed that a woman's love flows into a man's life "like a special sun, like grace" (p. 223). He asks for that kind of love from Meridian. She forgives Truman and pities him, but knows the "sun" and the "grace" in his life must come from his own search for wholeness. She sets him free, and in so doing, she frees herself of the bitterness and pain she has felt as a woman used and discarded:

> You are free to be whichever way you like, to be
> with whoever, of whatever color or sex you
> like—and what you risk in being truly yourself,
> the way you want to be, is not the loss of me.

She adds, however, that he is *"not free . . .* to think that she is a fool" (p. 223).

In the final chapter of the novel Walker shows Meridian emerging from her shack, free of headaches, seizures, guilt, bitterness, and confusion. Her hair is no longer thin; it is a soft wool that frames her "thin, resolute face." She is "strong enough to go" from the small town of Chickowema out into the world of health. In the eyes of Truman, we see the magnificence of Meridian's wholeness: "Meridian would return to the world cleansed of sickness." Truman will take her place in the small town, and tomorrow "the people would come and bring Truman food" (p. 226). Meridian does not have all the answers for Truman, as she does not have all the answers for herself, because the search for wholeness and for answers to the problem of human injustice is an individual search, in Barbara Christian's words, "a continuing process rather than an adventure that ends in a neat resolution." Truman's sickness clearly is a part of that "continuing process." Christian writes:

> Walker's ending suggests that even Meridian's
> dearly won salvation is not sure unless we others
> sort out the tangled roots of our past and pursue
> our own health. In other words, until the pattern
> of this society is transformed, no part of it is free

and it cannot be free unless each of us pursues our own wholeness. By making the end of the novel the beginning of another such quest, Walker invites us to use the novel as a contemplative and analytical tool in our own individual search. For the questions that she gives flesh to in the novel, questions that are rooted in this country's past, persist in the present.[26]

The differences between Sula's quest for a version of herself she could touch with a velvet glove and Meridian's quest for health are major ones. Meridian is a child of the race whose mind and vision of life are shaped by the collective consciousness of her people. Sula is the child of Eva and Hannah, whose lives, though clearly shaped by race, are more decidedly shaped by sex. *Sula* is, then, more about sexual consciousness than about racial struggle. The time of the novel—the thirties, forties, and fifties—and the setting—a small midwestern town—make it different from *Meridian*, which is set in the South during the height of the Civil Rights Movement. In spite of these differences, however, *Sula* and *Meridian* are very similar because both are stories of black women who will not be restricted to narrow definitions of themselves as women. This similarity cuts across time, place, and even circumstance. Sula challenges the assumption that a woman should be the "tuck and hem" of a man's garment. Meridian challenges the assumption that a woman should be a "special sun" in a man's life, and in the individual challenges, each woman creates "something else to be."

We can conjecture that had Sula lived in a different place, and certainly at a different time—one that offered the Civil Rights Movement, for example, as an outlet for her defiance and creativity—she might have been able to sustain her own version of self. Implicitly, Morrison's portrait is a criticism of an environment that offers no alternatives to wifehood and motherhood, to suffocation and sacrifice. A corollary to this observation is that, without the Movement and without an education, Meridian could have become like Mrs. Hill, a woman who knows suffocation is "all deliberate" but who lives nonetheless a life of blind sacrifice.

On another level, both *Sula* and *Meridian* are about the human need for wholeness, for in both novels we see how race and sex also fragment the lives of men. Ajax wants to be free to be himself no less than Sula does. Truman Held, in the final chapters of the novel, does penance for his failure to say no to external factors that name him. Unquestionably, their realities are no less eclipsed by race and sex than the realities of the women. We can say, then, that while the controlling statements in the two novels are about black womanhood, the subsidiary statements are about all people, regardless of sex or race: the "special sun" in our individual lives must come from within our souls and must challenge the darkness in which the essence of our humanity is hidden.

7

THE SPACE AND THE ENCLOSURE

THE COLLECTIVE VISION OF BLACK WOMEN

the most beauty that i am i am inside and so few
deign to touch i am a forest of expectation. the
beauty that i will be is yet to be defined.

what i can be even i can not know.

—*Carolyn Rodgers, "I Have Been Hungry," 1968*

Black people are often asked to prove their objectivity—to lean backwards from the person they are in order to convince others that they are not racially biased. Black writers have had a similar problem. They are legitimate as artists only if their visions stand the test of "universality," a catch-all term for anything that is not obviously black. In other words, they must prove that they are artists who just happen to be black. Black women critics face the same problem. If they hold their blackness or their womanness too tightly, they are guilty of subjectivity, of writing under a black woman's persuasion, which automatically negates any truths they might present. It does not matter in regard to blacks that white scholars are not asked to prove that they are writing from a "universal" perspective rather than a white perspective, and it does not matter in regard to women that male critics are given carte blanche privileges in their scholarship. What matters is that blacks and women are interrogated about their work and denied the privilege of invoking the Fifth Amendment.

When I have presented portions of this book to sexually and racially mixed audiences, I have experienced the predictable interrogation. I am asked, although Toni Morrison, Alice Walker, Toni Cade Bambara, Paule Marshall, Gayl Jones, Gwendolyn Brooks, and other major black women writers are significant artists, are they not the "chosen few" who made it into the literary establishment, which is influenced by the capitalist system? Is it not possible that they made it because they present a vision of black womanhood that the system wants and expects? The interrogation continues. Is it not possible that the similarities in their vision prove only similarity in the experiences of these women rather than a collective consciousness among black women? And how can we look closely at their works without talking about their lives? Who are they? Where did they live? Whom did they marry? Did they remain married? How many children do they have? Why do they write? For whom do they write?

Questions about feminist criticism are important, for it is only in open discussion that all of us grow in our understanding of sexual politics and double jeopardy. Even when the questions reek with racism and sexism, we should be patient with persons who are essentially doubtful about feminism and black women and attempt to offer answers. No one asks how representative is Richard Wright's vision of black life in the ghetto during the forties, and no one doubts that William Faulkner's picture of life in Yoknapatawpha is as authentic as a fictive picture can be. They, too, are the "chosen," no less than black women writers whose works have made it through the system are the "chosen." We accept their visions because we accept them as writers. In regard to women writers whose works I have discussed, we can accept their visions as representative of black women's reality because those visions corrobate, extend, and particularize the history of black women in this country as documented in the historical overview. If we begin there, perhaps it is only a short distance to accepting them as writers.

Yes, it is true that black women writers, like all writers, are vulnerable to the call from the capitalist system, which says, "Write what I want you to write and you will be published." Gwendolyn Brooks says that there are "black writers who are writing in such a way—they *think*—as to be 'accepted' by the white literary world runners," and sometimes it works.[1] Toni

Morrison speaks of "artificial black writing," which she calls
"slumming among black people."[2] If black writers have written
artificially about black life, black women writers cannot be excluded from game playing simply because they are women. But
neither should they be singled out for criticism. Often the response to their literature is but a response to the whole issue of
women's rights. For example, more than a few readers believe
that Ntozake Shange played the game in the play *For Colored
Girls Who Have Considered Suicide When the Rainbow Is Enuf*.
Why else, they ask, has it been so loved by white audiences
across the nation? They also believe that Alice Walker wrote *The
Color Purple* fully aware that lesbians in the feminist movement
have a very strong lobby in the world of publications. Why else,
they ask, did this book (which is not her finest work) receive the
Pultizer Prize? They see through a glass darkened by antifemi-
nism.

There is really no way to answer such charges and, in a sense,
to answer them is to dignify them. No one can prove that black
women writers under discussion in this book were not influenced
by the system just as their critics cannot prove that they *were*
influenced. The starting point of questions about black women's
literature must be respect for the integrity of the women as
writers. They alone among writers have produced against
difficult odds, for they are blacks, women, and artists. This triple
jeopardy explains why, as Claudia Tate writes,

> By and large black women writers do not write
> for money or recognition. They write for them-
> selves as a means of maintaining emotional and
> intellectual   clarity,   of   sustaining   self-
> development and instruction. Each writes be-
> cause she is driven to do so, regardless of
> whether there is a publisher, an audience or
> neither.[3]

These writers are individual artists who have different attitudes toward the creative process and the function of art. They
write consciously about the black experience because that experience shaped them into women, writers, and persons. Gwendolyn

Brooks believes in "blacks writing about black life, but she does not believe "in sitting down and saying, 'I'm going to use this poem as a vehicle through which life can achieve some order for black women'." She gets her ideas from life around her or she goes "into my interior."[4] Her writing begins with an interest in black people. Gayl Jones is interested in "telling stories that happen to be there . . . in relationships between men and women, particularly from the viewpoint of a particular woman, the psychology of women, the psychology of language, and personal histories."[5] For Alice Walker, writing is "about living." Her "whole program as a writer is to deal with history just so I know where I am."

> It was necessary for me to write a story like *The Third Life of Grange Copeland* . . . so I could, later on, get to *Meridian,* to *In Love and Trouble* and then on to *The Color Purple.*[6]

Like her sisters in art, Morrison also begins the "writing process that goes on all the time" where she is as a black person:

> When I view the world, perceive it, and write about it, it's the world of black people. It's not that I won't write about white people. I just know that when I'm trying to develop the various themes I write about, the people who best manifest those themes for me are the black people whom I invent. It's not deliberate or calculated or self-consciously black.[7]

Interest in the black experience, and particular interest in the black woman's experience, does not mean that the women writers do not enlarge the understanding of the human experience. Indeed, it is the human experience as seen through the eyes of black women that makes their work significant. To the charge that their works are mired in blackness and womanness and fail, therefore, to reach the universal, Tate's statement is the best response.

> Whether the subject of a book originates in personal experience, in observation, empathy, or imaginative projection is not nearly so important as the degree of truthfulness and sincerity with which a book is rendered. If a writer honestly depicts what he or she *really* feels, sees, and believes, . . . then a work breathes with its own self-sustaining vitality. It then possesses a truth that exceeds the limited experience that is depicted and is, therefore, applicable to life in general. The work . . . achieves universality.[8]

Finally, I am sensitive to the criticism that we cannot evaluate the women's visions of black womanhood without knowing who they are in their personal and private lives. I do not subscribe to the stance of new critics who study works independent of biographical information. We *can* learn a great deal about the origin of the visions from studying the lives of the women writers. For example, we might be more sensitive to Maud Martha's love of "daffodils" if we know that the work is in part autobiographical. In the novel gentle Mauda Martha responds to the problem of color for black women. In real life, gentle Gwendolyn Brooks asks, "Why in the world has it been that our men have preferred either white or that pigmentation which is as close to white as possible."[9] Reading about Toni Morrison the person introduces us to her fascination with "compelling" black women, her interest in nurturing characteristics of the black community, and her belief in a tradition of friendship among black women. This information might help us understand the community in *Sula* and, most especially, the relationship between Sula and Nel. Morrison says "there is no homosexuality" in the novel.[10] And, finally, the wealth of information about her personal and private life that Alice Walker has shared in various interviews and articles can help us understand differences among the women's visions in *The Third Life of Grange Copeland*, *Meridian*, and *The Color Purple*. And yet, as important as biographical information can be, our sensitivity as readers is not hampered for want of it. When art is honest, real, poignant, and masterfully written, it connects us to truths about our humanity even when we know neither the author's life nor her name. That is true about the compellingly powerful works of these black women writers.

In a real sense, the black women writers themselves should raise questions about my interpretations of their works. In my search for themes, do I fail to pay attention to form, structure, and language—the essentials of craft that distinguish them as *artists* rather than identify them as women who made a literary statement about a subject? Do I hold the works so closely under the light of my own interests that I inadvertently suggest the how and why of their writing? On the basis of what I see in their works, do I identify the "right" audience? And there are other questions.

Obviously, there is more truth and power in the twelve novels I have discussed than this book examines. I isolated parts of the whole, but like pieces of a puzzle that have their own color and shape, the parts are important only when they serve their purpose in the larger picture. But sometimes we come to appreciate the beauty and power of literature in the same way that we come to appreciate those of a masterful painting; compelling parts magnetically attract us to the painting, but once we stand close to the canvas, we see the richness and beauty of the total picture. It is often by way of the parts that we come to appreciate the whole.

The parts I isolated in the novels' pictures of humanity are race and sex, which are dominant concerns in American culture. The writers draw three different and distinct circles of reality in America, all three of which are shaped by capitalism. In one circle white people, mainly males, experience influence and power. Far removed from it is the second circle, a narrow space in which black people, regardless of sex, experience uncertainty and powerlessness. And in this narrow space, often hidden but no less present and real, is the third circle, a small, dark enclosure for black women only. It is in this enclosure that black women experience what Mary Helen Washington identifies as the unique marks of black womanhood—"isolation, loss, vulnerability, and victimization."[11]

To understand the dark enclosure, we must first understand the narrow space, for it is here that black women along wih their men share a collective history of oppression, exploitation, and often consummate victimization. It is here that they first learn the meaning of force, of conflict, and of unending struggle, all three of which affect the lives of those whom black women love—their husbands, their children, and other family members. And it is here that they develop approaches to life that affect the way they see themselves and the way they function in the enclosure. Indeed, in a real sense, what they experience in the enclosure is shaped by what they experience, with other black people, in the narrow space. Hence, the convincing argument that sex—or the reality in the enclosure—is the "lesser question" for black women.

Without pitting sex against race, or vice versa, the women novelists never equivocate on the harsh exigencies of life in the narrow space and never minimize how profoundly those conditions affect suffering in the small enclosure. Numerous instances have been discussed in the preceding chapters of this study. Pauline Breedlove, for example, suffers intensely because, in the narrow space of black powerlessness, her life is ravaged by stark poverty and by the effects of imposed inferiority. This fact alone explains her attitudes toward herself, toward her husband, and toward her children. Mariah Upshur says that her life "ain't been nothing but wind" because, in the narrow space, she is powerless against the malnutrition to which her children are subjected and against a superstructure of exploitation that questions her husband's manhood even as he demonstrates in his back-breaking work that he is twice over a man. Mem Copeland moves from one manure-filled barn to another because a vicious sharecropping system keeps black people, and especially black men, in servile dependence akin to slavery. And finally, Eva Peace has "no time" for loving her children because racism and poverty make bare survival a phenomenal task.

When we read these novels and others that illuminate the narrow space, we understand how profound is the suffering of black people. We see black women, along with their men, standing in the center of the space, laboring in darkness to open their lives to light. And we understand that since all their suffering begins in the narrow space, wider options for black women must be effected as much in the space as in the enclosure—and most definitely *first* in the narrow space. Black feminist thinkers of the seventies say as much when they write that black women will not gain their emancipation at the expense of their men or, more cogently, that wider options for black women, of necessity, mean wider options for black men. As separate as they are, the narrow space and the dark enclosure are inextricably bound together, for race, sex, and class are interdependent in white America.

However, since "double jeopardy" means, by definition, that there is a reality unique to black women, we must go beyond the narrow space deep into the dark center of the enclosure to understand the extent to which sexism exacerbates the effects of racism, or how the two work together as major determinants of the lives of black women. That journey begins, as Mary Helen Washington writes, when we attempt "to finger the grooves of . . . the scars" on the lives of *women* characters in selected black women's fiction. As we fingered those "scars" "until we [knew] the designs by heart,"[12] we made several interesting discoveries, some already mentioned. First of all, we discovered that black women's reality in the dark enclosure converges and diverges with their reality in the narrow space to the extent that the former is greatly exacerbated by the latter and never completely separate from it. Second, we discovered that while their reality in the enclosure is unique to them, black women often confuse what they experience in this special world with what all black people experience in the narrow space of uncertainty and powerlessness. And finally, we discovered that it is often in the enclosure that women experience their deepest and most permanent scars, for it is here that they are in conflict, not with a white-controlled system, but with black men who shatter their dreams of love and acceptance. This final discovery is perhaps the most distinguishing feature of black women's fiction. Written from a woman's perspective, which by definition illumines the enclosure, contemporary black women's fiction develops the thesis that black men, unwittingly or deliberately, participate in the victimization of black women. Alice Walker's title for her collection of short stores is, therefore, by far the most appropriate caption for portraits of the women characters. Without denying the darkness of the narrow space, the portraits emphasize the enclosure and reveal therein women "in love and trouble."[13]

In *The Street*, a classic protest novel of the forties, Ann Petry illumines both the narrow space and the enclosure in her attack on the capitalist system's exploitation of black people in ghettoes of the North. She establishes a cause-and-effect relation between what the system does to black men and what they in turn do to black women. The men are victims whom harsh reality causes to become victimizers of their women. They are not perceived, however, as the major oppressors of black women. Racism and poverty are. Therefore, when Lutie Johnson strikes Boots Smith in rage, she indicts him as a representative of many black men on "the street" who exploit black women, but she lands her heaviest blows on the system that places black men and black women as antagonists in the suffocatingly narrow space, creating thereby the special dark enclosure of pain for black women.

Emphasis on the capitalist system as the cause of conflict between black men and black women also shapes visions from the fifties, but the emphasis is less intense, given the waning of protest in that decade. In *Maud Martha*, for example, protest against race and class is subdued as Gwendolyn Brooks analyzes, from a positive perspective, the "kitchenette" culture of Southside Chicago, which is an economic half-step above the culture of "the street." Racism created the culture, but a strong sense of community and the workings of survival motions save Maud Martha from the despair and violence that engulf the characters in Petry's novel. Nothing, however, can save Maud Martha from the "grooves . . . of scars" made by the system's definition of beauty in white terms. The ache in her soul is a woman's ache because she cannot close the distance between her appearance and the idea of white beauty. When her husband is cold, insensitive, and even rejecting, she forgives him because he is a psychological captive of a white-oriented value system.

In *Brown Girl, Brownstones*, also from the fifties, Paule Marshall's sympathy for black men, indeed her illustration of the theory of the defeated black man, is expressed in the contrasting portraits of Deighton Boyce and his wife, Silla. Deighton is warm, gentle, and affectionate. Silla, on the other hand, is hard, distant, and fiercely ambitious. Her fury comes from the lingering pain of the death of her son but in a more immediate way from her frustrations with her husband's lack of ambition, his dance-and-play games with long shots for success, and his indiscreet infidelity. He dresses in silk shirts, spends days with his "concubine," and whittles away his future and his family's future on empty fantasies that can never be realized in white America. She works long shifts in the factory in the hope of saving enough money to buy a brownstone. Marshall writes of Silla with understanding, but of Deighton she writes with deep compassion, for he has been turned from pride and a sense of accomplishment by the omnipresence of white power, first in Barbados and then in Brooklyn.

As early as the late sixties, and most definitely by the seventies, the victimization of black men no longer obscured the harsh and heavy lines of the enclosure in which black women are placed. Black women writers, like black women activists, began to answer the question Mariah Upshur raises in *This Child's Gonna Live:* "but what about the colored *woman?*" In the first major black woman's novel of the decade, *The Third Life of Grange Copeland,* Alice Walker answers the question, but not without an understanding of what has happened to "the colored man." Her moving portraits of Grange Copeland and his son Brownfield, both victims of a vicious sharecropping system, are obviously attacks on the narrow space in which black people, regardless of sex, dance with only shadows of dreams and trudge wearily through a journey of hopelessness. Walker sympathizes with black men, but she does not excuse them for their destruction of their gentle and devoted wives. Grange is held accountable, and his conscience ravaged, for the suicide of his wife Margaret; and Brownfield, whose brutality lies at the center of the novel, is not forgiven for his murder of Mem. Toni Morrison in *The Bluest Eye* writes sympathetically of Cholly's pain as he moved violently on the black women in full view of mocking white men whose flashlight made a white circle on Cholly's nakedness, but his pain does not ease the loneliness and alienation Pauline feels in the cold steel town of Lorain. In these novels and others, black women are damaged persons not only because they are black and often poor but also because they mix the colors of their dreams in black men's cups of victimization and sexism. The line between sexual oppression and racial oppression is so thin as to be, at times, indistinguishable.

In novels written later in the seventies, victimization of black men is no longer the recognizable axis on which the abuse of black women turns and, accordingly, the assumption that sex is the "lesser question" is no longer without challenge. Sula's denigration of Jude, who seeks stroking and indulgence because "the man" is at his throat, is similar in tone to the writings of Barbara Sizemore, Frances Beal, Pauli Murray, and other feminist thinkers of the decade. However, whereas these thinkers admit that there are racially imposed shackles on the lives of black men, Sula seems to make mockery of the notion of injured black men. In her opinion, they have more than their share of love and attention and a chance for flight and freedom. When she sees victimization in "the Bottom," she sees black women, "spiders" on a rung, who are slowly and silently "dying" without having lived. Eva Medina, in Gayl Jones's *Eva's Man*, has a similar vision of black reality. In the black world in which she seeks "alternatives to brutality"[14] for black women, she sees women who are forced to become bitches or whores or, rejecting those images, "queen bees" and "Medusas" whose lives are synonyms for isolation and loneliness.

But there are no monolithic statements on sexism in the black experience. Not all black men victimize their women. Not all are cold, selfish, rejecting or, for that matter, broken. Walker writes of the sexism of Truman, who believes that women are to be "had," and if they are virgins prized, but "had" nevertheless, but she also writes with tenderness of the sensitivity of Mr. Hill, who cried when he broke into his wife's body. Marshall paints tenderness and affection into her portrait of Deighton Boyce, and Louise Meriwether writes of "Daddy's" laughter and the sweet tinkling of the piano. Jude speaks to Sula's mind and delights in having her on top of him. Bart Judson is an unselfish and humble man who is victimized by a manipulative and "ice" cold wife. Black men in black women's fiction are not always *the* enemy.

These positive portraits, however, are but variations on a theme of male insensitivity and exploitation. From Boots Smith's attempt in *The Street* to get *his* first to Davis' attempts in *Eva's Man* to put "the fork" in Eva's road, black men in the novels, as a rule, do not see black women beyond the services they render for others, most especially for men. They see a house cleaned, meals prepared and served, and children tended to, rather than the women who have performed the chores. They understand money problems and racial problems rather than the problems of their women that go beyond money and race. They see bodies to be had rather than minds to be respected and aspirations to be encouraged. They believe that husbands and wives should share the responsibilities associated with families, but they do not themselves share by performing traditional women's roles in the home. They understand that pain is real and deep, but they do not disengage themselves from their own pain long enough to recognize the pain their women suffer. In a word, they fail to see the small, dark enclosure within the narrow space. They do not know that they are sexist because being so is as basic to their reality as being black is an invitation to exploitation in white America. And significantly, they are not sexist because they are black or even because they are victimized. They are sexist because, as men, they are socialized to be sexist. Sexism has no respect for race or class, just as racism has no respect for sex.

It goes without saying that sexism is far more complex than love battles between men and women, just as racism is far more complex than the presence of "for black only" signs in our society. Along with racism and class, sexism is a part of an infrastructure that affects every aspect of a black woman's life. For this reason, it is important, as Zillah Eisenstein writes, to avoid "seeing sex or class, or race or class, or sex or race" and study instead "the process and relations of power."[15] It is equally important to avoid seeing male-female conflicts as the only manifestations of the sexual arm of "the process." But there is a logical explanation for what seems to be undeserved emphasis on male-female conflicts in the novels. The women writers, as artists, are interested in the particulars of a woman's life that define her in relation to others and, in doing so, define her within her own psyche. Given the cultural weight of a woman's "place," those particulars are dramatically vivid in the "inside" world. It is the inevitability of what Cleo Judson calls woman's "sphere" that keeps women apart from the "world" in which male power reigns often unchallenged.

The weight of the "sphere" in the black experience does not mean that women are confined to the home or that they never participate in the world of work outside the home. Unlike many of their white counterparts, black women leave the "sphere" to participate in the labor force, and in that force they work mainly as domestics, clerks, and operatives. There are no professional black women in the novels who are active participants in the "outside" world. Perhaps this is a shortcoming of the visions since in real life there are black women professionals, who are usually teachers, nurses, and social workers—jobs historically reserved for women. The focus of the writers, however, is on nonprofessionals, a focus that lends support to Claudia Tate's opinion that black women writers are "concerned with a kind of folk heroine and have not, as yet, dealt with the college-educated black woman who is, by fact of her education, encountering all kinds of additional problems."[16]

In portraits of these "folk heroines," women work because they have to work, not because they wish to be competitive in a man's world. They have been socialized as women, in spite of their race and perhaps in a more urgent way because of their race, to believe that they are keepers of the heart and the hearth, and they have learned through the ages that keeping the hearth dry and protected against storms necessitates their involvement in the world outside the home. For economic reasons, then, they function in the outside world, but their dreams, their visions of success, and their search for meaningful relationships were for and in the inside world. Their orientation to this inside world explains why many of the women experience their deepest disappointments in it. Given this fact of black women's reality, it is easy to understand why black men in the novels often emerge as agents of agony for the women.

And yet, black women's loyalty to their men is a recurring theme in the novels, a theme that is the other side of the theme of racial bonding. In none of the twelve novels studied do black women see white men as symbols of masculinity or sexuality. Pauline Breedlove's fantasy about being Jean Harlow is the only instance of a black woman looking longingly at a white man, but even here the white man is not sexually desired. In fact, as Morrison handles the fantasy, we see that Pauline is interested in being Jean Harlow because Harlow symbolizes power, beauty, and security. The love she receives from Clark Gable is only one expression of the contrast between her life and Pauline's life. Lutie Johnson is taught as a young girl that she should not let white men bother her, and as an adult woman she would rather lie with a snake than sleep with a white man. Significantly, when she attempts to borrow money for her son's bail, she goes to Boots Smith although she knows that it is Junto, the white man on "the street," who owns everything. A third example of the point being made is found in *Sula*. When people in "the Bottom" want to prove that Sula is evil incarnate, they spread the rumor that she has committed the worst sin of all: she has slept with white men. In all of the novels, black women are sexually attracted only to black men.

One of the results of studying race and sex in the same context is that triumph in one dimension of "double jeopardy" is juxtaposed, and in some instances, challenged by defeat in another. Women can challenge racial limitations on their reality and achieve in spite of them and, at the same time, submit to sexual limitations, or vice versa. This dynamic of failure and success—challenge and submission—is particularly dramatic in portraits of women who are mothers, since the legendary black woman of strength and achievement against insurmountable odds is more often than not a mother. If one looks through the veil of motherhood at the behavior of Mem Copeland in *The Third Life of Grange Copeland*, Meridian in *Meridian*, or Eva Peace in *Sula*, one sees the "sturdy black bridges" of which Carolyn Rodgers writes. They are the women who are "resilient and hardy," and like "midnight birds" they are "yearning and impatient."[17]

But in that they are bridges over the treacherous waters of race, class, and sex, the major chord of maternal triumph becomes only one of several chords in a sorrow song. Mem Copeland is an exemplary mother, but outside the role she is destroyed by male abuse. Meridian's grandmother has reason to recite her success in "turning corners and reachin' landins'" as a mother, but outside the role she tastes the acidity of her husband's hostility to wider options for women. And Eva Peace makes the phenomenal sacrifice of a leg for the welfare of her family, owning at first only three beets and $1.65 to her name and later a house of many rooms, but she is half a person because she encloses her feelings behind an impenetrable wall of hatred for the man who abandons her. Often, then, when the women soar as mothers into seeming triumph above race and class, their wings are clipped in flight and, sexually, they plunge into devastating agony.

Not all women are exemplary mothers, however. In *Meridian*, for example, Mrs. Hill anchors Meridian's spirit in guilt and her own maternal posture in distance, not because, racially, she has been forced to sacrifice her own life for the welfare of her daughter. Brilliantly, Alice Walker depicts Mrs. Hill as a woman whose serenity and independence have been robbed by the sexual role of mother. Thus she irons into her childrens' clothes the "starch" of her sexual anger and continues to cry inside, "It's all deliberate." Pauline Breedlove, as a mother, is psychologically cruel, adding her own brand of rejection to racial factors that make Pecola wish tragically for blue eyes. Morrison explains that Pauline is damaged by her inferior status as a poor black woman in a white world of wealth and also by her husband's failure (or inability) to compensate in their love relationship for what she experiences in the outside world. In these examples, and in others, the women are not negligent mothers. Indeed, they are "good" mothers in that they attend to the physical needs of their children, and, although they do not demonstrate affection, they love them. But they can not travel the emotional miles from indifference to involvement, from maternal frustrations to maternal fulfillment, because as blacks and as women, they are "damaged persons."

The maternal missions of the women characters reflect the double-edged nature of their reality and also the significance of their sexual vulnerability. Boys receive the message of preparation for survival and success in a white world, with the emphasis on dealing with "*the* man" and the system. For girls, it is a very different lesson, given the emphasis on winning in "man's" world rather than "*the* man's" world. Mrs. Medina and Eva's other mother give Eva one lesson for the future: "don't let men mess with you," suggesting that her identity as a woman rather than her identity as a black person is imbued with problems. Silla Boyce and Henrietta Coffin stress the importance of an education, and in the same breath they warn their daughters that their sexual vulnerability is the greatest threat to this goal. If socialization is a comment on reality, and it is, then one could argue that black women perceive sexual vulnerability, not racial oppression, as the greater danger in their lives. Racism is, of course, involved here, and in a major and decisive way. It determines where the women live, what kinds of jobs and salaries they receive, what monsters will stalk their children's future, how they and their men are treated and, as a result, how they are treated by their men—in a word, the parameters of their lives. But racism alone does not explain the women's sensitivity to their sexual vulnerability. This sensitivity supersedes race at the same moment that it intersects with race. It supersedes race because it is a biological fact that is not contingent on race. It intersects with race because one of the results of racism and sexism in the black experience is that black women are more physically vulnerable because they are perceived by the larger society and, more tragically, by their own men as devalued sex objects.

Their double identities, along with the problems of their men in white America, add another dimension to their socialization: they must be independent. Unlike most white women, they are taught that no one will adore them, revere them, care for them, and protect them. There are no pedestals in their reality and no crystal stairs. Only on themselves can they depend for their survival. Because they are black, they can expect nothing from white America except that which they manage to acquire through miracles, hard work, and sometimes game playing. And because they are female, they can expect very little from their men, even if they play a woman's game of coquettish indulgence.

Independence, however, is not the same as selfishness, and self-sufficiency is not a mirror image of egotism, for the women have the ability to be self-sacrificing at the same time that they are self-sufficient. This fact is an unchanging feature in the novels: the women are rarely seen doing for themselves. They are rarely happy in the "inside" world, but they are always there, serving their husbands and children. They do not shop for themselves, collect things for themselves, or spend time on themselves. Mariah Upshur's sigh, "no time to sew for myself," is a good description of the extent to which most of the women are depicted as other-directed. Somehow, all of them, regardless of class, manage in the crises of their personal lives to keep in focus their role as keepers of the "inside."

"The subject of the black woman's physical beauty," writes

Mary Helen Washington, "occurs with such frequency in the writings of black women that it indicates that they have been deeply affected by the discrimination against their skin and texture of their hair." The "color theme," she continues, "almost always plays at least a peripheral role in the lives of imaginative women created by black women writers."[18] Washington's thesis is supported by the color and hair problem in *The Bluest Eye, Maud Martha, Corregidora, The Living Is Easy,* and, for Mrs. Hedges, in *The Street.* But it does not surface in *Eva's Man; Sula; Brown Girl, Brownstones;* or *The Third Life of Grange Copeland.* Walker dismisses "color" as a problem when she writes of Mem's interpretation of color as something done to flowers.

One would be foolish, of course, to ignore the impact that the specter of white beauty has on the thinking of black women. It is an intrinsic part of their socialization, and even when they cope with their blackness, it is an ever-present ache in their souls. They know that they are devalued because they are black women. But without denying its weight in the lives of black women, the women writers move us beyond this problem to the larger and more complex problem of sexism, which can not be traced to color or other physical features. Sexism is not fed or created by men's interest in beauty, though their vanity makes them believe they should have only those women who are beautiful. Rather, sexism is fed by men's assumption that, as men, they should have dominant roles in society. To be sure, there is a mixed and intricate picture here, in which a multitude of factors are at play—color, hair texture, race, class,—and none can be extricated from the total picture without the truth being distorted. But we must be sensitive to proportion, as the women novelists are, and in our sensitivity, recognize that black women in the novels, though often not pleased with the way they look, experience "loss, isolation, vulnerability and victimization," even when they are beautiful, because they are hostages in a racist and sexist culture. Black men might use the color and hair problems as excuses for their abuse of black women, as does Brownfield when he reminds Mem that she is not white, but the single most decisive factor in their attitudes is their socialization in a sexist culture.

Perhaps William Grier and Price Cobbs are correct in writing of the absence of female narcissism in black women, for the women in the novels either have little interest in expressing their "femininity" in traditional frills and frivolities, in wardrobes of sheer garments and dressers cluttered with makeup that colors cheeks and enlarges eyes. Obviously, for poor black women, time and money are deciding factors. And yet, we can challenge the novels' failure to include in the portraits of black women, even those who are poor, the women's interest in their appearance. It is not true, as many of the authors imply, that this interest is subdued in black women. The flourishing market of special cosmetics for black women and cheap ones for poor black women proves otherwise. The cheap clothing stores that pepper black communities prove otherwise, as does the presence of beauty shops within shouting distance of one another. No woman who is socialized in this society of Mabelline eye cosmetics, silky fabrics, and alluring perfumes can fail to be affected in some way by the institutionalized and profit-oriented program of American femininity. We could argue, in fact, that black women, more than white women, might seek aids to femininity because they have been denied beauty in white America.

Black women's interest in being "pretty" and "attractive" in a "feminine" way is not completely excluded from the visions. In *Brown Girl, Brownstones* and in *Corregidora*, women are seen flocking to beauty shops where they sit for hours enduring the heat of metal or chemicals that will improve the appearance of their hair. In *The Street*, Lutie Johnson expresses her desire to be more than a struggling mother by flirting with a reflection of a "feminine" self in a mirror as she prepares to make her debut as a nightclub singer. The most convincing statement on the effect of the femininity market on black women is given by Toni Morrison, for she uses Sula's desire to be "feminine," as it is defined in American culture, as a sign of Sula's destruction. When Sula seeks to hold Ajax in a relationship of possessiveness, she joins other women in the beauty parlor, decorates her hair with ribbons, and scents the bedroom with fragrances. Seeing Sula behave like a typical woman, Ajax mounts her, rides through her pleasure, and abandons her.

While the novelists pay only minor attention to these concerns, they pay preeminent attention to other criteria of "femininity," criteria that determine how a woman should function rather than how she should look and, in a sense, that determine the darkness of the enclosure. The women in the novels want to be dainty, soft, winning, coquettish, demure, sweet—all criteria of "femininity." They want to be supportive rather than domineering, a major criterion of femininity. If it is true that black men are socialized to be sexist, it is also true that black women are socialized to be "feminine," or to internalize sexist assumptions about the appearance and behavior of a successful and desired woman. The novelists' visions support this fact as evidenced, among other examples, by Mrs. Hedges' concern about her enormous size, Eva's belief that women should coquettishly pamper their men rather than openly compete with them, and Nel's decision to be "the tuck and hem" of Jude's garment rather than "something else" more fulfilling.

Being a woman and being feminine are two different experiences in the novels, and it is the former that most engages the attention of the writers. To be a woman is to be legitimized in a relationship with a man. To be a woman is to be a mother, a wife, and/or lover. To operate outside these roles often brings censure from the community. To challenge these roles is to enclose oneself in loneliness and isolation. This was the dilemma of Eva Medina. In a sense it was the dilemma of Mrs. Hill, who functioned in the roles of wife and mother without acknowledging their significance. It was the dilemma that made Sula, who would create a different version of herself, a pariah in "the Bottom." And it was the cultural lesson, accepted by most black women, that made Eva explain that what Sula needed to do most was to make babies. To live outside these roles is certain death for women.

Like their white counterparts, black women are victims of the concept of romantic love. They, too, have sung the songs, recited the poems, seen the movies, and read the true romance magazines about "the man I love." They too, have been fed from the "staples"[19] of American mythology about the magic of romantic love. Because of their location in the narrow space of powerlessness, perhaps they need the magic in a special way, but ironically, it is often because of this location that they discover there is no magic at all. Toni Morrison best explains the tragedy of this concept in the lives of black women. Like the concept of physical beauty, she writes, the concept of romantic love is a destructive force in civilization. It is presented as such in most of the novels. It colors Pauline Breedlove's fantasies and poses her idle at a country fence waiting for a man to make her whole. It causes Josie to forget her victory over a community of exploitative men and rush head-on into victimization at the hands of that special man. It makes Nel relinquish her claim on the right to create "something else to be," and it turns Sula 180 degrees from independence, freedom, and unlimited expression of self. For the women, to be loved by a man is to know one is alive.

Belief in the concept of romantic love does not, however, make the women empty-headed, dizzy, pining souls who are stagnant in life, singing the blues for a man who has gone. Men come into their lives, often they conquer, often they exploit, often they leave having conquered, but in their leaving they cannot look back at women so devastated by disappointment in love that they cease to function. With the exception of Margaret, in *The Third Life of Grange Copeland*, who commits suicide, the women rise from the ashes of unrequited love and male abuse to put the pieces of their lives back in place. The scars are real, deep, and lasting. Often the women never love again or they box their lives in loneliness and isolation, in cynicism and hostility. But they continue to be pragmatic women who get on with the business of living and coping. Their resilience in the enclosure is forged by their reality in the narrow space, for what they experience as blacks prepares them to confront problems peculiar to them as women.

In the novels written in the seventies, the sexuality of women, or more specifically, their experience with sexual lovemaking is treated with honesty, frankness, and bitterness. Again, race, class and sex are involved in the quality of the experience, for "coitus is never in a vacuum."[20] The myth of the sexually talented and sexually eager black woman is examined critically, resulting in the conclusion that black women are sexually active on one hand and spiritually frustrated on the other hand. Josie bumps and grinds with great skill, but she wants more than the pleasure of the act itself. She wants to be cleansed, and that takes love, acceptance, and tenderness. Sula sleeps with men but gets no pleasure from the experience because their monotonous love tricks deny the existence of her mind. Mrs. Hill can not separate the act from the consequences of the act—pregnancy and mother-hood—which imprison her in unfulfilling, noncreative duties. Meridian finds the nights with Eddie only exercises in duty and mechanics because he is too limited to understand that there is a larger world of possibility than the one they know in the small Mississippi town. And finally, at the extreme end of the spectrum is Cleo Judson, whose still face mocks the "busyness" below be-cause men are her enemies "because they are male." Sex in many of the relationships is an unremarkable experience that comes with the role of wife.

These black novels make no allusions to new definitions of fe-male sexuality similar to those that are made in many white feminist writings in the seventies. Criteria for orgasms are not treated from a biological or physical perspective. Sexual gym-nastics are neither the problem nor the solution, for black women are not searching for new ways of making love. The old ways work when one essential about their personhood is in place; and when that essential is in place the women experience what Toni Morrison in *Sula* calls "the silence of orgasm." Predictably, the essential is recognition of the women's need to be appreciated and loved and respected, to be valued not for what they do, but for what they are as persons. Mem enjoys lovemaking with Brownfield when he basks in her intelligence, in her humanity, and in her character, which makes her outstanding in the commu-nity. Meridian is bored by nights with Eddie, but in her first coitus with Truman, she ascends into bliss because she believes he loves her, respects her mind, and more importantly, is com-mitted to the noble cause of the struggle. The strongest state-ment of the significance of this woman's essential in lovemaking is given in Morrison's portrait of Sula. When Ajax listens to Sula and respects what she says, Sula forgets the eclipsed joy of mas-turbation and ecstatically plunges into thrilling rides above Ajax. For men, coitus is merely physical. For black women, when it brings pleasure, it is a harmonious blend of what they can physi-cally enjoy and what they emotionally need and desire. There-fore, black men in the novels are sexually potent only when they stroke the souls of women as expertly as they stroke the thighs.

The collective and individual visions of the women, regardless of time, class, or region, are pictures of victimization, isolation, loneliness, and loss. The women understand that theirs is a difficult and complex reality. However, like Pauline Breedlove in *The Bluest Eye* and Min and Mrs. Hedges in *The Street*, to name three, the women sometimes fail to understand that what they experience as women is a cultural phenomenon. They perceive the sexual dimensions of their suffering, but they do not always realize that other women are in the enclosure with them. Rather, they see the enclosure, real though it is in their lives, as the result of their peculiar reality.

Other women, however, understand that they are not alone in the enclosure, just as they are not alone in the space. They understand that other black women turn the same corners and tip-toe through the same morass of limitations and powerlessness. But understanding the problem is one thing and talking about the problem is another altogether. In most instances, their anger is turned inward, and black men, as a result, rarely have an opportunity to hear women out on matters that are peculiar to the reality of "double jeopardy." Women turn their anger inward because they are socialized to believe that their agony is second to the agony of the race and second to the agony of their men. Consequently, they often persevere and suffer in silence. And for those unique women such as Mariah Upshur, Sula Peace, Eva Medina, and Eva Peace, turning anger outward results in further isolation, estrangement, and deeper agony.

What is more surprising about the portraits is that even when the women understand that they share a sisterhood of oppression, they often do not act on the belief that "sisterhood is powerful." They do not come together to talk about their common history and their common reality. When they do attempt to communicate as *women*, they fail to sustain the sisterhood. Mariah Upshur and Vyella in *This Child's Gonna Live* are kindred souls, seeking wider options for their lives, but the intensity of sexism and religious backwardness in Tangierneck keeps them in separate camps. Meridian and Anne Marion in *Meridian* touch each other's version of self, but the versions are in conflict on an issue that is fundamental to the black liberation struggle in which both are involved. And finally, Sula and Nel in *Sula* are so close they are like "two throats and one eye," but what they are as sisters is ultimately destroyed by Nel's acquiescence to woman's "place" in a web of spiders and Sula's intense desire to cut the web where it holds women dangling from the frailest of threads.

In her second work, *Midnight Birds* (1980), Mary Helen Washington writes that "one of the most important themes in women's literature [is] women's reconciliation with one another."[21] She gives as an example of this theme the final act of Ntozake Shange's choreopoem, *For Colored Girls*. In the scene of reconciliation, seven women characters who have experienced different kinds of abuse come together and sing, "i found god in myself and i loved her fiercely." Washington writes that "reconciliation [in the play] is finally and completely a feminine and a feminist act."[22] *Sula*, also, Washington writes, is a work in which this theme is developed. She quotes Morrison on this point:

> But black women have always had that, they have always been emotional life supports for each other. That's what I was trying to say in Sula, when Nel discovered that it was not her husband that she had missed all those years, but her friend Sula.[22]

While it is true that there has been a "communal network"[24] in the lives of black women, it is also true that there has been hostility among them. This paradox is ignored by some black feminists as they write of the power of sisterhood. In some ways, failure to acknowledge that the corrupt society in which we live has created tension among black women is not unlike failure of black women prior to the seventies to acknowledge publicly that some black men oppress black women. Both are the results of a "sacred cow"[25] attitude toward black women and black men, respectively. In the larger truth, we must include some discussion of a breakdown in the "communal network"[26] once black women stop being "young girls" and become competitors in the adult world for men, for jobs, for status in organizations, and for status in the community. Audre Lorde writes of the failure of black women to acknowledge the anger, hostility, and suspicion we have against each other. "It is easier," she explains, "to examine anger in situations less emotionally loaded, for instance in relationships with white women, which do not threaten genuine self-exposure," but few black women in this country give to their sisters "acceptance, gentleness, enough space to consider change, room to be wrong." Her honesty is a cry for healing:

> I don't like to talk about hate. But the anger
> between Black women is the tip of an iceberg,
> the understructure of which is hatred. From the
> moment she is born, a Black woman in America
> becomes vulnerable to hatreds that amount to a
> societal death wish—for her color, for her sex,
> for her effrontery in daring to presume she has
> any right to live in racist sexist America. . . .
> Echoes of this hatred return as anger in our deal-
> ings with each other, for each of us bears the face
> that hatred seeks.[27]

Unless we deal with this hatred, we will be guilty, as Mary Helen Washington writes in her first book, *Black-eyed Susans*, and seems to contradict in her second book, *Midnight Birds*, of taking a "sacred cow" attitude toward black women, We will "settle for some idealized nonsense about black women and remain deprived of real characters from whom we could learn more about ourselves."[28]

The novels analyzed in this book do not have a "sacred cow" attitude toward black women, for several of them allude to tension among women characters. In fact, the deeper we travel into the authors' visions, the more we realize that the hardships of black life sometimes push women apart and arrange them in the narrow space and in the dark enclosure as antagonists. A theme hinted at but not developed in the novels, is that black women sometimes participate in the victimization of other black women. Josie ignores the agony of Mem by stretching herself into Brownfield's life. The women in the church flagellate Mariah Upshur verbally and physically and keep her forever in doubt about her morality. The concubines of Deighton Boyce and James Coffin are not ignorant of their participation in the destruction of families that involve not only wives, but children as well. Regardless of the reason that drives Sula to make a point about the empty lives of women in "the Bottom," she is the cause of Nel's agony. And finally, Mrs. Hedges, who realizes that women are vulnerable because they are women, lures her sisters in oppression into the worst trap of all—prostitution.

Hostility between black women and white women is understandably well developed in the novels, for white women symbolize the American ideal of beauty, and through their relationships with white men they hold the strings of power and influence. In fact, in the novels, white women rather than white men often represent the enemy. Nancy Hoffman is therefore correct in advising white women who teach black American literature to be prepared to be "the enemy."[29] And yet, even on the issue of white women, there is no monolithic statement in the novels. In the forties, white women are madams. In the fifties, they are women of beauty, floating like abstractions in the "other" world. But in the seventies, they are sometimes only passing subjects of conversations or they are not mentioned at all. In *Meridian*, which suggests a new treatment of white women, they are sisters in oppression. Lynn Rabinowitz, whom Alice Walker depicts with compassion and understanding, is victimized because she is white in a world of black rage and female in a movement dominated by sexist men. Walker's sensitivity to Lynn's tragedy supports Washington's thesis that "wrongs acknowledged and challenged, silence broken, signal a distinct change for the relationship between black women and white women."[30]

The women's coping mechanisms vary from novel to novel, but all of the women bleed, and real tears wash salt into gaping wounds. Margaret Copeland is driven to suicide, and Lutie Johnson and Eva Medina to murder. Cleo Judson schemes and plays games to maximize her chances for more power and influence. Pauline Breedlove becomes a self-righteous woman whose religion saves her from insanity. Josie bumps and grinds her way into economic security, playing the game and losing even as she wins. Eva Peace retreats from the world of spontaneous and honest feelings, and her granddaughter, Sula, strikes out against every vestige of sexism, or any phenomenon that will keep her from "catching the slant of life." Regardless of their mechanisms for coping, all of the women, except Lutie Johnson in *The Street*, are at their weakest in their need for love. The tragedy of their lives as black women is that they are socialized to believe that they will ultimately be abandoned, neglected, mistreated, or abused by men, and ultimately most of them are.

What they desire as black women is not unfamiliar in studies of the black experience. They want to be relieved of the strains of poverty. They want their children's horizons unfettered by anything other than their own potential and dreams. They want their men to realize the fullest expression of manhood. In a word, they want to be free to live outside the narrow space. What they desire as black *women* is expressed very well by Washington. They want "solitariness, a space and time for themselves, they want to be free of male domination, the need to be the Angel in the House at the cost of [their] creativity."[31]

It is necessary that we understand, however, that these desires do not mean that the women characters are feminists. Sula, however, articulates the feminist belief that a woman should "make myself." The artists write from a feminist perspective, but their characters are like most black women in real life. They are essentially traditional in their approach to life. They do not seek new definitions of sexual roles. Most of them, in fact, are willing to observe the old rules, if, in doing so, they are free of victimization. Their desires for wider options, when examined closely— both in the narrow space and in the dark enclosure—are essentially what Gayl Jones calls "alternatives to brutality." They want love, acceptance, respect, and, for several women, the freedom to express their creativity. Even when they realize that the "old rules" are by definition obstacles to these desires, most of the women would rather take their chances with the "old rules" and struggle in small ways for a new reality. They live what most women live—lives of contradiction. For black women, unlike for other women, the contradiction is the result of their loyalty or conditioning (or both) in the space and in the enclosure.

In her prefaces to *Black-Eyed Susans* (1974) and *Midnight Birds* (1980), Washington writes of distorted images of black women that "abound like weeds in this society."[32] Only in fiction written by black women, she posits, is the complexity of black womanhood truthfully and sensitively presented, for as "dynamic interpreters of their own lives," black women writers choose "some brand-new" images of black women: "black-eyed susans" of "hardiness and resilience" and "midnight birds" of "yearning and impatience."[33] This statement should not be construed to mean that black women writers ignore and discard traditional images that have constituted a national mythology about black womanhood. As artists, they understand that while "self and image are not the same . . . they can not live apart from each other."[34] Images, even when they are false, are the public mirrors in which we first see ourselves as others see us and, are, therefore, the starting places for our definitions of ourselves. If we deny the existence of public images before they are replaced by more truthful ones, "the self becomes a jibbering ghost, immured in its watchtower, unable to reach the world."[35] Moreover, public images are so fundamental a part of our reality that to repudiate them totally is tantamount to repudiating a part of ourselves.

The selection of new images of black women must be seen as a first and very necessary step toward bringing together in the same place public images of black women and the women's authentic selves in the anticipation, though never the certainty, that the authentic selves will gain a firmer hold in the national consciousness than the images. However, it is a first step and, as such, it must rely on old images. For this reason, it is not true that "one does not see in the black woman as portrayed by the black woman writer any such perversions as the super sex object, or the domineering matriarch, or the evil black bitch."[36] In fiction, as in real life, some black women *are* those so-called "perversions," for myth and truth, image and self, are often one and the same reality. Pauline Breedlove in *The Bluest Eye* is at times a self-effacing mammy. Josie in *The Third Life of Grange Copeland* and Hannah Peace in *Sula* are at times super sex objects. And Cleo Judson in *The Living Is Easy* often behaves like a castrating matriarch and, sometimes, like "an evil black bitch."

The presence of these women in black women's fiction does not altogether contradict Washington's thesis that black women writers choose new images of black women. Rather, it heightens our appreciation for the special way the writers use old images as they draw bold lines of black women's humanity. In their inside rendering of familiar, traditional, or even stereotypic images, we find complex and sensitive women who, as individuals, are larger than the images and more sensitive to their humanity than national interpretations of black women suggest. The unique contributions of black women's fiction to our understanding of black women's reality is, therefore, not new images, but a new and deeper understanding of old images and familiar myths. The writers move us through images and myths so that they can enlarge hidden dimensions where matriarchs, mammies, super sex objects, and even evil black bitches, in the sphere of the authentic self, are often "black-eyed susans" and "midnight birds."

Perhaps discussions of these "perversions" and feminist analysis of literature are mutually exclusive, especially if we as black feminist writers take the position that our task is to counter negative statements about black women with positive statements, or create new myths about black women that would render old myths powerless. Such self-consciousness and deliberate creation of myths, however, would be tantamount to an overkill and, as well, misrepresentation of truth. We succeed in raising the consciousness of black people in general by admitting that there are, in fact, problems within the race that must be addressed, regardless of their cause. And we succeed in raising the consciousness of black women in particular by admitting that we have internalized myths about our reality. As a result, we sometimes see ourselves as others see us and we sometimes suffer from low self-esteem. We cannot cure an illness by denying that we suffer from its symptoms.

And yet, illness is not all there is to our reality as black people in white America. There is a strong sense of ourselves as a community of people with a rich heritage, a positive present, and a promising future. We want to see our health and our wholeness as the foreground and background of artistic pictures of the black experience. We know there are black women in real life who are not chosen as models for imaginary characters in much of the fiction written by black women today. We have lived with them in our communities. We have worshiped with them in our churches and studied with them in our schools. We have ridden the back of the bus with them, spent hours of laughter with them in beauty shops, and gossiped with them in neighborhood laundromats. We have grown up with their daughters and married their sons. We have seen them age, slowly and with dignity, and we have heard them remind us, affectionately, that they knew us when we were all legs and pigtails. No one ever abandoned them or beat their heads, and they never abandoned or abused their loved ones. They were never unsure of their goals or visibly depressed by any aspects of their lives. They were, as my mother says of herself, women with "a single eye on success." Some of them were prim and proper women who decorated church pews with colorful hats and white gloves. They never missed school meetings, they took their time fingering fruit in white-owned stores, they blushed when they talked about their husbands, and they preened when they talked about their daughters and sons. Some of them were exceedingly vain women who never knew that black women are not supposed to be beautiful. And still others were proud women who, like my grandmother, wore their blackness and independence at cocksure angles of defiance. They lived in insular black communities where there was warm laughter, where there was gentle nurturing, where there was protection from the world outside. They never opened their doors to social workers or traveled downtown to welfare offices for food stamps or more forms on top of forms. In more than a few cases, at least in the Deep South, many of them never knew "madams." Rather, they knew poor white women across the tracks and around the corner with whom, in spite of segregation, they sometimes shared stories about children (a game of boasting that black women often won), swapped mason jars, hoed in adjacent gardens, cut patterns from discarded newspapers, and "talked Bible." And there were professional black women who lived in the "pretty" houses we passed as we walked the long way to segregated schools past the "better" schools closed to us. They were the school teachers, social workers, secretaries, funeral parlor receptionists, piano teachers, and wives of doctors or lawyers. By definition, their lives were complex and, from the perspective of nonprofessional blacks, most intriguing. And there were the men who, together with these women, built strong families capable of overcoming adversity with dignity. They were role models of hard work, decency, and caring for young boys and examples of good husbands for young girls who fantasized about marriage. They never raped their daughters, abused their wives, or failed to be vigilant in their guard over the lives of all the children in the community. Where are these flesh and blood people from our childhood and our adulthood?

As the collective vision of black women's novels shows, these people *are* in the literature, but they share the canvas with negative images that disturb us and, more painfully, that "prove" myths about the black experience to be truths articulated by our own writers. And so, we desire to select proper material for black artistic visions. But there has never been a time in the history of literature when readers select material for writers. There will never be a time. There can never be a time. There should never be a time. Nor has there ever been a time when all readers have been satisfied with all the literature of a culture. If black women writers dealt mainly with laughter, black readers would ask about our pain. If they dealt mainly with professional blacks, we would speak of the dignity of the poor. If they wrote of tenderness in love relationships, we would remember the many instances of sexual exploitation we witnessed or heard talked about in our communities. If they wrote mainly of achievements without struggle and pain, we would charge them with forgetting from whence they came. As black readers, we can wish for that "other" story (and there is always that "other" story), but we should evaluate literature only on the basis of its connection to truth and its ability to help us see humanity and the human experience with deeper insight and sensitivity. We cannot deny that the visions of the women writers discussed in this book are familiar, poignant, powerful, and real.

Perhaps our desire for the "other" story is a subconscious wish for material that would make us feel better about what *other* people are told about our reality, not about what *we* know to be real and whole. Perhaps, too, it is a desire for material that would better serve "personal and political presuppositions." Deborah McDowell discusses the danger of this control and cautions black feminist critics against leaning on "one individual persuasion." She speaks mainly to lesbian critics, but her points apply to all feminist critics. We must guard, she writes, against reading literature

> as though it were polemic. . . . Using literature
> to make what is essentially a political point, we
> find ourselves virtually rewriting a text, ignor-

ing certain aspects of plot or characterization, or over-simplifying the action to fit our "political" thesis. Then we are neither practicing honest criticism nor saying anything useful about the nature of art, or about art, or political persuasion, for that matter.[37]

I agree with McDowell, but I believe there are few, if any, discussions on any subject that can not be construed as political in nature and intent. This is particularly true of discussions about subjects rarely handled in scholarly disciplines. That which is new or different is perceived in the mainstream of scholarship as political. *No Crystal Stair* is "political" in that it is a revisionist approach to criticism about black women's literature. It challenges the assumption that black women writers write only about the black experience, not about the black *woman's* experience. My "individual persuasion," then, has been obvious: to convince, or persuade, the reader that "double jeopardy" is a dominant theme in the writings of selected black women writers from 1946 to 1976.

This "persuasion" did not require a rewriting of any of the texts, for in all of the novels discussed *race* and *sex* draw distinct lines of the women's realities. The writers illuminate the dark enclosure of sex at the same moment that they move us through the narrow space of race. What we learn in their visions is the irrefutable fact about the lives of most black women in white America. Life for them "ain't been no crystal stair." We feel the razor-sharp points of "tacks," trace the difficult journeys from "landins'" to "corners," struggle in the "dark" with complex women in search of freedom and dignity. The women have reason to explode and build for themselves a place in the sun, for the enclosure is the farthest distance from the large circle of power and influence. And yet, perhaps because of their condition in the enclosure, they are almost always struggling to improve the quality of life in the narrow space. They rear children, stroke or struggle with their men, battle with other black women, stay sane, and continue to dream. They are "tall" and "impervious," and when we *see* them beyond myths, we are "renewed."[38]

AFTERWORD

By the mid-1960's, when the intellectual currents of the Black Revolution were becoming apparent, the demand for a "new Black History" was already being heard. The leading proponents of "Black Consciousness" seemed to say that the pride, respect, and self-esteem that were vital to their movement necessitated a revision of the way blacks had been treated in traditional American history as well as in traditional Negro history.

However, once black history and black studies were established as proper enterprises throughout most of American academia, new questions arose as to their meanings and orientations. Was black history, for example, simply a darker imitation of traditional white history, i.e., was it simply the story of great, black men? In other words, like mainstream American history, was it both elitist and sexist?

Many in the "new Black History Movement" obviously wanted to believe that black history was different. And, there could be persuasive arguments that black history was classless, since almost all blacks, since slavery, had shared common degrading experiences. Similarly, it could be argued that there was no place for sexism in black history, because of the toils and oppression of men, women, and children alike.

With respect to sex, it was, indeed, true that in the colonial and antebellum eras, the names of Phillis Wheatley, Sojourner Truth, and Harriet Tubman were seen frequently alongside those of Jupiter Hammon, Richard Allen, and Frederick Douglass. In the postbellum periods, Ida Wells Barnett, Anna Cooper, and Mary Church Terrell emerged, as did Booker T. Washington, John Hope, and W. E. B. DuBois. And in the present times, Fannie Lous Hamer and Coretta Scott King have found a place in our history with Malcolm X and Martin Luther King, Jr.

Therefore, it has been argued that the equality of the sexes, at least in leadership, can be seen much more clearly among blacks than among whites. On the other hand, there have been pictures of the dominating black matriarch, both in slavery and freedom,

247

and of the ruthless, brutal, and shiftless black male, especially in freedom.

In *No Crystal Stair*, Gloria Wade-Gayles is very conscious of American history and black history in general and of black women's history and studies in particular. She skillfully employs a knowledge of economics, sociology, and psychology in her quest to understand and help others understand the place of black women in American life and history from the end of the Second World War to the crest of the civil rights movement and, more especially, their unique reality in American culture.

The period she has chosen is an ideal one to demonstrate the emergence of new vicissitudes in the black experience, which continue to dominate black lives, even today. This period, of course, is the time of the last great migration from the South, the opening of new political and economic opportunities in the North, the birth of the modern civil rights era, and the explosion of Black Revolution and Black Consciousness. As in earlier times, we see in these periods strong, black, female leadership, both in individuals from Mary McLeod Bethune to Fannie Lous Hamer, and in organizations from the Neighborhood Union to the National Council of Negro Women. On the other hand, none of these reached the public significance of Martin Luther King, Jr., or the male-dominated NAACP. And many important black women, such as Etta Moten of the Southern Christian Leadership Conference (SCLS), remain almost invisible.

So it was that black women scholars in the last five or ten years have been able to point out correctly that, even at leadership levels, the roles of black women have often been subordinated, at least in historical and other literature, to those of black men. But more importantly, these scholars have tended to suggest that black women, generally, suffer disabilities and discriminations on account of both race and sex, suffering some of the latter at the hands of black men. These occurrences and their effects on the social, physical, mental, and fiscal well being of black women have been, as Wade-Gayles recounts, the subjects of numerous scholarly works by black and white women in recent days.

No Crystal Stair is a welcome addition to this growing body of literature, particularly because of the different approaches and perspectives it brings and the judicious balance it achieves. Many of the previous studies on black women have been flawed because they have been too one-dimensional. Some have been strictly fictional; othrs have been mainly historical; some have had an anti-male tone. A few have tried to link black women and white women in a common tale of oppression. Wade-Gayles harmoniously interfaces fiction with the latest and most reputable of historical, economic, psychological, and sociological studies to create the real environment out of which black women come.

While recognizing the special disabilities and responses of black women in American society and the role that black men have played in some of that oppression, the work commendably points to the real culprit—a system of exploitative capitalism, controlled by white males. And in this exploitation, the grievances of black women and white women are not identical, for white women do not suffer the legacies and the realities of white racism.

In this book, then, we have the best of two worlds—an updated synthesis and analysis of race and sex as expressed in a wide selection of black women's novels as well as a scholarly treatment of those two variables in the life and history of contemporary black women. Although, indeed, this study confirms that black women have not climbed a crystal stair, it does illuminate the paths they have been treading in their quest for self-fulfillment and racial and sexual equality.

ALTON HORNSBY, JR.
Editor, *Journal of Negro History*

NOTES

Introduction

1. *Signs* 6 (Winter 1980): 282.
2. This quote comes from Annis Pratt's "The New Feminist Criticisms: Exploring the History of the New Space," in *Beyond Intellectual Sexism: A New Woman, A New Reality,* ed. Joan T. Roberts (New York: David McKay, 1976), p. 10.
3. Barbara Smith, "Toward a Black Feminist Criticism," *Conditions: Two,* 1977: 27–28.
4. Ibid., p. 32.
5. Deborah McDowell, "New Directions for Black Feminist Criticism," *Black American Literature Forum* 14 (October 1980): 153.
6. Ibid., p. 158.
7. Cheri Register, "Literary Criticism," *Signs* 6 (Winter 1980): 270.
8. McDowell, "New Directions," p. 156.
9. Ibid., p. 155.
10. Mary Helen Washington, Introduction, *Black-Eyed Susans: Classic Stories by and About Black Women* (Garden City, N.Y.: 1971), p. 4.

Chapter 1

1. Langston Hughes, "Mother to Son," in *Black Writers of America: A Comprehensive Anthology* ed. Richard Barksdale (New York: Macmillan, 1972), p. 518.
2. Lerner, *Black Women in White America,* p. ix.
3. Michele Wallace, "Black Macho and the Myth of the Super Woman," *Ms.* 4 (January 1979): 45.
4. "The Combahee River Collective: A Black Feminist Statement," in *Capitalist Patriarchy and the Case for Socialist Feminism,* ed. Zillah Eisenstein, p. 365.
5. Eisenstein, "Relations of Capitalist Patriarchy," p. 47.
6. See Beverly Guy-Sheftall, "Interdisciplinary Approaches to Incorporating Southern Black Women's History into the Study of American History" (Paper presented at the Annual Conference of the Association for the Study of Negro Life and History, Philadelphia, October 1981).

7. Elizabeth Cady Stanton, quoted in Chafe, *Women and Equality* p. 47.

8. Maya Angelou, *I Know Why the Caged Birds Sing* (New York: Random House, 1970), p. 92.

9. Elizabeth Cady Stanton, quoted in Chafe, *Women and Equality*, p. 46.

10. For an interesting discussion of the problems created by this analogy, see Hooks's *Ain't I a Woman*.

11. Chafe, *Women and Equality*, p. 46.

12. Beal, "Double Jeopardy", p. 343.

13. Hernton, *Sex and Racism in America*, p. 125.

14. Diane Lewis, "A Response to Inequality," p. 347.

15. Frances E. W. Harper, quoted in Chafe, *Women and Equality*, p. 54.

16. "Combahee River Collective," in *But Some of Us Are Brave: Black Women's Studies*, ed. Hull, et al., p. 16.

17. This phrase is Georgia Douglas Johnson's description of the task of the black woman writer. See Jay Saunders Redding, *To Make a Poet Black* (College Park, Md.: McGrath, 1939), p. 25.

18. "Ar'nt I a woman?" was the poignant refrain of Sojourner Truth's historic speech at the Women's Convention in Akron, Ohio, in 1853. The speech is considered the first recorded feminist address delivered by a black woman.

19. Zora Neale Hurston, *Their Eyes Were Watching God* (Boston: Lippincott, 1937; reprint, Greenwich, Conn.: Fawcett, 1965), p. 16.

20. Wright, *This Child's Gonna Live*, p. 11.

21. Dance, "Black Eve or Madonna?" p. 123.

22. Chafe, *Women and Equality*, p. 59.

23. Barbara Smith, "Doing Research on Black American Women," p. 4.

24. Olsen, *Silences*, p. 6.

25. Alice Walker, quoted in "Combahee River Collective," in *But Some of Us Are Brave*, p. 163.

26. Langston Hughes, *The Big Sea* (New York: Hill and Wang, 1940), p. 228.

27. Alice Walker, "Stripping Bark from Myself," in Walker, *Goodnight Willie Lee* (New York: The Dial Press, 1978), p. 23.

28. "Combahee River Collective," in *But Some of Us Are Brave*, p. 18.

29. Claudia Tate, ed., *Black Women Writers at Work* (New York: Continuum, 1983), p. xix.

30. Ibid., p. xx.

Chapter 2

1. See Brisbane, *The Black Vanguard.*

2. Chafe, *The American Woman,* p. 136.

3. Ibid., p. 139.

4. Ibid., p. 142.

5. Ibid., p. 143.

6. Delores Aldridge, "Black Women in the Economic Marketplace," p. 52.

7. Chafe, *The American Woman,* p. 142.

8. See Chafe, *The American Woman,* and Franklin, *From Slavery to Freedom.*

9. Chafe, *The American Woman,* p. 191.

10. Lerner, *Black Women in White America,* p. 239.

11. Brisbane, *The Black Vanguard,* p. 87.

12. Information on court cases, demonstrations, and numbers of black male and black female leaders in a synthesis of data found in Hornsby, ed., *The Black Almanac,* pp. 80–104.

13. A good study of the burdens of black women in northern ghettos is Horace Cayton and St. Clair Drake, *Black Metropolis,* vols. 1 and 2 (New York: Harcourt, Brace & World, 1945).

14. Chafe, *Women and Equality,* p. 94.

15. Chafe, *The American Woman,* p. 210.

16. Helen Deutsch, from *The Psychology of Women,* vol. 1, quoted in Chafe, *The American Woman,* p. 209.

17. Sochen, *Movers and Shakers,* p. 202.

18. Chafe, *The American Woman,* p. 231.

19. Harley and Terborg-Penn, *The Afro-American Woman,* p. 24.

20. Null, *Hollywood,* p. 121.

21. After her role in *Mildred Pierce* (1945), Butterfly McQueen vowed that she would never play the degrading role of Aunt Jemima again. She kept that promise.

22. Herbert Gutman, quoted in Hooks, *Ain't a Woman?,* p. 84.

23. Sochen, *Her Story: A Woman's View of American History,* vol. 2 (New York: Alfred Publishing, 1974), p. 368.

24. Christian, *Black Women Novelists,* p. 90.

25. Hooks, *Ain't I a Woman,* p. 86.

26. Frances E. W. Harper, quoted in Chafe, *Woman and Equality,* p. 54.

27. This information is a synthesis of facts found in Hornsby, *The Black Almanac*, pp. 80–104.

28. DuBois, *The Souls of Black Folk*, p. iv.

29. Sizemore, "Sexism and the Black Male," p. 4.

30. U.S. Department of Labor, *Handbook of Labor Statistics*, pp. 75–79.

31. Walter Allen, "Family Roles, Occupational Statuses and Achievement Orientation Among Black Women in the United States," p. 679.

32. Pauli Murray, "Jim Crow and Jane Crow," p. 597.

33. Margaret Wright, "I Want the Right to Be Black and Me," in *Black Women in White America*, ed. Lerner, p. 607.

34. Murray, "Jim Crow and Jane Crow," p. 596.

35. Rodgers, "I Have Been Hungry," in Rodgers, *How I Got Ovah*, pp. 49–50.

36. Michele Wallace, "A Black Feminist's Search" in *But Some of Us Are Brave*, ed. Hull, p. 6.

37. Hernton, *Sex and Racism in America*, p. 7.

38. Ibid., p. 17.

39. Chafe, *Women and Equality*, pp. 110–111.

40. Hooks, *Ain't I a Woman*, p. 110.

41. Ibid., pp. 109–110.

42. Amiri Baraka, in Hooks, *Ain't I a Woman*, p. 95.

43. Wallace, "A Black Feminist's Search," p. 10.

44. Lee, "BLACKWOMAN," in Lee, *Don't Cry, Scream*, p. 55.

45. Miller, "Farewell to Liberals," p. 437.

46. Silberman, "Crisis in Black and White," pp. 438–439.

47. Lewis, "A Response to Inequality," p. 349.

48. Sizemore, "Sexism and the Black Male," p. 4.

49. See Aldridge, "Black Women in the Economic Marketplace," pp. 48–62.

50. Murray, "Jim Crow and Jane Crow," p. 587.

51. Bambara, *The Black Woman*, p. 7.

52. Angela Davis quoted in Lynch, "Notes on Black Women Writers of the Past Two Decades," p. 52.

53. Chisholm, "Sexism and Racism: One Battle to Fight," p. 125.

54. Chisholm, *Unbought and Unbossed*, p. xxi.

55. Hamer, "It's in Your Hands," p. 609.

56. Friedan, *The Feminine Mystique*, p. 55.

57. Hooks, *Ain't I a Woman?*, p. 124.

58. Angela Davis, *Women, Race and Class* (New York: Random House, 1981), p. 70.

59. Rich, "Disloyal to Civilization: Feminism, Racism, and Gynephobia," p. 23.

60. Hooks, *Ain't I a Woman?*, p. 124.

61. "Combahee River Collective," in *But Some of Us Are Brave*, ed. Hull, p. 19.

62. Wallace, quoted in "Combahee River Collective," in *But Some of Us Are Brave*, ed. Hull, p. 18.

63. Robert Staples, "The Myth of the Black Matriarchy," *The Black Scholar* 1 (January–February 1970): 9.

64. Stokely Carmichael, quoted in Morgan, "Know Your Enemy," p. 35.

65. Lewis, "Response to Inequality," p. 351.

66. Beal, "Slave of a Slave No More," p. 9.

67. Sizemore, "Sexism and the Black Male," p. 3.

68. Nikki Giovanni, "Beautiful Black Men," in *The Black Poets*, ed. Dudley Randall (New York: Bantam, 1971), p. 320.

69. Walker, "He Said Come," in Walker, *Revolutionary Petunias* (New York: Harcourt Brace Jovanovich, 1971), p. 50.

70. Sizemore, "Sexism and the Black Male," p. 10.

71. Wallace, *Black Macho and the Myth of the Superwoman*, p. 75.

72. Ibid., p. 79.

73. Ibid., p. 83.

74. See the results of the Virginia Slims poll on black women's support of women's liberation in Chafe, *Women and Equality*, p. 125.

75. Chafe, *Women and Equality*, p. 147.

76. "Combahee River Collective," in *But Some of Us Are Brave*, ed. Hull, p. 19.

77. Truth, "I Suppose I Am About the Only Colored Woman," p. 566.

Chapter 3

1. Rich, *Of Woman Born*, p. 15.

2. Ibid., p. 23.

3. Monta Crane and Betty Scott, compilers, *Along the Way* (Cushocton, Ohio: Shaw-Barton, 1977), p. 16.

4. Simone de Beauvoir, quoted in Sochen, *Movers and Shakers*, p. 201.

5. Rich, *Of Woman Born*, p. 5.

6. Ibid., p. 39.

7. Eisenstein, "The Relations of Capitalist Patriarchy," p. 47.

8. Rich, *Of Woman Born*, p. 20.

9. Ibid., p. 24.

10. Ibid.

11. Ladner, *Tomorrow's Tomorrow*, p. 63.

12. Robert Staples, "The Myth of Black Matriarchy," in *The Black Family*, ed. Robert Staples (Belmont, Calif.: Wadsworth Publishing, 1971), pp. 158–159.

13. Thompson, *Sociology of the Black Experience*, p. 81.

14. Maya Angelou, quoted in *Jet* (December 13, 1973), p. 48.

15. Andrea Benton Rushing, "Comparative Study of the Idea of Mother in Contemporary African and African-American Poetry," in *Frances, Zora and Lorraine*, ed. Juliette Bowles (Washington, D.C.: Howard University Press, 1979), p. 3.

16. Carolyn Rodgers, "It Is Deep," in *Sturdy Black Bridges*, ed. Roseann Bell et al. (New York: Doubleday, 1979), p. 377.

17. Dance, "Black Eve or Madonna?, p. 127.

18. Ibid., p. 131.

19. Thompson, *Sociology of the Black Experience*, p. 81.

20. Christian, *Black Women Novelists*, p. 205.

21. Ibid., p. 240.

22. Walker, *Meridian*, p. 39. Subsequent references to this work appear in the text.

23. See Jeffers, *Living Poor*.

24. Christian, *Black Women Novelists*, p. 220.

25. Walker, "In Search of Our Mothers' Gardens," p. 64.

26. Morrison, *Sula*, p. 80. Subsequent references to this work appear in the text.

27. Christian, *Black Women Novelists*, p. 220.

28. Ibid., p. 138.

29. Morrison, *The Bluest Eye*, p. 5. Subsequent references to this work appear in text.

30. Steptoe, "Intimate Things in Place: A Conversation with Toni Morrison," p. 478.

31. Rich, *Of Woman Born*, p. 168.

32. Jeffers, *Living Poor*, p. iv.

33. Rich, *Of Woman Born*, p. 151.

34. Jesse Bernard, *Marriage and Family Among Negroes*, p. 108.

35. Christian, *Black Women Novelists*, p. 146.

36. Ibid., p. 68.

37. Ibid.

38. Gwendolyn Brooks, *Maud Martha*, p. 5. Subsequent references to this work appear in the text.

39. Meriwether, *Daddy Was a Number Runner*, p. 169. Subsequent references to this work appear in the text.

40. Marshall, *Brown Girl, Brownstones*, p. 4. Subsequent references to this work appear in the text.

41. Steptoe, "Intimate Things in Place," p. 478.

42. Mari Evans, quoted in Rushing, "Idea of Mother," p. 5.

43. Steptoe, "Intimate Things in Place," p. 478.

44. Wallace, *Black Macho and the Myth of the Superwoman*, p. 66.

45. Montagu, *The Natural Superiority of Women*, p. 12.

46. Lounsberry and Honet, "Principles of Perception in Toni Morrison's *Sula*," p. 128.

47. Ibid.

48. Christian, *Black Women Novelists*, p. 180.

49. Ibid., p. 182.

50. "Interview with Alice Walker," in *Interviews with Black Writers*, ed. O'Brien, p. 192.

51. Walker, *The Third Life of Grange Copeland*, p. 44. Subsequent references to this work appear in the text.

52. Zora Neale Hurston, *Their Eyes Were Watching God* (Greenwich, Conn.: Lippincott, 1937; Fawcett, 1965), p. 16.

53. Daryl Dance, "Father May Bring Home the Bacon, But He Don't Cut No Ice: The Economic Plight of the Father Figure in American Literature;" in *Journal of Afro-American Issues* 3 (Summer/Fall 1975): 298.

54. Karenga, "In Love and Struggle," p. 18.

55. Cleaver, *Soul on Ice*, p. 72.

56. Shulamith Firestone, *The Dialectic of Sex: The Case for Feminist Revolution* (New York: William Morrow, 1970), p. 108.

57. Hernton, *Sex and Racism in America*, p. 61.

58. Washington, *Black-Eyed Susans*, p. xxii.

59. Toni Morrison, quoted in "Artists without Art Form," *Conditions: Five*, p. 53.

60. Walker, "In Search of Our Mothers' Gardens," p. 66.

61. Interview with Alice Walker, *Encore* 2 (April 1973): 41.

62. McCray, "The Black Woman and Family Roles," p. 72.

63. Smith in *Frances, Zora and Lorraine: Essays and Interviews on Black Women and Writing*, ed. Juliette Bowles (Washington, D.C.: Howard University Press, 1979), p. 33.

64. Jessie Bernard, "The Impact of Sexism and Racism in Employment Status and Earnings" in Lewis, "A Response to Inequality," p. 361.

Chapter 4

1. Noble, *Beautiful, Also*, pp. 75–76.

2. Ibid., p. 75.

3. Ibid.

4. See Null, *Hollywood*.

5. Douglas Turner Ward, *Happy Ending* (1966), in Noble, *Beautiful, Also*, p. 83.

6. Louis D. Stone, "What It's Like to Be a Colored Woman," *Washington Post*, November 13, 1966, quoted in *Black Women in White America*, ed. Lerner, p. 217.

7. Noble, *Beautiful, Also*, p. 75.

8. Morrison, *The Bluest Eye*, p. 109.

9. Petry, *The Street*, p. 127. Subsequent references to this work appear in the text.

10. Brownmiller, *Against Our Will*, p. 5.

11. Lincoln, "Who Will Revere the Black Woman?" p. 82.

12. French, *The Women's Room*, p. 120.

13. See William Ryan, *Blaming the Victim* (New York: Pantheon Books, 1971).

14. "The Combahee River Collective: A Black Feminist Statement," in *Capitalist Patriarchy and the Case for Socialist Feminism*, ed. Eisenstein, p. 363.

15. Rosen and Davidson, eds., *The Maimie Papers*, p. xxv.

16. Walker, "Interview with Alice Walker," in *Interviews with Black Writers*, ed. O'Brien, p. 192.

17. Walker, *The Third Life of Grange Copeland*, p. 39. Subsequent references to this work appear in text.

18. Schultz, "'Free in Fact and at Last,'" p. 332.
19. *Ibid.*
20. Ibid., p. 335.
21. Bischoff, "The Novels of Toni Morrison," p. 21.
22. Ibid., p. 22.
23. Walker, "In Search of Our Mothers' Gardens," p. 66.
24. Franklin, *From Slavery to Freedom*, p. 620.
25. See E. Franklin Frazier, *The Negro Family in the United States* (Chicago, University of Chicago Press, 1939).

Chapter 5

1. Robert Hayden in *Frances, Zora and Lorraine*, ed. Juliette Bowles (Washington, D.C.: Howard University Press), p. 45.
2. Statement by Beulah Gloster of Morehouse College in a conversation on the condition of women in April of 1974.
3. Carolyn Rodgers, "poems for some black women," in *How I Got Ovah*, pp. 47–48.
4. Bone, *The Negro Novel in America*, p. 180.
5. Schraufnagel, *From Apology to Protest*, p. 42.
6. Gayle, *The Way of the New World*, p. 196.
7. Beatrice Royster, "The Ironic Vision of Four Black Women Novelists," Ph.D. diss., Emory University, 1975, p. 158.
8. Ibid., p. 154.
9. Petry, *The Street*, p. 7. Subsequent references to this work appear in the text.
10. Ivy, "Ann Petry Talks About Her First Novel," p. 198.
11. Vernon Lattin, "Ann Petry and the American Dream," p. 69.
12. Ibid., p. 70.
13. Gayle, *The Way of the New World*, p. 194.
14. Richard Wright, *Native Son* (New York: Harper and Row, 1940; Perennial Classics, 1966), p. 215. For an interesting discussion of Wright's treatment of black women characters, see Sylvia Keady's study, "Richard Wright's Women Characters and Inequality," *Black American Literature Forum* 10 (1976): 123–126.
15. Royster, "The Ironic Vision," p. 155.
16. Truth, p. 566.
17. Royster, "The Ironic Vision," p. 171.
18. Bone, *The Negro Novel*, p. 187.

19. Ibid.

20. William H. Robinson, Introduction to West, *The Living Is Easy*, p. ii. Subsequent references to this work appear in the text.

21. Bone, *The Negro Novel*, p. 188.

22. Ibid.

23. Ibid., p. 187.

24. Ibid., p. 188.

25. Ibid.

26. Hyde, "Tomboyism," p. 74.

27. Wright, *This Child's Gonna Live*, p. 15. Subsequent references to this work appear in the text.

28. Wright, quoted in Rush and Meyers, eds., *Black American Writers Past and Present*, p. 791.

29. Nella Larsen, *Quicksand* (New York: Alfred A. Knopf, 1929), p. 174. Subsequent references to this work appear in the text.

30. Tate, *"Corregidora,"* 140.

31. Gayl Jones, *Corregidora*, p. 25. Subsequent references to this work appear in the text.

32. Tate, *"Corregidora:"* p. 140.

33. Ibid., p. 141.

34. Ibid., p. 139.

35. Ibid.

36. Steptoe, "Intimate Things in Place," p. 478.

37. Jones, quoted in Rush and Meyers, eds., *Black American Writers Past and Present*, p. 440.

38. "Gayl Jones: An Interview," *The Massachusetts Review* 18 (1977): 701.

39. Ibid.

40. Jones, *Eva's Man*, p. 121. Subsequent references to this work appear in the text.

41. "Gayl Jones: An Interview," pp. 700–701.

42. Ladner, *Tomorrow's Tomorrow*, p. 109.

43. Lerner, ed., *Black Women in White America*, pp. 163–164.

44. Bell Hooks, *Ain't I a Woman*, p. 59.

45. Tate, "An Interview with Gayle Jones," p. 146.

46. Sonia Sonchez, "Poem No. 7," in *Frances, Zora and Lorraine*, ed. Juliette Bowles (Washington, D.C.: Howard University Press, 1975), p. 51.

47. Evelyn Heinz, ed., *Anais Nin: A Woman Speaks* (Momence, Ill.: Swallow Press, 1975), p. 44.

Chapter 6

1. Roseann Bell and Bettye Parker, "Introduction: The Analytical Vision," in *Sturdy Black Bridges* ed. Roseann Bell et al. (New York: Doubleday, 1979), p. 133.
2. Washington, "An Essay on Alice Walker," in *Sturdy Black Bridges*, p. 133.
3. Ibid.
4. Walker in *Interviews with Black Writers*, ed. O'Brien, p. 192.
5. Weems, "Artists Without Art Form," p. 56.
6. Smith, "Toward a Black Feminist Criticism," p. 166.
7. Bischoff, "The Novels of Toni Morrison," p. 21.
8. Ibid., p. 22.
9. Steptoe, "Intimate Things in Place," p. 476.
10. Ibid., p. 480.
11. Smith, "Toward a Black Feminist Criticism," p. 168.
12. Ibid., p. 168.
13. Ibid., p. 170.
14. Steptoe, "Intimate Things in Place," p. 477.
15. Rich, *Of Woman Born*, p. 151.
16. Christian, *Black Women Novelists*, p. 209.
17. Ibid., p. 215.
18. Ibid., p. 218.
19. June Jordan, "What Would I Do White?" in *Black-Eyed Susans*, ed. Washington, p. xviii.
20. Christian, *Black Women Novelists*, p. 207–208.
21. W. E. B. DuBois coined the term "double consciousness" in *The Souls of Black Folks*, 1898.
22. Christian, *Black Women Novelists*, p. 210.
23. Ibid., p. 218.
24. Ibid., p. 184.
25. Ibid., p. 185.
26. Ibid., p. 235.

Chapter 7

1. Gwendolyn Brooks in Claudia Tate, ed., *Black Women Writers at Work* (New York: Continuum, 1983), p. 45. This is an invaluable collection of interviews of contemporary black women. Because it is the only work of its kind and also because the interviews are rich in information about the writers' lives and, of equal importance, their views of their art and the creative process, I have depended on it heavily in this chapter.

2. Morrison in Tate, ed., *Black Women Writers at Work*, p. 118.

3. Tate, ed., *Black Women Writers*, p. xviii.

4. Brooks, ibid., pp. 47–48.

5. Jones, ibid., p. 95.

6. Walker, ibid., p. 185.

7. Morrison, ibid., p. 118.

8. Tate, ed., ibid., p. xviii.

9. Brooks, ibid., p. 44.

10. Morrison, ibid., p. 118.

11. Washington, *Midnight Birds*, p. xiv.

12. Ibid.

13. The phrase "in love and trouble" is the title of Walker's collection of short stories about the burdens peculiar to black women. It is an appropriate phrase for the historical conflict between black men and black women that was seeded in racism and class and is exacerbated by sexism.

14. Tate, "Interview with Gayl Jones," p. 147.

15. Eisenstein, "The Relations of Capitalist Patriarchy," p. 47.

16. Tate, "Interview with Gayl Jones," p. 147.

17. Washington, *Midnight Birds*, p. xiv.

18. Washington, ed., *Black-Eyed Susans*, p. xv.

19. This word was used by Frederick Douglass for the rhetoric and images that the slaveholding culture of the South used to imprison the minds of blacks. It is an appropriate term for the rhetoric and myths that are used to imprison the minds of women and of men as well.

20. Kate Millett *Sexual Politics* (New York: New American Library, 1969), p. 31.

21. Washington, *Midnight Birds*, p. xvi.

22. Ibid., p. xvii.

23. Ibid., pp. xvi–xvii.
24. Ibid., p. xvii.
25. Washington, ed., *Black-Eyed Susans*, p. xxxi.
26. Washington, *Midnight Birds*, p. xvii.
27. Audre Lorde, "Black Women's Anger," *Essence*, October 1983, p. 90.
28. Washington, ed., *Black-Eyed Susans*, p. xxxi.
29. Hoffman, "White Women, Black Women," p. 22.
30. Washington, *Midnight Birds*, p. xx.
31. Ibid.
32. Washington, ed., *Black-Eyed Susans*, p. ix.
33. Washington, *Midnight Birds*, p. xiv.
34. Janeway, *Between Myth and Morning*, p. 170.
35. Ibid.
36. Washington, ed., *Black-Eyed Susans*, p. xi.
37. Deborah McDowell, "New Directions for Black Feminist Criticism," *Black American Literature Forum* 14 (Winter 1980): 155.
38. Mari Evans, *I Am a Black Woman* (New York: William Morrow, 1964), pp. 11–12.

SELECTED BIBLIOGRAPHY

Primary Sources

Brooks, Gwendolyn. *Maud Martha*. New York: Harper and Row, 1953.

Jones, Gayl. *Corregidora*. New York: Random House, 1975.

————. *Eva's Man*. New York: Random House, 1976.

Marshall, Paule, *Brown Girl, Brownstones*. New York: Random House, 1959.

Meriwether, Louise. *Daddy Was a Number Runner*. New York: Pyramid, 1970.

Morrison, Toni. *The Bluest Eye*. New York: Pocket Books, 1976.

————. *Sula*. New York: Bantam Books, 1973.

Petry, Ann. *The Street*. Boston: Houghton Mifflin, 1946.

Walker, Alice. *Meridian*. New York: Harcourt Brace Jovanovich, 1976

————. *The Third Life of Grange Copeland*. New York: Harcourt Brace Jovanovich, 1970.

West, Dorothy. *The Living Is Easy*. New York: Arno Press, 1948.

Wright, Sarah. *This Child's Gonna Live*. New York: Dell, 1969.

General Works

Ahern, Dee. *The Economics of Being a Woman*. New York: Macmillan, 1976.

Aldridge, Delores. "Black Women in the Economic Marketplace: A Battle Unfinished." *Journal of Social and Behavioral Sciences* 21 (Winter 1975): 48–62.

"Alice Walker Talks About Black Women." *Encore*, April 1973, pp. 41–42.

Allen, Walter. "Family Roles, Occupational Statuses and Achievement Orientation Among Black Women in the United States." *Signs* 4 (Summer 1979): 672–679.

Angelou, Maya. *Gather Together in My Name*. New York: Random House, 1974.

Bambara, Toni Cade, ed. *The Black Woman*. New York: New American Library, 1970.

———. "On the Issue of Roles." In *The Black Woman*, edited by Toni Cade Bambara, 101–110. New York: New American Library, 1970.

Bardwick, Judith, and Elizabeth Dowan. "Ambivalence: The Socialization of Women." In *Women in Sexist Society*, edited by Vivian Gornick and Barbara K. Moran, 85–90. New York: Mentor, 1971.

Baxandall, Rosalyn, et al., eds. *America's Working Women: A Documentary History, 1600–Present*. New York: Vintage Books, 1976.

Beal, Frances. "Double Jeopardy: To Be Black and Female." In *Sisterhood Is Powerful*, edited by Robin Morgan, 340–352. New York: Random House, 1970.

———. "Slave of a Slave No More." *The Black Scholar* 6 (March 1975): 2–10.

Bernard, Jesse. *Marriage and Family Among Negroes*. Englewood Cliffs, N.J.: Prentice Hall, 1966.

Billingsley, Andrew. *Black Families in White America*. Englewood Cliffs, N.J.: Prentice Hall, 1966.

Bird, Caroline. *Born Female: The High Cost of Keeping Women Down*. New York: David McKay, 1968.

Bischoff, Joan. "The Novels of Toni Morrison: Studies in Thwarted Sensitivity." *Studies in Black Literature* 6 (Fall 1975): 21–26.

Blackburn, Regina. "In Search of the Black Female Self: African-American Women's Autobiographies and Ethnicity." *Women's Autobiography*. Edited by Estelle Jelinke, 133–148. Bloomington, Ind.: Indiana University Press, 1980.

Blackburn, Sara. "You Still Can't Go Home Again." Review of *Sula*, by Toni Morrison. *The New York Times Book Review*, December 30, 1979, p. 2.

Blauner, Robert. *Racial Oppression in America*. New York: Harper & Row, 1972.

Bloch, Ruth. "Untangling the Roots of Modern Sex Roles: A Survey of Four Centuries of Change." *Signs* 4 (Winter 1978): 237–252.

Bond, Jean Carey. "The Media Image of Black Women." *Freedomways* 15 (1975): 34–37.

Bone, Robert A. *The Negro Novel in America*. New Haven, Conn.: Yale University Press, 1958.

Brisbane, Robert H. *Black Activism*. Valley Forge, Pa.: Judson Press, 1974.

———. *The Black Vanguard*. Valley Forge, Pa.: Judson Press, 1970.

Brownmiller, Susan. *Against Our Will: Men, Women and Rape*. New York: Bantam Books, 1975.

Chafe, William H. *The American Woman: Her Changing Social, Economic, and Political Roles, 1920–1970.* New York: Oxford University Press, 1972.

———. *Women and Equality: Changing Patterns in American Culture.* New York: Oxford University Press, 1977.

Chisholm, Shirley. "Race, Revolution and Women." *The Black Scholar* 7 (December 1971): 17–21.

———. Racism and Anti-Feminism." *The Black Scholar* 1 (January/February 1970): 40–47.

———. "Sexism and Racism: One Battle to Fight." *Personnel and Guidance Journal* 51 (October 1972): 123–216.

———. "Women Must Rebel." *Voices of New Feminism.* Edited by Mary Lou Thompson, 207–216. Boston: Beacon Press, 1970.

———. *Unbought and Unbossed.* Boston: Houghton Mifflin, 1970.

Christian, Barbara. *Black Women Novelists: The Development of a Tradition, 1892–1976.* Westport, Conn.: Greenwood Press, 1981.

Clark, Joanna. "Motherhood." *The Black Woman,* edited by Toni Cade Bambara, 6. New York: New American Library, 1970.

Cleaver, Eldridge. *Soul on Ice.* New York: McGraw-Hill, 1968.

Cole, Johnetta, "Black Women in America: An Annotated Bibliography." *The Black Scholar* 2 (December 1971): 42–53.

———. "Culture: Negro, Black and Nigger." *The Black Scholar* 1 (June 1970): 40–46.

Cornelisen, Ann. *Women of the Shadows.* Boston: Little, Brown, 1976.

Cornillon, Susan, ed. *Images of Women in Fiction: Feminist Perspectives.* Bowling Green, Ohio: Ohio University Press, 1972.

Cowley, Joyce. "Pioneers of Women's Liberation." In *Voices of the New Feminism,* edited by Mary Lou Thompson, 83–86. Boston: Beacon Press, 1970.

Dance, Daryl. "Black Eve or Madonna? A Study of the Antithetical Views of the Mother in Black American Literature." In *Sturdy Black Bridges,* edited by Roseann Bell et al., 123–132. New York: Doubleday, 1979.

Davis, Angela. "Rape, Racism and the Capitalist Setting." *The Black Scholar* 10 (April 1978): 38–42.

———. "Reflections on the Black Woman's Role in the Community of Slaves." *The Black Scholar* 3 (December, 1971): 7–9

Dill, Bonnie. "The Dialects of Black Womanhood." *Signs* 4 (Spring 1979): 543–555.

DuBois, W. E. B. *The Souls of Black Folk*. Boston, 1898. Reprint. New York: Fawcett, 1963.

Eisenstein, Zillah R., ed. *Capitalist Patriarchy and the Case for Socialist Feminism*. New York: Monthly Review Press, 1979.

———. "Some Notes on the Relations of Capitalist Patriarchy." In *Capitalist Patriarchy and the Case for Socialist Feminism*, 46–53. New York: Monthly Review Press, 1979.

Ellison, Ralph. *Invisible Man*. New York: Random House, 1952.

Evans, Sara. *Personal Politics: The Roots of Women's Liberation in the Civil Rights Movement and the New Left*. New York: Alfred Knopf, 1979.

Exum, Pat Crutchfield, ed. *Keeping the Faith: Writings by Contemporary Black American Women*. Greenwich, Conn.: Fawcett, 1974.

Fanon, Frantz. *Black Skin, White Masks: The Experience of a Black Man in a White World*. New York: Grove Press, 1967.

Ferguson, Mary Anne. *Images of Women in Literature*. Boston: Houghton Mifflin, 1973.

Fisher, Paul, and Ralph Lowenskin. *Race and the News Media*. New York: Praeger, 1967.

Foster, Frances. "Changing Concepts of the Black Woman." *Journal of Black Studies*, June 1973, pp. 433–452.

Franklin, John Hope. *From Slavery to Freedom*. New York: Random House, 1969.

French, Marilyn. *The Women's Room*. New York: Jove, 1977.

Friedan, Betty. *The Feminine Mystique*. New York: W. W. Norton, 1963.

———. *It Changed My Life*. New York: Dell, 1976.

Gayle, Addison. *The Way of the New World: The Black Novel in America*. Garden City, N.Y.: Doubleday, 1973.

Giele, Janet Z. *Women and the Future*. New York: Macmillan, 1978.

Gornick, Vivian, and Barbara K. Moran, eds. *Woman in Sexist Society: Studies in Power and Powerlessness*. New York: Mentor, 1971.

Grant, Joanne, ed. *Black Protest: History, Documents, and Analyses 1619 to the Present*. Greenwich, Conn.: Fawcett, 1968.

Green, Marjorie. "Ann Petry Planned to Write." *Opportunity* 24 (Spring 1946): 78–79.

Grier, William, and Price Cobbs. *Black Rage*. New York: Basic Books, 1968.

Hamer, Fannie Lou. "It's in Your Hands." In *Black Women in White America*, edited by Gerda Lerner, 609–614. New York: Random House, 1972.

Hare, Nathan. "Revolution Without a Revolution: The Psychology of Sex and Race." *The Black Scholar* 9 (April 1978): 12–17.

Harley, Sharon, and Rosalyn Terborg-Penn, eds. *The Afro-American Women: Struggles and Images.* New York: Kennikat Press, 1978.

Hatch, James, ed. *Black Images on the American Stage: A Bibliography of Plays and Musicals, 1770–1970.* New York: Drama Books Specialists, 1970.

Hernton, Calvin. *Coming Together: Black Power, White Hatred and Sexual Hang-ups.* New York: Random House, 1971.

———. *Sex and Racism in America.* New York: Grove Press, 1965.

Hoffman, Nancy. "White Women, Black Women: Inventing an Adequate Pedagogy." *Women's Studies Newsletter* 5 (Spring 1977): 21–24.

Hood, Elizabeth. "Black Women, White Women: Separate Paths to Liberation." *The Black Scholar* 4 (April 1978): 8–13.

Hooks, Bell. *Ain't I a Woman? Black Women and Feminism.* Boston: South End Press, 1981.

Hornsby, Alton, ed. *The Black Almanac.* New York: Barron's Educational Series, 1972.

Hull, Gloria, et al., eds. *But Some of Us Are Brave: Black Women's Studies.* Old Westbury, N.Y.: Feminist Press, 1982.

Hyde, Janet. "Tomboyism." *Psychology of Women Quarterly* 2 (Fall 1977): 73–75.

Ivy, James. "Ann Petry Talks About Her First Novel." In *Sturdy Black Bridges*, edited by Roseann Bell et al. New York: Doubleday, 1979.

Jackson, Jacquelyn. "Black Women in a Racist Society." In *Racism and Mental Health*, edited by Charles Willie et al. Pittsburgh: University of Pittsburgh Press, 1972.

———. "A Partial Bibliography on or Related to Black Women." *Journal of the Study of Behavioral Sciences* 21 (Winter 1975): 90–135.

Janeway, Elizabeth. *Between Myth and Morning: Women Awakening.* New York: William Morrow, 1974.

Jeffers, Camille. *Living Poor.* Ann Arbor, Mich.: University of Michigan Press, 1967.

Jordan, June. "All About Eva: A Review of Gayl Jones's *Eva's Man.*" *The New York Times Book Review*, 16 May 1976, pp. 36–37.

Joseph, Gloria, and Jill Lewis. *Common Differences: Conflicts in Black Feminism and White Feminist Perspectives*. Garden City, N.Y.: Anchor Books, 1981.

Kapai, Silla. "Dominant Themes and Techniques in Paule Marshall's Fiction." *College Language Association Journal* 16 (September 1972): 49–59.

Kaplan, Sydney Jane. "Review Essay: Literary Criticism." *Signs* 4 (Spring 1979): 514–527.

Karenga, Ron. "In Love and Struggle: Toward a Greater Togetherness." *The Black Scholar* 6 (March 1975): 16–28.

Keizs, Marcia. "Themes and Styles in the Works of Paule Marshall." *Black American Literature Forum* 9 (Fall 1975): 67–76.

King, Mae. "The Politics of Sexual Stereotypes." *The Black Scholar* 4 (March/April 1973): 12–23.

Klagsburn, Francine, ed. *The First Ms. Reader*. New York: Warner, 1973.

Klotman, Phyliss. "Dick and Jane and the Shirley Temple Sensibility in *The Bluest Eye*." *Black American Literature Forum* 13 (Winter 1979): 123–125.

Koontz, Elizabeth. "Women as a Minority Group." In *Voices of the New Feminism*, edited by Mary Lou Thompson, 38–44. Boston: Beacon Press, 1970.

Ladner, Joyce. *Tomorrow's Tomorrow*. New York: Doubleday, 1972.

LaRue, Linda. "The Black Movement and Women's Liberation." *The Black Scholar* 1 (May 1970): 36–42.

Lattin, Vernon. "Ann Petry and the American Dream." *Black American Literature Forum* 15 (Summer 1978): 68–70.

Lee, Don. *Don't Cry, Scream*. Detroit: Broadside Press, 1969.

Lerner, Gerda, ed. *Black Women in White America: A Documentary History*. New York: Random House, 1972.

Lewis, Diane. "A Response to Inequality: Black Women, Racism and Sexism." *Signs* 3 (Winter 1977): 339–361.

Lincoln, Abbey. "Who Will Revere the Black Woman?" In *The Black Woman*, edited by Toni Cade Bambara, 80–84. New York: New American Library, 1970.

Loewenberg, Bert James, and Ruth Bogin. *Black Women in Nineteenth-Century American Life*. University Park: The Pennsylvania State University Press, 1976.

Lounsberry, Grace, and Grace Honet. "Principles of Perception of Toni

Morrison's *Sula." Black American Literature Forum* 13 (Winter 1979): 124–129.

Lynch, Acklyn. "Notes on Black Women Writers of the Past Two Decades." In *Frances, Zora and Lorraine: Essays and Interviews on Black Women and Writing*, edited by Juliette Bowles, 45–49. Washington, D. C.: Howard University Press, 1979.

Lynch, Hollis R. *The Black Urban Condition: A Documentary History, 1866–1971.* New York: Thomas Y. Crowell, 1973.

Lyons, Harriet. "Female Eroticists: Stirrings of Sexuality." *The Village Voice,* 27 April 1972.

Mainardi, Pat. "The Politics of Housework." In *Sisterhood Is Powerful,* edited by Robin Morgan, 23–26. New York: Random House, 1970.

Mapp, Edward. "Black Women in Films." *The Black Scholar* 4 (March/April 1973): 42–46.

McCray, Carrie. "The Black Woman and Family Roles." In *The Black Woman,* edited by LaFrances Rodgers-Rose, 56–60. Beverly Hills, Cal.: Sage Publications, 1980.

Meriwether, Louise. "Half a Man: Emasculation of the Negro Man." *Negro Digest* 14 (October 1965): 4–13.

Miller, Loren. "Farewell to Liberals." In *Black Protest: History, Documents, and Analyses,* edited by Joanne Grant, 427–483. New York: Fawcett, 1968.

Millett, Kate. "Sexual Politics in Literature." In *Sisterhood Is Powerful,* edited by Robin Morgan, 311–336. New York: Random House, 1970.

Montagu, Ashley. *The Natural Superiority of Women.* New York: Macmillan, 1968.

Morgan, Robin. "Know Your Enemy: A Sampling of Sexist Quotes." In *Sisterhood Is Powerful,* edited by Robin Morgan, 31–36. New York: Random House, 1970.

Murray, Pauli. "Jim Crow and Jane Crow." In *Black Women in White America,* edited by Gerda Lerner, 584–588. New York: Random House, 1972.

———. "The Liberation of Black Women." In *Voices of the New Feminism,* edited by Mary Lou Thompson, 87–102. Boston: Beacon Press, 1970.

Myers, Carol. *Women in Literature: Criticism of the Seventies.* Metuchen, N.J.: Scarecrow Press, 1976.

Noble, Jeanne. *Beautiful, Also, Are the Souls of My Black Sisters.* Englewood, N.J.: Prentice-Hall, 1978.

———. "Negro Women and their Education." *Journal of Negro Education* 26 (Winter 1957): 15–21.

Null, Gary. *Hollywood: The Negro in Motion Pictures.* New York: Citadel Press, 1975.

O'Brien, John, ed. *Interviews with Black Writers.* New York: Liveright, 1973.

Ogunyemi, Chikwenye. "Sula: A Nigger Joke." *Black American Literature Forum* 13 (Winter 1979): 130–134.

Olsen, Tillie. *Silences.* New York: Delta/Seymour Lawrence, 1965.

Pettigrew, L. Eudora. "Women's Liberation and Black Woman." *Journal of Social and Behavioral Sciences* 23 (Spring 1977): 146–161.

Piercy, Marge. Review of *Meridian,* by Alice Walker. *New York Times,* 23 May 1976, pp. 5–12.

Reid, Inez. *"Together" Black Women.* New York: Emerson Hall, 1971.

Rich, Adrienne. "Disloyal to Civilization: Feminism, Racism and Gynephobia." *Chrysalis* 7 (1979): 10–27.

———. *Of Woman Born: Motherhood as Experience and Institution.* New York: W. W. Norton, 1970.

Roberts, J. R., ed. *Black Lesbians: An Annotated Bibliography.* Tallahassee, Fla.: Naiad, 1981.

Rodgers, Carolyn M. *How I Got Ovah.* New York: Doubleday, 1976.

Rodgers-Rose, LaFrances, ed. *The Black Woman.* Beverly Hills, Cal.: Sage, 1980.

Rosenblatt, Roger. *Black Fiction.* Cambridge, Mass.: Harvard University Press, 1974.

Rosen, Ruth, and Sue Davidson, eds. *The Maimie Papers.* New York: Feminist Press, 1977.

Royster, Beatrice. "The Ironic Vision of Four Black Women Novelists." Ph.D. diss., Emory University, 1975.

Ruby, Kathryn. "The Feminine Aesthetic: New Avenues." *Margins* 7 (August/September 1973): 3–4.

Rush, Thelma, and Carol Myers, eds. *Black American Writers Past and Present: A Biographical and Bibliographical Dictionary.* Metuchen, N.J.: Scarecrow Press, 1975.

Schraufnagel, Noel. *From Apology to Protest: The Black American Novel.* Deland, Fla.: Everett Edwards, 1973.

Schultz, Elizabeth. "'Free in Fact and at Last': The Image of the Black Woman in Black American Fiction." In *What Manner of Woman*, edited by Marlene Springer, 337–347. New York: New York University Press, 1977.

Silberman, Charles. "Crisis in Black and White." In *Black Protest: History, Documents, and Analyses*, edited by Joanne Grant, 436–440. New York: Fawcett, 1968.

Sizemore, Barbara. "Sexism and the Black Male." *The Black Scholar* 4 (March/April 1973): 2–11.

Skeeter, Sharyn. "Black Women Writers: Levels of Identity." *Essence* 4 (May 1973): 3–10.

Smith, Barbara. "Beautiful, Needed, Mysterious." *Freedomways* 14 (First Quarter 1977): 69–72.

———. "Doing Research on Black American Women." *Women's Studies Newsletter* 4 (Spring 1976): 4,5,7.

———. "Notes for Yet Another Paper on Black Feminism, Or Will the Real Enemy Please Stand Up?" *Conditions: Five*, 1979: 12–18.

———. "Toward a Black Feminist Criticism." In *But Some of Us Are Brave*, edited by Hull, pp. 167–175.

Sochen, June. *Movers and Shakers: American Women Thinkers and Activists, 1900–1970*. New York: Quadrangle, 1974.

Stack, Carol. *All Our Kin: Strategies for Survival in a Black Community*. New York: Harper and Row, 1974.

Staples, Robert. "The Myth of the Impotent Black Male." The *Black Scholar* 9 (April 1978): 2–9.

Steptoe, Robert. "Intimate Things in Place: A Conversation with Toni Morrison." *Massachusetts Review* 9 (Autumn 1977): 473–484.

Sternberger, Janet. *The Writer on Her Work*. New York: W. W. Norton, 1980.

Tate, Claudia. "*Corregidora:* Ursa's Blues Medley." *Black American Literature Forum* 13 (Winter 1979): 139–140.

———. "An Interview with Gayl Jones." *Black American Literature Forum* 13 (Winter 1979): 142–149.

———. *Interviews with Black Women Writers*. New York: Continuum, 1981.

Thompson, Daniel. *Sociology of the Black Experience*. Westport, Conn.: Greenwood Press, 1974.

Thompson, Mary Lou, ed. *Voices of the New Feminism*. Boston: Beacon Press, 1970.

Truth, Sojourner. "I Suppose I Am About the Only Colored Woman." In *Black Women in White America*, edited by Gerda Lerner, 566–571. New York: Random House, 1972.

U.S. Bureau of the Census. *The Social and Economic Status of the Black Population, 1974*. Washington, D.C.: Government Printing Office, 1974.

U.S. Department of Labor. *Handbook of Labor Statistics, 1978: Bulletin 3000*. Washington, D. C.: Government Printing Office, 1979.

Walker, Alice. "In Search of Our Mothers' Gardens." *Ms.* 2 (May 1974): 64–70, 105.

Wallace, Michele. *Black Macho and the Myth of the Super Woman*. New York: Dial Press, 1978.

Ware, Cellestine. *Woman Power: The Movement for Women's Liberation*. New York: Tower, 1970.

Washington, Mary Helen, ed. *Black-Eyed Susans: Classic Stories by and About Black Women*. Garden City, N.Y.: Doubleday, 1975.

———. *Midnight Birds: Stories of Contemporary Black Women Writers*. New York: Anchor Books, 1980.

Weems, Renita. "Artists Without Art Form." *Conditions: Five* 1979: 8–13.

Woolf, Virginia. *A Room of One's Own*. New York: Harcourt Brace, 1929.

PERMISSIONS

INDEX

A

Angelou, Maya, 8, 59–60
artistic yearnings, 138, 195–196
Aunt Jemima (image of), 5, 28–29

B

Bambara, Toni Cade, 11, 16, 41, 185
Beal, Frances, 9
beatings, 70, 110, 119, 154
Bethune, Mary, 31
black male-female relationships, 83–86, 88–91, 93, 98–101, 102–113, 129–135, 141
black men, 83–85, 86, 88–91, 93, 98–101, 102–113, 129–135, 141, 152–153, 156, 158–159, 161, 163–165, 166, 168–169, 171, 225–227
black men characters,
   Ajax, 191, 197–199, 233, 236
   Boy-Boy, 99–101
   Boyce, Deighton, 88–91, 224–225, 239
   Breedlove, Cholly, 69–78, 140–142
   Coffin, "Daddy," 83–86, 239
   Copeland, Brownfield, 103–112, 131–135, 154
   Copeland, Grange, 102, 131–135, 225
   Held, Truman, 206–209, 210, 212–213
   Judson, Bart, 158–160, 163
   Jude, 101–192, 193–194
   Thomas, Mutt, 173–175
   Upshur, Jacob, 166–168, 171
Black Power Movement, 20, 35, 37

black women activists, 25–26, 30–31, 40, 43; feminists, 6, 7, 47–54; politicians, 31–32, 40–42; writers, 12–16
black women as daughters, 57, 66–69, 78–80, 84–86, 87–100, 129, 135, 139–140, 158–164, 175–180, 186–190
black women as lovers, 72–73, 104, 191–199
black women as mothers, 57–113, 130–136, 146–157, 158–164, 165, 172
black women as wives, 57–113, 158–164, 165–172
black women in the labor market, 22–27, 33
black women in the media, 28–30, 47
black women in scholarship, 40–42
black women in relationships with black men, 10, 11, 37–39, 50
black women in relationships with white women, 4–9, 27–28, 35–37, 45–47
black women novelists
   Gwendolyn Brooks, 17, 217, 219–220
   Gayl Jones, 17, 176–177, 219
   Paule Marshall, 17, 95–96
   Louise Meriwether, 17
   Toni Morrison, 17, 184–187, 217, 220
   Ann Petry, 17, 150, 157
   Alice Walker, 7, 103, 111, 184–186, 219
   Dorothy West, 17, 157
   Sarah Wright, 17, 165
Black Women Organized for Action (BWOA), 47–49

black women protagonists
    Boyce, Selina, 86–98
    Breedlove, Pauline, 67–78, 79–
        81, 136–141, 225, 228, 230,
        235, 242
    Breedlove, Pecola, 67–78, 139–
        140
    Coffin, Francie, 83–86
    Coffin, Henrietta, 83–86
    Copeland, Mem, 103–117, 225,
        228
    Corregidora, Ursa, 171–175
    Hill, Meridian, 64–67, 185, 199–
        215, 228
    Hill, Mrs., 63–67, 230, 234, 236
    Johnson, Lutie, 148–157, 224,
        228, 233, 240
    Judson, Cleo, 157–165, 227,
        240, 242
    Josie, 103–104, 128–135, 240,
        242
    Maud Martha, 79–83
    Medina, Eva, 175, 177–183,
        226, 230, 237
    Min, 118–124
    Nel, 190–192, 193, 204, 234, 235
    Peace, Eva, 98–102, 188–190,
        204, 222, 228, 229, 234, 240
    Peace, Hanna, 190, 242
    Peace, Sula, 186–199, 204, 214–
        215, 233–237
    Upshur, Mariah, 165–171, 222,
        224–225, 231, 237, 239
black women's independence, 231
black women's loyalty to black
    men, 228–229
Bluest Eye, The, 67–68, 136–144,
    225, 242
Brooks, Gwendolyn, 17, 217, 219–
    220
Brown Girl, Brownstones, 86–98,
    224, 233
Brownmiller, Susan, 5

C

capitalism, 3, 6, 7, 12, 224

childbirth, 75–76, 83
Chisholm, Shirley, 40–43
Christian, Barbara, 29, 67, 102,
    213
Civil Rights Movement, 20, 31–
    33, 35–37, 39, 47, 54, 204,
    206–207, 209
Cleaver, Eldridge, 107, 206
Combahee River Collective, 6
Corregidora, 171–175, 233

D

Daddy Was a Number Runner,
    83–86
Dance, Darryl, 6–61, 106
Davis, Angela, 6, 42, 45
de Beauvoir, Simone, 27, 57–58
domestics, 115–117, 137–140
double jeopardy, 4–6, 8, 9, 14

E

Eisenstein, Zillah, 47, 67
Eva's Man, 175–183, 226

F

"femininity," 233–234
Freidan, Betty, 27, 45

G

Guy-Sheftall, Beverly, 7

H

Hamer, Fannie Lou, 43–44
Harper, Frances E. W., 10–11,
    12, 30
Hooks, Bell, 37–38, 42, 45, 46

I

insanity, 78

J

Jones, Gayl, 17, 176–177, 219
Jordan, Barbara, 42

L

lesbianism, 11, 18, 45, 53, 173, 175, 182–183, 195, 218
Living Is Easy, The, 157–164, 242
Lorde, Audre, 238
love, 70, 81–82, 104–106, 161

M

McDaniel, Hattie, 28
McQueen, Butterfly, 28
Mammy, 5, 9, 29
Marshall, Paule, 17, 95–96
Maud Martha, 79–83, 224
Meridian, 62–67, 199–214, 229
Meriwether, Louise, 17
Morgan, Irene, 25
Morrison, Toni, 17, 184–187, 217, 219–220
motherhood as institution, 57–59
murder, 112, 134–135, 152, 182
Murray, Pauli, 34, 41

N

Nation of Islam, 37–38
National Black Feminist Organization (NBFO), 47–49
novels, black women's
  Bluest Eye, The, 67–68, 136–144, 225, 242
  Brown Girl, Brownstones, 86–98, 224, 233
  Corregidora, 171–176, 233
  Daddy Was a Number Runner, 83–86
  Eva's Man, 175–183, 226
  Living Is Easy, The, 157–164, 242
  Maud Martha, 79–83, 224
  Meridian, 62–67, 199–214, 229
  Street, The, 117–128, 148–156, 223
  Sula, 98–102, 186–199, 214–215, 226, 233, 242
  Third Life of Grange Copeland, The, 102–113, 128–136, 225, 229, 242
  This Child's Gonna Live, 165–171, 225

O

Olsen, Tillie, 14

P

Parks, Rosa, 31
passing, 18
Petry, Ann, 17, 150, 157
poverty, 7, 165–168
pregnancy, 63, 72, 74, 129, 201–202
prostitution, 124–127, 130–131, 143

R

rape, 68, 77, 152, 179
religion, 142, 167, 168
Republic of New Africa (RNA), 38
Rich, Adrienne, 46, 58
Rushing, Andrea Benton, 60

S

Sapphire (image of), 5, 29–30
sex, 71, 132, 160–161, 169, 182, 195, 197–198, 200–201
sexual abuse, 119, 152, 172–173, 177–179, 190–192
Shange, Ntozake, 12, 238
Sipuel, Ada, 26
Sizemore, Barbara, 49
Smith, Barbara, 13, 190, 195
Stanton, Elizabeth, 8, 45
Street, The, 117–128, 148–156, 233

Student Nonviolent Coordinating
    Committee (SNCC), 34, 35,
    42, 43, 49
suicide, 91, 132, 223, 240
Sula, 98–102, 186–199, 214–215,
    226, 233, 242

T

Tate, Claudia, 16, 173, 228
Terrell, Mary Church, 28, 30
Third Life of Grange Copeland,
    The, 102–113, 128–136, 225,
    229, 242
This Child's Gonna Live, 165–
    171, 225
Truth, Sojourner, 3, 56

W

Walker, Alice, 17, 103, 112, 184–
    186, 219
Wallace, Michele, 38, 41, 48, 99

Washington, Mary Helen, 56, 221,
    223, 238–241
Wells-Barnett, Ida, 28
West, Dorothy, 17, 157
white feminists, 4–5, 7–9, 27, 45–
    46, 49, 52–54
white men, 126, 127, 132–133,
    151, 153, 160, 193–194
white men characters
    Junto, 126–128, 151
    Captain Chispley, 132
white standard of beauty, 73, 78,
    80–83, 124–125, 128, 137, 158,
    224, 231–233
white women, 119, 123, 124, 131–
    132, 133, 139, 150, 153, 155,
    159–160, 168, 206–207
white women characters
    Miss Bannie, 168–169
    Mrs. Pizzini, 123
    Rabinowitz, Lynn, 204, 209,
    240
Women's Movement, 20, 44–47
Wright, Sarah, 17, 165